Perspectives on
Talk and Learning

NCTE Yearbook Committee 1988

Perspectives on Talk and Learning

Edited by

Susan Hynds
Syracuse University

Donald L. Rubin
University of Georgia

National Council of Teachers of English
1111 Kenyon Road, Urbana, Illinois 61801

Staff Editor: David A. Hamburg

Cover Design: Carlton Bruett

Interior Design: Tom Kovacs for TGK Design

NCTE Stock Number 3252-3020

Library of Congress Cataloging-in-Publication Data

Perspectives on talk and learning / edited by Susan Hynds, Donald L. Rubin.
     p.   cm. — (NCTE forum series)
     Includes bibliographical references.
     ISBN 0-8141-3524-2
     1. English language—Study and teaching. 2. Oral communication.
3. Interaction analysis in education. 4. Language arts. I. Hynds, Susan. II. Rubin, Donald L. III. National Council of Teachers of English. IV. Series.
LB1576.P544   1990
372.6'044—dc20
                                           90-33763
                                             CIP

Contents

III Talking across Cultural Boundaries

Foreword

This collection is the third volume in a series commissioned by the NCTE Executive Committee during the late 1980s and created by the NCTE Yearbook Committee under the guidance first of Ben Nelms and then of Margaret Early, chairs. The Forum Series (originally the NCTE Yearbooks) was conceived as an opportunity for discussions of the central issues of pedagogy and policy that affect English teachers across teaching levels. In the first volume, *Consensus and Dissent*, edited by Marjorie Farmer, contributors examined many of the conflicting pressures—political, curricular, institutional—on the professional lives of English and language arts teachers. The second volume, *Literature in the Classroom*, under the editorship of Ben Nelms, advanced the professional conversation about the place of literature in the English curriculum. An especially timely work, it managed to weave a useful and influential discussion from the rather disparate strands of reading theory, literary criticism, and classroom practice. Timeliness, in fact, has been one of the most satisfying things about the Forum Series thus far. For each of the first two volumes, the committee not only selected discussions with deep significance for our profession, but also managed to catch those discussions as their significance was still emerging. I'm optimistic that these volumes have found their audiences at a most receptive moment, at a moment when the scholarship and plain good sense represented in them could have their best effect.

With the present collection, *Perspectives on Talk and Learning*, the committee has another timely volume to offer. For some time, scholarship in a variety of disciplines has been uncovering the importance of oral language in learning. Freire's description of a "culture of silence" among the sociopolitically oppressed urges us to examine the culture we foster (and sometimes impose) in the classroom. Tannen's complex insights on oral-based cultures admonish us to be aware of the dominance of essayistic literacy in academic discourse and the difficulties that that dominance may create for many students. Work with basic writers, with elementary writers, work in collaborative learning, in dialogue journals, writing centers, and workshops, all point to the usefulness of drawing on the vitality of students' oral language as we coach them toward growth in other literacies. We are coming to appreciate the role that oral language plays in the learning process and to agree with Rubin, who says (in *Consensus and Dissent*) that "speaking and listening instruction are clearly central to what ought to be going on in English and language arts classes."

So now seems an appropriate time to frame a systematic discussion of talk and learning in the English curriculum, and that is what Susan Hynds and Donald L. Rubin have done with this volume. Of course, no single work can offer an exhaustive treatment of a subject so vast and complex, but we hope that in the forum between these covers you'll hear many significant voices. We hope you'll find yourself drawn into the discussion. We hope you'll allow this forum to affect your own perspective on talk and learning.

Michael Spooner
Senior Editor for Publications

1 Introduction: Ways of Talking about Talking and Learning

Donald L. Rubin
University of Georgia

Eight-year-old Emily is explaining why it has taken her so long to come down to the kitchen at dinner time:

> I was looking in the mirror and talking and . . .
> Just I was talking and I couldn't stop talking once I got started.

Her mother does not accept that explanation at face value. She wants to know what Emily was talking about to the mirror that was so crucial as to hold up everyone else's meal. Emily responds:

> Talking about stuff. Kinda . . . ME-TALK!

Emily's remark about ME-TALK reminds us that, whatever else talk is or can become, it is at its heart an exuberant affirmation of self. Babies babble with canny conversational intonation, and they do it for the sheer pleasure of making those mouth sounds that assert their stake in the mysterious but alluring club of mouth-sound-makers, the same club in which their parents and elder siblings all seem to hold membership.

As adults, most of us are capable of ignoring junk mail that accumulates on our desks, capable of slamming a door and ignoring a vestibule closet on the verge of regurgitating its delicately balanced clutter. Few of us, however, are capable of ignoring the insistent invitation of a telephone ringing. We cannot resist the summons to talk. Talk compels. Talk compels because in every casual conversation, every answer shouted out in class, as well as in every rehearsed public presentation, there is a substrate of ME-TALK—an affirmation of our own fundamental human identity.

At the opposite extreme of self-affirming ME-TALK is what Paulo Freire (1970), an advocate of the pedagogy of emancipation, calls "the

1

culture of silence." Oppressed people have nothing to say. Their talk is limited to instrumental functions needed to get done the concrete tasks at hand. Their talk does not support the "critical consciousness" needed to see oneself and one's world from a broader perspective. One reason why some people's talk may be limited in this fashion is that social institutions—too often schools—sometimes seize control of minority groups' language options. Thus, for example, Native American children attending public schools have been historically forbidden from speaking their native languages.

Even majority language youngsters, however, may have nothing to say because no one has cultivated in them the kind of talk that supports critical consciousness; they may be denied the kind of talk that helps to transform or reconstruct their experiences from a reflective stance.

As an unhappy example of how some classrooms create a nonreflective culture of silence, consider this brief interaction in a kindergarten class. Ms. F is working with students on labels for spatial relationships. Glancing at a well-worn teachers' guide, she asks Anita to use two animal figures to demonstrate a spatial relationship:

> OK, Anita. Now it's your turn. Will you show me
> THE COW IS BEHIND THE PIG?

With deliberation, Anita places the cow and pig flank-to-flank, the broad side of the pig facing Ms. F and her. Ms. F corrects her:

> No, that's not right. I said, "THE COW BEHIND THE PIG."

Clearly confused, Anita tries reversing the position of the two animals, this time facing the broad side of the cow, then returns the animal figures to the same position in which she had put them originally. During this manipulation, Anita is uttering a long, drawn "Ummmmm . . ." But she finds no words to help herself transform this double-bind situation. It seems either Anita must reject her teacher's authority, or else she must reject her own common sense. Again, Ms. F rejects Anita's solution:

> No, that's not right either. You put the cow BESIDE the pig, and I
> wanted BEHIND. This is BEHIND.

Ms. F places the cow's head touching the pig's tail. Anita makes one attempt to explain her reasoning:

> It's in back . . . .

Ms. F cuts her off; explanations are out of order:

BEHIND. This is BEHIND. Try to remember that for next time. OK, now, who can come up here and show me IN FRONT OF?

Anita does not appear really upset or crushed by this incident, just a little more glazed over. She is getting used to the culture of silence being constructed in this classroom. Pretty soon, when she does answer a question on another occasion, it will not be in her own voice. She will speak in some alien school intonation, "THE COW IS BESIDE THE PIG."

Freire, though primarily concerned with literacy learning, recognizes that "speaking the word"—authentic dialogue, in particular—is the key to transcending the bounds of immediate perceptual experience, the key to going beyond the information given. By speaking the word, by the power of talk, we are able to transform knowledge and, ultimately, transform our lives. One of the most significant rights humankind possesses, therefore, is "the right to have a voice" (Freire 1970, 213).

Speaking the word, then, is knowledge producing as well as ego affirming. James Britton (1970) similarly captures the centrality of speech to learning and to personal growth by asserting that "talk is the sea upon which all else floats." We internalize talk, and it becomes thought. We externalize talk, and it becomes our link to social reality. We elaborate talk, and it becomes our bridge to literacy. Like the sea, talk is the environment that first incubates and then nurtures our development.

Talk is like the sea in yet another sense. A traditional homily tells us that fish would be the least likely creatures to ever become aware of water. For those of us who teach, talk surrounds us and it also constitutes our primary mode of action. It is our medium, our atmosphere, and also our substance. And it is therefore invisible to us much of the time. Because talk is invisible to us, we rarely treat it as a matter of deliberate concern for teaching and learning. Of course, students do learn about talk in classrooms, but the lessons they learn may not be ones we would choose to teach if we thought about it. Sometimes students learn more about silence than about talk, for example, and more about hearing than about listening.

In order to render talk more visible and therefore more subject to reflective teaching, it is helpful to develop some vocabulary—ways of talking and thinking about talk. That is what this book is all about. The chapters that follow illuminate the nature of student talk, teacher talk, and the talk that fuels processes of learning in classrooms. They provide tools for educators—tools with which to observe and understand the wide range of oral communication events. Several of the chapters also highlight the role of talk as a curricular object in language arts instruction and in other content areas. They show the qualities of classroom talk that lead to growth in reading, writing, listening, and thinking. Still other chapters explore cultural diversity in the structure and uses of talk, and explore also the consequences of those diverse speech styles for students who may discover in schools alien expectations of what counts as good talk.

This introductory chapter sketches some fundamental dimensions of oral communication which are revisited in various guises in the later sections of the volume. It first presents three complementary approaches—interaction analysis, style analysis, and function analysis—for categorizing the broad range of talk in which we engage. The chapter next proposes two particular dimensions of talk—the epistemic function and the communalizing function—as especially important for understanding the interaction of talking and learning in schools. Finally, the plan for the remainder of the volume is briefly previewed.

Some Characteristics of Talk

Widening Circles of Interactants

One simple way to categorize types of talk is by describing the range of audiences with whom we can interact. We can engage in inner speech, talking to ourselves, and that is intrapersonal communication. We can talk to a single other person, and that is conversation. (When that conversation is planned ahead of time and motivated by some instrumental purposes, it becomes an interview.) When we participate in a well-defined network composed of several known individuals, we are engaging in small group discussion. When we participate with a larger, more heterogenous, and more loosely collected group of people, there is usually a more definite separation and inequality between the roles of speaker and listener: while one person monologues, the others do not. In that case, we are engaging in public communication. When talk is technologically mediated, so that there is no certain way of knowing which audience members are tuned in to our message at any given time, we are broadcasting.

In the past, typical classroom communication tended to rely on public communication models. Teachers talked, students listened—or if they did not listen, at least they did not talk. Teacher-centered instruction gave students little turn-taking power. The timing, the structure, the content of student talk was sometimes so circumscribed, that

even when students did vocalize, the situation could hardly be regarded as dialogue. When power relations in classrooms are vastly
asymmetrical, students are not likely to feel much *response-ability*.

In the alternative model students participate in the full spectrum of
interaction roles. Teachers do not hold exclusive gatekeeping power
over speaking rights. Students participate in decisions regarding who
gets to talk and in what direction lessons develop. Collaborative projects and activities result in classrooms in which students engage in a
great deal of small group communication, and at any given time, students can be found working with their peers in finding, defining, and
solving their own learning challenges. The teacher's role becomes one
of consultant, facilitator, or coach. This alternative model of shared
classroom talk allows students and teachers to mutually *negotiate* their
curriculum; many examples of negotiating curriculum will be found
throughout this volume.

Oral Language

As we move between narrower and wider circles of interaction—from
muttering to ourselves to declaiming archivally "for the record"—we
switch our language style. Musing to ourselves or to those with whom
we are most intimate, our language tends to be elliptical, choppy,
stream of consciousness, with a single word carrying a constellation of
meaning. Expounding to diffuse or psychologically distant audiences,
in contrast, we talk in a literate style which is linguistically very similar
to the style of written documents (Rubin and Kantor 1984).

In this regard, the actual channel in which a message is delivered—
speaking or writing—has less effect on language style than does the
rhetorical context and intent of the message (Rubin and Rafoth 1986;
Tannen 1985). Still, it is useful to point to the style of *prototypical* speech
events, the style of unplanned, face-to-face interaction. (For recent
reviews of this topic, see, for example, Horowitz and Samuels 1987;
Rubin 1987.)

In prototypical oral language, speakers compose "on the fly." They
are at the mercy of time pressures and memory constraints. Since
speech leaves behind no permanent trace to which they could return
at their leisure, speakers are limited in their ability to revise and limited
in the complexity of their constructions. Moreover, speakers are usually more focused on their personal concerns with the topic or with
their audience, and less attentive to structural aspects of their discourse. In all, then, oral style contains markers of personal involvement such as first- and second-person pronouns and reliance on pre-

sent tense. It is also marked by loose structuring—coordinate conjunctions and word repetitions—instead of more integrated structures such as dense subordination and noun clusters (Chafe 1982).

As a prototypical example of oral style in a learning community, consider Joby's contribution to a meeting of his Presidents' Day Task Force. He and three other sixth graders have been assigned the job of choosing a president around whom the class will organize a series of projects. The group has already rejected the "standard" choices of great presidents: Washington, Lincoln, Kennedy. One has suggested Ronald Reagan, but Joby demurs:

> Yeah, easy for research. But it's almost too much. I everywhere it's Reagan this and Reagan that. Like I got this stuff and he's cool. Andrew Jackson and so. So not too many people will know about Andrew Jackson. And he was a tough guy. People were pissed at him, fancy government people, 'cause he partied so much at his inauguration. And it wasn't your regular government guys, see, wear coonskin hats and all stuff and he rides this horse, this big white horse, right into the fanciest part of the White House. Shut up, Franco, I'm trying to be serious here. He's cool. And like this book, it shows you can be just plain folks. Andrew Jackson, he's a Southerner. And like Ronald Reagan: Yeah! Like he's some kind of everybody thinks he's God. So I say him.

Multiple Functions

As this excerpt from Joby's talk shows, children learn to accommodate their styles to the type of interaction in which they are engaging (peer group discussion in this case), according to the channel of communication in which they are operating (oral or written), and also according to their aims or purposes. Joby's purpose was clearly to persuade. Another way of thinking about types of speech, then, pertains to the purposes of speech, what functions are being accomplished through talk.

Roman Jacobson (1960) devised a useful catalogue of speech functions by noting, first of all, that all communication situations involve (1) a speaker transmitting a (2) message to (3) an audience through (4) a channel (5) by means of some language or code, and that all of this takes place in some larger (6) context.

Talk that focuses on the speaker fulfills the (1) *expressive* or *emotive* function. Talk that highlights the message as an object of attention is (2) *poetic*. When speakers try to influence their audiences in one way or another (persuading, informing, entertaining), they are engaging in (3) *instrumental* or *conative* talk. If the function of the interaction is simply to make sure that channels of communication are open—as when we talk about the weather or make vague plans to "get together" or decide to run our meeting by parliamentary procedure—then the function is (4) *phatic* or *ritualizing*. If the purpose of the talk is to evaluate or describe the nature of the very code we use to communicate (which is function of this entire volume), then the talk is (5) *metalinguistic*. Finally, (6) *referential* talk functions to tell us something about the nature of the world.

The referential function dominates most school discourse. Teachers (and occasionally students, too) talk about the natural resources of Belize, colloidal suspensions found in common foods, and the symbolic significance of the river in Conrad's *Heart of Darkness*. Increasingly, however, educators are learning that all of the other functions of talk also yield valuable outcomes. In literacy learning, for example, expressive or emotive discourse provides entry to composing processes, and is central to developing meaningful responses to literature. Conative or instrumental talk links writers and readers with sense of audience and rhetorical intent. And since metalinguistic awareness is prerequisite to emerging literacy, talking about their own talk, words, sentences, and the like is especially important to primary-grade children.

Although it is possible to point to the dominant function of an utterance, it is more realistic to recognize that any given utterance probably serves several of these functions simultaneously. A high school student combines expressive and instrumental elements along with referential functions in his response to the death scenes in *Romeo and Juliet*:

> I tell you, I think Romeo got what he deserved. He was a jerk in the whole play, but at the end when he kills himself, I don't even feel sorry that he did it by mistake. 'Cause that's just the chicken thing to do. 'Cause I've felt that way, like there's no other way so you might as well, you know? And probably everybody knows somebody who went ahead and did it. Or if you don't know somebody, you know about somebody, a friend of a friend or something. So like if I did it every time I was feeling that way, I'd be a goner six or seven times over. Yeah, well, I wouldn't'a hadda read *Romeo and Juliet*, but it's dumb. You just wait it out no matter how bad it gets and sooner or later it gets to be not such a big deal, not so big.

Communalizing and Epistemic Functions of Talk

Categorizing the functions of talk as either expressive or instrumental or referential or the like is useful for examining individual utterances.

It helps us think about discourse microscopically, one unit at a time. But to think about the broader functions of talk within human development, or less grandiosely within a curriculum, it helps to adopt a more macroscopic view.

Rubin and Kantor (1984), for example, reflect much contemporary educational thought in observing that children's oral (and written) language develops in tandem with their developing social awareness and their ability to reconstruct experience. Corresponding to social awareness, the *communalizing* function of talk "adjusts ideas to people and people to ideas" (Burke 1950). Corresponding to reconstruction of experience, the *epistemic* function of talk shapes the speaker's own perceptions of the world and represents them as knowledge.

To better understand what the communalizing function of talk embraces, it is helpful to think about the polar opposite actions included in this dimension. On the one hand, we can use talk to *intimate* information to a listener. When we intimate, we are speaking indirectly, assuming rich shared associations with our conversational partner, and attributing to our listener an affirmative goodwill effort to retrieve our intended meaning. Clarity is less important than solidarity. A seventh-grade peer tutor intimates to her classmate the procedure for dividing by fractions:

> Like before you multiplied the top and the top then the bottom. They're shaking hands I guess she said. This time it's . . . kiss my feet!

In contrast to intimating discourse is using talk to *articulate*. When we articulate, we make connections, explicate coherence, assume diverse backgrounds among our listeners, and attribute little prior motivation for response-ability on their parts. In articulating talk, the speaker forges relationships through language, reaches out and impels hearers to become listeners through seductive audience-centered strategies such as previewing, internal summaries, and organizational cues. In a referential communication accuracy exercise designed to cultivate articulate talk, a fourth-grade student tape-records his description of an abstract design so that some unknown listener could draw the design based on his description:

> To start off, I'm going to describe the outside shape, and then I'll tell you about the lines that zigzag inside the shape. But don't draw anything until I run through it one time kind of in general. Then I'll come back and tell it all to you again in more detail. So first the outside shape, it's going to be like an egg shape except one end

has this half-circle cut into it. So the basic egg shape is about as long as your thumb, and at its widest it's . . . .

The epistemic function of talk is likewise clarified by showing its extremes. On the one hand, talk can *reproduce* knowledge. When we reproduce knowledge, we are re-citing, we are preserving the content and structure of some body of information with as much fidelity as we can muster. Our concern is with detail and accuracy and quantity. When one health education teacher conducts a class "discussion" based on textbook readings about human reproduction, the whole interaction has the flavor of an interrogation.

T: OK, now what do we call the sperm and the egg?

Henry: Fertilizing?

T: No. Fertilization is what takes place. What are they?

Henry: Oh, yeah, they're cells.

T: No. I mean what kind of cells are they? Jeff?

Jeff: The sperm and the egg? Zygotes?

T: No. Zygotes is later. Who knows this? Alan Luttan?

Alan: They're germs, right?

T: Germ cells or the other word is "gametes." Next. What is it after the sperm fertilizes the egg?

Jeff: That's the zygotes.

T: Zygote, right. Now in what part of the female reproductive tract does fertilization happen? This is back in what we read yesterday, no, on Tuesday.

There is a tendency to regard knowledge-reproducing talk like that used in this health education lesson pejoratively as mere parroting. Note, however, that this negative view may be culture bound. Traditional oral-based cultures often prize the knowledge-reproducing talk of a bard or griot far more than the originality that Western industrialized societies claim to cultivate.

In addition, there is a role for knowing and reciting discrete facts, a role for expertise, in classroom talk. Kieran Egan (1979) makes a compelling argument that, especially at certain stages of development, students have an obsession with facts: naming Super Bowl quarterbacks, pop singers' discographies, lyrics to hamburger chain advertising jingles, characters in baroquely complex fantasy comic books. This obsession is not necessarily unhealthy, for without some fact-base, children cannot continue their development as generalizers and pat-

Donald L. Rubin

tern detectors. Sometimes well-meaning teachers eager to turn out problem solvers rather than encyclopedists do their students a disservice when they denigrate the importance of knowledge-reproducing talk in a blanket fashion.

Rather than reproducing knowledge, some talk functions to *transform* knowledge (similar to Bereiter and Scardamalia's 1987 distinction between "knowledge telling" and "knowledge transforming"). We use talk to transform knowledge when we sift through observations and evaluate some information as more important than some other, or when we compare two claims and arrive at some new synthesis. Or we transform knowledge when we take some schema or metaphor or template that applies to one domain of experience and apply it to a new domain. Talk that transforms knowledge yields the critical consciousness that Freire (1970) discussed, the power to see oneself and one's world from more than just a single perspective. Consider this portion of a ninth-grade class discussion arising from the story "Flowers for Algernon," about a mentally handicapped person. The students here are collaboratively transforming the meaning of this literary event:

> *Anna:* The thing about the story to me is that it shows sometimes people with lots of brains can be mean and people without much brains can have more heart than the smart ones. Those scientists could've cared less.
>
> *Dong:* When you think about being smart—you said the smart ones—it all depends because someone is always going to be smarter than you are. Well, in the middle Charlie was.
>
> *Roger:* Also, Charlie wasn't so dumb. Well, I mean even when he was dumb the people who were supposed to be smarter were really acting dumber because they never tried to see Charlie as a regular person. He had feelings and stuff. Like Dong said no matter how smart you are. But also no matter how dumb you are. Even when you feel real inferior, you might not be so inferior as some of the people who think they're the superior ones. Know what I mean?
>
> *Anna:* So really I guess the story is saying there's different ways of being smart. Being smart in school is not, it's just one way. Probably it's just as important to be smart to let you see people for like everybody is worthwhile.

Diversity in Communalizing and Epistemic Talk

It is the literate bias of formal education that leads teachers to value articulate, transformational talk above all other types. All epistemic

VARIETIES OF CLASSROOM TALK

Communalizing Functions

	Intimate	*Articulate*
Reproducing **Epistemic** **Functions**	Examples: teasing, some language play	Examples: oral reports, announcements, theater
Transforming	Examples: peer problem-solving groups	Examples: class debates, group presentations

talk, however, knowledge-reproducing as well as knowledge-transforming, can play a useful role in classroom learning. Similarly, there is a place for intimating as well as articulating talk. The chart above lays out some common classroom activities according to these functions. Using such a matrix, teachers can inventory their curricula and classroom practices to ensure that they support a full range of talk.

Plan of This Book

Learning to Talk and Talking to Learn

Any model of learning has to take into account both the trajectory of the learner's cognitive development and also the orbit of the subject matter to be learned. For a successful rendezvous between learner and subject, teachers must carefully calculate a host of factors, engineering their classroom climate and curriculum, and patiently waiting for clear conditions. The first section of this volume—"Learning to Talk and Talking to Learn"—adopts just this stance.

In "Speaking Creatures in the Classroom," Judith Lindfors starts from the perspective of human development. Similar to the concepts of communalizing and epistemic functions developed in this introductory chapter, Lindfors demonstrates that children develop as talkers first "to connect with others" and then "to understand the world." Superimposed upon both these drives to talk is the need—as in Emily's ME-TALK—"to reveal oneself."

Douglas Barnes takes the complementary approach to Lindfors in his chapter, "Oral Language and Learning." Barnes begins with an analysis of typical classroom talk: teacher controlled, alien from what children already know about talk and about their worlds, and ultimately ineffective as a medium of learning. When students are given free rein to bring to bear the richness of their naturally developed speech, as in collaborative learning projects, however, they are able to construct new meanings in what they study and especially in their reading. Like two tunnelers, each working from the opposite shore, the language developmental and the curriculum developmental perspectives happily meet in the middle. Both point to the power of authentic, exploratory talk to drive learning.

Talk in the Learning Community

The second section of the book, "Talk in the Learning Community," details the ways in which students and teachers interact. Some chapters in this section point to the nature of collaborative discourse among students, and to the impact of such collaboration on learning outcomes. Other chapters highlight particular kinds of classroom speech events or activities (e.g., dramatic improvisation).

In "Negotiation, Language, and Inquiry: Building Knowledge Collaboratively in the Classroom," Cynthia Onore opens a window on one second-grade class, like second-grade classes across the nation, learning about the Pilgrims at Thanksgiving season. What is perhaps extraordinary about this class, however, is that the teacher forgoes a model of "motivating the students" in favor of a climate in which "[T]hrough talk and collaboration the teacher's intention and the child's intention are allowed to become shared."

From the point of view of teacher-talk, questions are the primary vehicles that shape classroom talk. Theresa Rogers, Judith Green, and Nancy Nussbaum, in "Asking Questions about Questions," analyze why some styles of questioning lead to authentic dialogue among the entire learning community, whereas other styles of questioning result in painful interrogations. From the parallel point of view of student-talk, language which is elaborated, cohesive, and rich in metalinguistic awareness betokens the ability to transform knowledge, betokens school success. Lee Galda and A. D. Pellegrini, in "Play Talk, School Talk, and Emergent Literacy," show the genesis of this kind of student-talk in the play of preschool children.

In primary grades, the playfulness and sociality of talk remains of primary importance to children, even as they are being initiated into the wonders of literacy. Conversation is the wellspring of early school learning in a number of respects. In "Talking Up a Writing Community: The Role of Talk in Learning to Write," Anne Haas Dyson shows how, in a classroom that permits interaction among children, talk provides the "social energy," the gravitational pull that allows students to work in concert. Talk also serves as an "analytic tool" to help children manipulate language itself, and as a "social consequence" of literacy activities, to talk about what they have written.

Whereas Dyson addresses mainly writing as the incidental focus of children's conversation (they could as easily be talking about artwork or block building), Anne Ruggles Gere, in "Talking about Writing Groups," analyzes talk produced in instructional groups deliberately set up to promote writing. In peer writing groups, students create a metalanguage for talking about discourse. In groups designed for collaborative writing, they must also create social organizational schemes for dividing the labor of producing a joint text.

The impact of different modes of small group interaction in promoting literacy learning is likewise the subject of "Reading and Response to Literature: Transactionalizing Instruction" by Stanley Straw. Straw distinguishes between "interactive" and "transactive" group talk as students work together in discovering and creating meaning in literature.

Much work in learning communities, such as those described by Gere and Straw and other authors in this volume, takes place between students. Teachers, of course, are also key members in classroom learning communities. In "Teacher/Student Talk: The Collaborative Conference," Muriel Harris attends to the ways in which a teacher can enter into authentic dialogue with individual students. Harris describes several roles a teacher may adopt: partner in a search, uncritical listener, coworker. In the specific context of writing conferences, teacher dialoguing helps students "see the relationship between the verbal world they live in and the paper they write on."

This ability and willingness to bring one's understanding of social interaction to bear in school learning is likewise the subject of Susan Hynds's chapter, "Talking Life and Literature." Like Harris, Hynds points to the pivotal role of the teacher in promoting an interaction style in which students are able to match the world of literature against the world of their primary experience. When student talk is directed toward honest responses to literature rather than toward teacher-centered knowledge brokering, students enact rich and meaningful literary experiences.

In the history of our civilization, as well as in each of our personal histories, literary experience is strongly linked to oral performance. Poems are songs to be sung. Books are stories to be heard. In "Student Performance of Literature," Elizabeth Fine shows that the deepest understanding and response to literature arises out of performance.

Fine claims a number of advantages in recapturing the orality of literary experience. Among these advantages, she notes, "performance is a holistic activity that rescues literature from the fragmenting tendency of criticism."

In performance, learning is enlivened by nonverbal enactment. Knowledge becomes action. Like the literary performance which Fine describes, dramatic improvisation is a powerful tool for learning. In "Dramatic Improvisation in the Classroom," Betty Jane Wagner describes two kinds of dramatic improvisation: story drama and theme-oriented drama. Students learn through enacting their roles, of course. But in addition, considerable learning takes place by virtue of the preliminary discussion that must be conducted in preparing the improvisation. Oral performance implies a speaker, a text—improvised or not—and, most naturally, a listener. In "Learning to Listen and Learning to Read," Sara W. Lundsteen calls our attention to the centrality of listening processes to learning in content areas as well as in language arts. Listening is not just one monolithic process. Instead, we listen differently—just as we speak differently—depending on the function we are trying to accomplish. Listening critically, for example, demands a different approach than does listening aesthetically, say, to literature read aloud. Students can enhance their range and effectiveness in listening by acquiring certain metacognitive strategies.

Lundsteen advocates that we treat listening as an object of curriculum, an object of deliberate instruction. In many schools and school systems, some accommodation is made for an object of curriculum known as "speech." Often the image we have of speech class is based on a public speaking model: the speech-a-week model. But many other models of speech curriculum are available (Halliday 1979). Phil Backlund writes in "Oral Activities in the English Classroom" of an eclectic collection of speech activities. To be sure, some speech activities are aimed at promoting formal, articulate talk. But Backlund shows that oral activities are eminently suited to the more general learning objectives of promoting social knowledge, self-knowledge, and content knowledge. To meet these objectives, Backlund contends, students must discover the efficacy of talk; their talk must make a real difference in the way things are.

Talking across Cultural Boundaries

The final section of the book, "Talking across Cultural Boundaries," considers language variation as a force that can enrich learning processes. Often variation from some norm of standard speech is regarded as a source of interference that teachers must help students overcome. Well-intentioned and linguistically sophisticated educators may recognize that nonstandard language varieties are no less valid from any structural or communicative criterion. Yet attitudinal biases in the mainstream community preclude speakers of nonstandard varieties from equal access to socioeconomic opportunity. Therefore, these sympathetic teachers argue, the humane policy is to give nonstandard speakers the option to adopt standard speech for those occasions when they choose to interact outside their immediate communities.

This bilingual/bidialectal position is naive with respect to the dynamics of second language learning and language evaluation. To learn a nonnative language variety is not merely some technical achievement. Instead, it betokens an attitudinal accommodation to the value structure of the "target" culture (Lambert 1967).

Moreover, linguistically mediated stereotypes merely reflect more deep-seated stereotypes. The etiology of prejudice is not substituting /d/ for /th/. Instead, prejudice serves certain psychological and social functions, protecting one's ego against admissions of failure, for example (Brislin 1981). Polishing one's pronunciation will not eliminate negative stereotypes. Improving conditions of social and economic justice might, however.

Finally, what some people find "wrong" or offensive with nonstandard language varieties is not entirely linguistic. Cultures vary in how they tolerate and express conflict, what they consider embarrassing and what is fit for a good public laugh, what counts as respect and what counts as standoffishness. These larger features of communication style, of rhetoric and discourse patterns, may be far more potent in triggering intercultural anxiety and distrust (Kochman 1974).

Lisa Delpit, in her chapter, "Language Diversity and Learning," adopts a similar line of reasoning in considering whether nonstandard language varieties might interfere with school learning. According to Delpit, educators' obsession with the discrete linguistic features of Black Vernacular English is misguided. A child is not precluded from understanding cause-and-effect relationships simply because she says, "Every time I test something sour, the litmus paper turns blue." Instead, a child from a nonstandard speaking community might be disadvantaged in a mainstream culture school because she has acquired different conventions for what to talk about and how to go about gaining access to an interaction.

In "Bilingual ESL Learners Talking in the English Classroom," Sarah Hudelson likewise asks us to distinguish between different sources of speech variation, in this case among nonnative speakers of English. On the one hand, ESL learners struggle to make themselves understood in a language which is overlaid upon their more spontaneous mode of expression. In most cases, interference from purely linguistic sources can be overcome by goodwill efforts toward understanding. On the other hand, even when nonnative English speakers acquire a good deal of linguistic proficiency, their norms for classroom participation may still diverge from the "standard" for school talk. Like Delpit, Hudelson shows that their very diversity can be a source of communicative strength for minority language users.

In the closing chapter of this volume, Jerrie Cobb Scott reaches similar conclusions about the significant impact of "nonstandard" norms for interaction among minority culture youngsters. Scott reports a project in which inner-city middle school students create a classroom language community for the purpose of carrying out a project of real concern to the children. Paralleling the thinking of other contributors to this volume regarding the promise of negotiated curriculum, authentic dialogue, collaborative discourse, and dramatic improvisation, the project provides students with an environment that invites talk and invites talk about talk. Here, students practice the epistemic and the communalizing functions of talk, and attention to language form and structure need not occupy focal awareness.

The contributions to this volume, it is apparent, are diverse indeed—just as talk itself is an instrument of marvelous diversity. And yet, within that diversity in content and emphasis, there lies remarkable consistency in the spirit of these chapters. If the collaborators to this volume—for this volume surely is an instance of collaborative discourse—speak with one voice, that chant calls us to

1. Nurture our students' ME-TALK.

2. Cast off oppressive cultures of silence by learning to speak the word.

3. Exploit varied opportunities for talk.

4. Discover talk as efficacious, as function.

5. Encourage students to build learning communities, to negotiate curriculum among themselves and with their teachers.

6. Celebrate diversity among speech communities.

The contributors to this volume hope that readers hear the echoes of these themes in its pages. Most of all, the contributors here are calling upon educators to adopt a deliberate, reflective stance toward oral communication and listen to the talk of children and young adults as they learn about themselves, each other, and their world.

Works Cited

Bereiter, C., and M. Scardamalia. 1987. *The Psychology of Written Composition*. Hillsdale, N.J.: Lawrence Erlbaum.

Brislin, R. W. 1981. *Cross-Cultural Encounters*. New York: Pergamon Press.

Britton, J. 1970. *Language and Learning*. Harmondsworth, England: Pelican Books.

Burke, K. 1950. *A Rhetoric of Motives*. New York: Prentice-Hall.

Chafe, W. 1982. "Integration and Involvement in Speaking, Writing, and Oral Literature." In *Spoken and Written Language*, edited by D. Tannen, 35–54. Norwood, N.J.: Ablex.

Egan, K. 1979. *Educational Development*. New York: Oxford.

Freire, P. 1970. "The Adult Literacy Process as Cultural Action for Freedom." *Harvard Educational Review* 40: 205–21.

Halliday, M.A.K., ed. 1979. *Teaching Speech Today: Six Alternative Approaches*. Skokie, Ill.: National Textbook.

Horowitz, R., and S. J. Samuels, eds. 1987. *Comprehending Oral and Written Language*. San Diego: Academic Press.

Jacobson, R. 1960. "Linguistics and Poetics." In *Style in Language*, edited by T. Sebeok, 350–77. Cambridge, Mass.: The MIT Press.

Kochman, T. 1974. "Orality and Literacy as Factors of 'Black' and 'White' Communication Behavior." *Linguistics: An International Review* 136: 91–117.

Lambert, W. 1967. "A Social Psychology of Bilingualism." *Journal of Social Issues* 23: 91–109.

Rubin, D. L. 1987. "Divergence and Convergence between Oral and Written Communication." *Topics in Language Disorders* 7, no. 4: 1–18.

Rubin, D. L., and K. J. Kantor. 1984. "Talking and Writing: Building Communication Competence." In *Speaking and Writing*, edited by C. Thaiss and C. Suhor, 29–74. Urbana, Ill.: National Council of Teachers of English.

Rubin, D. L., and B. A. Rafoth. 1986. "Oral Language Criteria for Selecting Listenable Materials: An Update for Reading Teachers and Specialists." *Reading Psychology* 7: 137–52.

Tannen, D. 1985. "Relative Focus of Involvement in Oral and Written Discourse." In *Literacy, Language, and Learning*, edited by D. Olson, N. Torrance, and A. Hildyard, 124–47. Cambridge, England: Cambridge University Press.

I Learning to Talk and Talking to Learn

2 Speaking Creatures in the Classroom

Judith Wells Lindfors
University of Texas at Austin

Talk is part of our very biological heritage by virtue of our membership in the human species. Talk is an imperative for us. It is an imperative for us to connect with others through talk, it is an imperative for us to explore our worlds through talk, and it is an imperative for us to express our self-hood through talk. Are our classrooms places in which speaking creatures flourish according to their nature, or are they places in which the imperative for talk is quashed?

Now here is something to think about:

> There is good evidence for the special evolution of those capacities preserved in the genetic code which makes us mature into speaking creatures.... In the case of Homo sapiens, it can be shown that our oral and respiratory systems did not just evolve to serve functions of eating and noisemaking, but to serve the particular functions of producing articulate speech. Chimpanzees... cannot learn to speak because they are not built to do so.... (Slobin 1979, 114–15)

But *we* are "built to do so." This is a very powerful idea: that other animal species make noises, but only our species speaks. It is not possible to say *why* we evolved into speaking creatures, but we can identify some important ways that our ability to talk empowers us. Talk helps us to accomplish our most deeply human purposes: to connect with others, to understand our world, and to reveal ourselves. These purposes are children's no less than they are ours. As full members of our speaking species, children—from infancy onward—develop and use talk to carry out these deep and continuing purposes.[1]

To Connect with Others

From birth, we are social beings. By two months of age, the child clearly differentiates between persons and objects and clearly prefers persons (Trevarthen 1977). Presented with a human face (a real one or a representation) and a real or represented object, the infant selects the human face. The preverbal infant reaches out very effectively to others in his or her social world through gesture, facial expression, vocalization. But it is no coincidence that many adults regard the child's first *word* as a major milestone. Why? Perhaps the adult senses the increase in communication power that talk gives a child. With only nonverbal means of expression, the child would be severely limited in carrying out many social purposes such as inviting others to do things with him, offering to do things for others, thanking people, apologizing, joking, arguing, complimenting—all communication acts which are more "interactional" than "informational" (Fillmore 1976, 659), acts that have more to do with maintaining and furthering social relationships than with conveying information. All are acts which are more fully accomplished through talk than through nonverbal means.

It is, of course, possible to reach out to others in written language. I think of the child giving out valentines or passing a note to a friend when the teacher isn't looking or sending birthday party invitations. In all of these, the child's connecting with others is accomplished by means of written language. But again we find that the expressive channel of talk has a special and particularly powerful role to play in the child's reaching out to others. Talk is social in its very essence. Though some talk is for self, most of it is for and with others. And though some talk is for public performance, most of it is for conversation. In conversation people come together. In fact, conversation is quite literally a coming-together, for one requirement of talk is that participants be physically close enough that they can hear one another. We have been reminded often that the power of writing is that it communicates across time and across distance. In contrast, the special power of talk lies in its immediacy. Talk is here-and-now, immediate, spontaneous, minute-to-minute. Me and you. Us. Together right here, right now.

In talk, people are together in another important way, also. Conversation is jointly constructed by the participants. Each picks up on what the other says and carries it a little further. Many people have called conversation a game. Clearly it is not a game of solitaire, but a game that several people play together. Each one's move depends on the partner's moves. Each participant takes the other(s) into account, trying to assure that the others understand what she says and also that she understands their talk. And each participant tries to keep the interaction going—your turn, my turn; back and forth; initiate and respond. A conversation is a text that people construct *together*, and conversing is an activity that people do *together*. As the following jointly constructed conversation between a mother and her 19-month-old daughter indicates, children become active participants in the joint construction of conversation early.

> (The child has finished her lunch and is still sitting in her high chair. *M* is mother; *C* is child.)
>
> C: ha-hoooooo-he (spoken in a high, sing-song voice)
>
> M: (singing) "Hi ho, hi ho, it's off to work we go."
>
> C: (blowing attempt at whistling)
>
> M: (whistles next line of song) (sings) "Hi ho"
>
> C: miomiomiowaaaa ("mirror mirror mirror wall")
>
> M: (very dramatically) "Mirror, mirror on the wall, who's the fairest of them all?
>
> C: owaa wiaawa mio*waa*miowa
>
> M: (very dramatically) "Mirror, mirror on the wall," the wicked old queen says that in *Snow White*. "Mirror, mirror on the wall."
>
> C: eh-eh-eh-eh (falling intonation, stairstep fashion)
>
> M: (witch voice) "Eh-eh-eh. Would you like an apple, deary?"
>
> C: ahba ("apple")
>
> M: She takes an apple. Snow White takes an apple.
>
> C: uh-oh ("uh-oh")
>
> M: What happens when Snow White takes an apple? Then what happens? What happens with Snow White? She takes an apple and falls asleep forever.
>
> C: oh dis ("kiss")
>
> M: Uh-hm. And then the prince comes and gives her a kiss. Yeah. And he comes on his white horse.
>
> (Lindfors 1987, 207)

Clearly this conversation is built out of the shared world of the participants. That's the way conversations are. The mother does much to support the child's participation. But the following conversational excerpts between two English three-year-olds demonstrate that young children can build conversations together, without the help of an adult.

> (The two children are playing with toy cars.)
>
> C-1: That's my red car, John.
>
> C-2: But it isn't really.
>
> C-1: Well, I was playing with it. I had it first.
>
> C-2: Oh, well, which shall I have then? I'm going to have the blue one and I'm going to race it.
>
> C-1: Mine's racing too—round it goes.

C-2: Push your car faster, Mark, like this. Wow————wow ————mine's going as fast as anything—as anything and fast as a train.

C-1: Mine's going fast as a rocket—whooooosh.

C-2: Watch out, Mark—my car's coming fast. I think there'll be a crash—make yours come to mine.

C-1: Yes, there will be a big crash. Mine's coming—watch out— brrrrr there————there crash.

C-2: Oh, an accident, an accident! My car's on fire!

C-1: Fetch the fire engine————the cars are burning all up.

C-2: And the people are getting all burnt up too! (He takes up a lorry and makes fire engine noises.) Er-Er. Er-Er—here's the fire engine coming.

C-1: Bring it here, John, by the cars. Put the water on.

C-2: Get out the thingummy—the long thing. You know.

C-1: Yes. Whooooosh—all water going on the fire. Er-er—the ambulance is coming to take the people to hospital.

(Tough 1974, 17–18)

————

(Now they are looking at a shoe box with the intention of making it into a garage.)

C-1: Well, you know, garages have to have doors.

C-2: Sometimes they don't.

C-1: Garages have to have doors that will open and shut.

C-2: My grandad has one and he puts his car in and that hasn't doors.

C-1: But a garage has doors—and you lock the door so nobody can take it, the car, you see.

C-2: My grandad has a car thing and it hasn't doors on. It just keeps the rain off you.

C-1: Oh, well. Shall we make a garage or a car thing like your grandad's?

C-2: Well, I don't know how to put doors on.

C-1: I would think of glue or pins or something like that.

C-2: No. Put it this way up, see? And cut it.

C-1: Yes, that might be all right.

C-2: Right, Mark, right. I'll get the scissors.

(Tough 1974, 21)

In the first excerpt, the boys' action and talk are mutually supportive, whereas in the second excerpt, their talk stands more on its own; but in both they are building a meaningful social event together. Conversation, from infancy onward, is a profoundly social, connecting act.

If this is so, why is it that children's conversation finds so little support in classrooms? In many of the classrooms I visit, the only kind of talk that is sanctioned is "performance talk"—"individual distinction talk"—in which a child, called on by the teacher, answers her known-answer question. I hear teachers reprimand children for talking when they "should be working," for talking when they "should be listening," for talking "too loud," for talking "in the wrong place," for talking "about the wrong thing," for talking "to the wrong person," for talking "without raising your hand," for talking "too much."[2] Where and when and how, then, does a child talk with friends in class? Of course, conversation among the children *does* happen; the social urge is irrepressible. But it happens without the teacher's blessing and, too often, surreptitiously.[3] Typically there is much support for performance talk, but the talk that serves that deeply human purpose of connecting with others often finds little support in the classroom.

Often . . . but not always. In some classrooms, connecting-with-others talk is valued and encouraged. Listen to this group of kindergarten children and their teacher. The teacher has asked the children, "How do you know if somebody likes you?" Before long the children, through their talk, are sharing remembered experiences.

> *Deana:* Jill, remember when you and me were in your father's car sucking our thumbs?
>
> *Jill:* Oh, yeah. That was so much fun. My daddy kept singing, "Rock-a-bye baby in the treetop." Remember?
>
> *Fred:* Hey, Wally. Remember at Eddie's birthday party we put those metal kettles on our heads?
>
> *Tanya:* Lisa, remember when I first came to your house and I didn't know where the bathroom was? And then we put the boats in the bathtub?
>
> *Teacher:* Are you children saying that you know someone likes you if you remember nice things you did together?
>
> *Ellen:* Remember when we were looking for the black kitty at your house, Kim? And we said, "Here, kitty, here's kitty" and we were laughing so much?
>
> *Kim:* And it was in the closet? I remember that.
>
> *Warren:* Kenny, remember in nursery school we brought snow inside in our hats and the teacher was laughing?
>
> *Kenny:* Hey, let's do that again, okay?

(Paley 1981, 151–52)

"Speaking creatures" indeed! How powerfully the expressive medium of talk serves these children's social purposes—that medium which is immediate, instantly available to all, and invites all to construct "text" together. These children's connecting talk is welcomed and valued in this classroom, which is largely why these children have so much of shared experience to draw on in their talk.

In its carrying out of social acts (like inviting or arguing), in its immediacy, and in its joint activity in conversation, talk seems to be the expressive channel par excellence for the social beings children are. But there is another side to this social power of talk. Like most powerful instruments, it is double-edged. My son reminded me of this fact in a particularly striking way when he was about five. I had sensed an approaching conflict between him and another child and I had quickly given the standard reminder, "Remember, Erik, we don't hit. Hitting hurts other people and we don't do that. We use words instead." And he said quietly, more to himself than to me, "Yeah, but words hurt more." He was right, of course, and I had no reply. The power of talk: the power to heal and the power to hurt; the power to bring us into relationships with others, but also to exclude us from those relationships.

> You can't play.
> I'm not going to invite you to my birthday.
> It's *our* secret; we're not telling *you*.
> You're not my best friend anymore.

We've heard it so often in the talk of children, perhaps hear it still in echoes from our own childhood. And the power of talk to include and to exclude is not only in what children say, but also in particular ways of talking. To share a group's ways of speaking is often to be *in* that group, while to speak in other ways is to be an outsider to that group. Children know this, of course, and that is why they often invent special speaking codes and styles (e.g., pig Latin, slang) which designate some as *in* group and others as *out* group. But many different ways of speaking exist that were not deliberately invented for purposes of including or excluding others, but which have the effect of including or excluding, nonetheless. The particular pronunciations one uses, one's particular words and ways of combining them, the expressive flourishes one uses (or does not use)—all of these mark an individual as from "our" place, time, social background or from some "other." So too do one's ways of using talk—how and in what situations one tells a story or a joke, or asks a question, or issues an invitation—all these and many more ways of using talk indicate group membership.[4] You're one of us; you're not one of us. You belong, but *you* don't. "I talk like you" becomes "I am like you" becomes "I like you."

And so talk gives children social power—to connect with or include others, but also to separate from or exclude others.

To Understand the World

A host of words come to mind designating language acts we engage in as we attempt to better understand our world: inquire, explain, inform, wonder, generalize, clarify, confirm, . . . The list is a long one. It is possible to engage in these acts in writing. However, talk may contribute to a child's building of understanding in special ways.

Just as children's use of talk to connect with others is evident early in their lives, so too is their use of talk to explore their world, to make sense of it. Britton goes so far as to suggest that a child begins "with the drive to explore the world he is born into," and that speech early becomes its "principal instrument" (Britton 1973, 93). He may be right. Child language research has documented that, in the one-word stage (i.e., when a child's "sentences" are limited to a single word, often with an accompanying action or gesture), the child is already using these single word utterances to inquire (Dore 1975; Halliday 1977). It is easy even for an outsider to hear the difference between the child's "Daaaaady" (calling) and "Daddy?" (with rising intonation and a quizzical look).

As the child's language system becomes more complex, her talk serves even more powerfully to help her make sense of the world. Listen to this two-year-old as she uses her short, simple sentences (two or three heavy content words strung together) to find out about the old-to-new continuum.

> (The child is in the bathtub playing with toys.)
>
> C: Gammy make those? (Refers to bathtub toys.)
>
> M: No. Gammy didn't make those.
>
> C: Gammy got those?
>
> M: No. Mommy and Daddy got those.
>
> C: Oh. Brand new?
>
> M: No, they're old.
>
> C: Throw away?
>
> M: Well, we may think about it. They're not really good blocks. Maybe Santa Claus'll bring you some better blocks. OK?

C: OK. (Child indicates another toy.) Gammy Gammy gave those me?

M: Yes, your Gammy gave those to you.

C: Oh. Brand new?

M: Uh-huh. They're brand new. Remember, they came in that package? Before Thanksgiving?

C: (Child indicates a different toy.) Mommy Daddy get those?

M: Yeah.

C: Oh. Old?

M: Not too. Got them to go on the airplane to see Gammy. 'Member?

C: OK.

M: They're pretty new. Pretty new.

C: Pretty new?

M: Uh-huh.

C: (Child indicates a different toy.) Those new?

M: No, those are old.

C: OK. (Child indicates a different toy.) Those, that old?

M: Pretty old.

C: Pretty old?

M: Uh-huh.

C: Those old? Gammy give it me?

M: No, Gammy didn't give those to you. Mommy and Daddy got those.

C: Oh. Those brand new?

M: No, they're old.

C: Still brand . . . still . . . still brand new?

M: No, they're not still brand new. They're old.

(Urzúa 1977, quoted in Lindfors 1987, 262–63)

Many children put their sense-making talk to good use in storyreading situations, as the following four-year-old does while her mother reads her a bedtime story.

> (Mother is reading a story that involves a rabbit and a squirrel sleeping in a tree.)
>
> M: (reading) "But the red squirrel pushed and shoved him until they were both settled snug and peaceful, high up in the tree under the stars."
>
> C: Where do rabbits really sleep?
>
> M: In their holes.

C: Under the ground?
M: Uh-huh. "The next day—"
C: Where do squirrels sleep?
M: In their trees.
C: Do they have nest-es?
M: They build nests in trees.
C: Squirrels do too?
M: Uh-huh.
C: But, who lays eggs?
M: Birds.
C: Ducks do too.
M: Well, ducks are birds. Fish lay eggs.
C: Huh-uh! (meaning no)
M: Yes, they do. Right in the water.
C: What else?
M: Uh, what else lay eggs? Turtles lay eggs.
C: Huh-uh!
M: They do. Go ask Daddy. They do![5]

(Lindfors 1987, 263)

It would seem that Margaret Donaldson is right: "We are, by nature, questioners. We approach the world wondering about it, entertaining hypotheses which we are eager to check" (Donaldson 1979, 67). One four-year-old recognized his own questioning tendencies; he told his mother, "I'm a why-er, you are a because-er" (Chukovsky 1968, 31)!

If the urge to make sense of the world runs so deep in children, and if their talk is such a powerful tool for their exploration, why is it that, in the classrooms I visit, I hear so much of performance talk and so little of exploratory talk? Why so much of a "tamed and house-trained curiosity" and "a tamed and house-trained language to match"?

> Young children have a curiosity and an urge to find out about the world. They pry into corners, turn over stones, stare at cranes, explore empty houses and comb rubbish dumps. All too often this curiosity is not sanctioned in school and their attention is directed instead to barren collections of information which give no hint of the excitement of discovery and doubt. Small wonder then if their language becomes barren too. It is only those affairs which create real preoccupation which can make them reach out for the language to express new understanding, new questions and new perceptions. This is the language of curiosity. It may express itself as a set of observations or be explicitly speculative but it is always the result of the child's own probing into the working of the world

... It should not be the business of school to produce a tamed and house-trained curiosity and, inevitably, a tamed and house-trained language to match. (Rosen and Rosen 1973,28)

We have become so accustomed to the "tamed and house-trained" talk of most classrooms that we may not even notice it. Nowhere is it more prevalent than in what is erroneously called "whole group *discussion.*" Here is an example from a third grade.

> *T:* Who remembers what we call these things that hang down from the ceiling? Do you remember ... (pause) ... what we just saw ... on the slides? ... (pause) ... Okay, I'm going to say it, and say it after me. Stalactites. They have to hang on tight. Stalactites. Everybody.
>
> *Cs:* Stalactites.
>
> *T:* Okay, now we can see something else in this picture. It starts in the bottom. Who remembers the name for these? They go up from the floor ...
>
> *Cs:* Stalagmites.
>
> *T:* Then, we see something that goes from the bottom of the cave all the way to the top, or from the top all the way to the bottom. Who remembers the name for this?
>
> *C:* I know. I know.
>
> *T:* What is it?
>
> *C:* Stalagmites.
>
> *T:* Well, a stalagmite starts at the bottom ... what could be coming off the bottom?
>
> *C:* Stalagmites.
>
> *T:* Stalagmites. And what could be coming down from the top?
>
> *Cs:* Stalactites.
>
> *T:* Good, stalactites. And what could be maybe starting at the bottom and going up to the top and starting at the top and going all the way to the bottom? What could be called that? . . . (pause) ... do you remember? Columns. Let's say that.
>
> *Cs:* Columns.
>
> *T:* Columns.[6]

(Lindfors 1987, 79)

But exploratory talk—sense-making talk—can happen in whole group discussion. Again it is Paley and her kindergarten class that provides the example.

> (Warren is Chinese and Akemi is Japanese.)
> *Teacher:* If you were in charge of the world, would you make only one language or many languages, the way it is now?

Tanya: One language. Oh yes! Then I could understand everyone in the whole world.

Eddie: No, let it stay this way so different countries keeps on being not the same. Then you take trips to see what those countries are like and how they talk.

Ellen: I like the world the way it is but I don't like fighting.

Teacher: Is that because they have different languages?

Ellen: Well, if they can't understand each other they might think good words sound like bad words.

Wally: She means like if someone says, "Let's play," in French, then in Chinese they might think he said, "Let's fight."

Warren: Keep it this way because if you're Chinese you would have to learn English.

Teacher: Would English have to be the language everyone learns?

Warren: I don't know what God likes to talk. Wait, I changed my mind. Let everyone say the same language. Then when my mommy and daddy speak quietly I could understand them.

Tanya: I changed my mind too. Better *not* have the same language. Here's why: whenever this whole world had the same language everyone would say they want *their* language to be the one everyone has to have. Then everyone would blame someone else for giving them the wrong language.

Akemi: If everyone speak Japan, everyone have to live there. My country too small for the big America.

Warren: Everyone can come to China. It's much bigger. Let Chinese be the language. No, I changed my mind. Let my mommy and daddy talk English *all* the time.

(Paley 1981, 119–20)

No tamed and house-trained language here!

A teacher might ask, "How can I teach my students to use exploratory talk?" But a deeper question that we all should be asking is, "What have we done in our educational system to bring about the extraordinary situation in which children—who from birth onward are relentless in their use of talk to make sense of their world—do not use their talk this way in classrooms, the very places which our society has established for the express purpose of increasing children's understanding and control of the world?" We must have worked very hard to achieve this! It is not a matter of "teaching a child how to use language in exploring"; it is simply a matter of inviting his well-developed exploratory talk into the classroom. There are two major ways teachers do this, and both involve forgetting about the talk itself and focusing instead on what is being *done*. If the teacher focuses on that, the talk takes care of itself. First, what has the teacher provided for the children to *do*? It must be something they care about, something that *matters*. Matters to *them*. If we watch and listen, children will tell us what matters to them. It's in the stories they tell us, the T-shirts they wear, the books they choose. There is nothing for children to explore, nothing for them to make sense of, in an experience that does not matter to them. The stalactites "discussion" is a good example. Vacuous labels go back and forth, but there is nothing real—there is no caring, no "ownership" (Graves 1983). Like well-trained parrots, the children provide memorized labels on cue. Tamed and house-trained talk; no exploration here. No meaning-making is apparent in the children's talk because there is no meaning to be made.

But in the kindergarten discussion the children are making meaning. They are working with a hypothetical problem which is engaging. They care about the question the teacher has posed. They care enough to sustain the discussion, to listen to one another's ideas, to reflect, to consider implications, to build on one another's contributions, to change their minds, to provide support for their suggestions, to explain their ideas, to stay on the subject, to take others' perspectives into account—in short, they care enough to do the very things we often say five-year-olds don't do. But children, even young ones, will use their talk in the making of meaning if we provide situations in which there is something to make meaning of, something to engage in, something to explore.[7]

The second way teachers invite children's exploratory talk into the classroom is to *themselves* actively engage in exploration and the talk it requires. There is no point thinking that our students will be explorers if we are not (any more than there is any point in thinking that they will be readers or writers if we ourselves are not readers or writers). It simply will not happen. Smith calls it "demonstration" when a teacher shows "how something is done" by actually engaging in doing that thing herself, for her own real reasons (Smith 1981, 108). In this case the "something" is exploring the world, making sense of it. Of course we use our talk as we do this; our children will too. That is what language is—a system that does for us the work that we are trying to do. Again, the differences in the first and second whole group discussions are striking. The teacher in the first demonstrates specific-label eliciting (What is this called? Here is a hint. Repeat after me.); the teacher in the second demonstrates playing with ideas.

Jerome Bruner recalls Miss Orcutt, his fifth-grade teacher. She played with ideas, too, as she demonstrated "negotiating the world of wonder and possibility."

> I recall a teacher, her name was Miss Orcutt, who made the statement in class, "It is a very puzzling thing not that water turns to ice at 32 degrees Fahrenheit, but that it should change from a liquid into a solid." She then went on to give us an intuitive account of Brownian movement and of molecules, expressing a sense of wonder that matched, indeed bettered, the sense of wonder I felt at that age (around ten) about everything I turned my mind to, including at the far reach such matters as light from extinguished stars still traveling toward us though their sources had been snuffed out. In effect, she was inviting me to extend *my* world of wonder to encompass *hers*. She was not just *informing* me. She was, rather, negotiating the world of wonder and possibility. Molecules, solids, liquids, movement were not facts; they were to be used in pondering and imagining. Miss Orcutt was the rarity. She was a human event, not a transmission device. (Bruner 1986, 126)

Miss Orcutt knew she did not have to "teach" Bruner and his classmates how to use talk to explore their world. They had been exploring through their talk for as long as they had *had* talk. She only needed to provide the engaging experience and the demonstration, and the talk would take care of itself.

Children's talk, inside and outside of the classroom, is a powerful means of furthering their understanding of the world. But again the power of talk is double edged. Just as surely as talk can further understanding, so it can also impede it and even create misunderstanding. Talk can clarify, but it can also confuse. Talk can free thinking, but it can also constrain it. I think right away of situations in which our teacher talk does not enhance a child's understanding. I think of the occasions when we thrust our empty verbalization into a meaning void. I think of the occasions when we "explain" a situation from our own perspective rather than from the child's and thus confuse rather than clarify the issue. I think of the teacher talk that moves the child through the preordained curriculum (calling the activity "teaching"), all the while forgetting that the child's agenda is to creatively construct understanding out of her active, exploratory engagement with the world (an ongoing activity called "learning"). The "moving-right-along" talk conflicts with and constrains the "I-wonder-how-come" talk.

The issue is not whether talk in the child's world—her own talk and the talk of others—can play a powerful role in her understanding. The issue is, rather, how that power of talk is to be used: to clarify or to confuse; to enhance understanding or to impede it; to further exploration or to constrain it; to invite speculation or to discourage it.

To Reveal Oneself

With the birth cry the individual says, "I am." That's only the beginning. Every individual continues throughout life, saying in ever more
sophisticated and diverse ways, "I am; I am *myself*, a unique being in
the world. Here is my mark." The distinctive marks we make are many:
a unique thumbprint, signature, way of walking. Not surprisingly, it is
talk that is an especially important way for children to reveal themselves and to make their marks—talk, so effortlessly and richly developed so early in their lives. Children, like the rest of us, reveal themselves in *what* they say. They tell us what they like and do not like (and
why), what they think they are and are not good at, what they hope
does and does not happen. But they also reveal themselves in how
they talk about these things. Some sociolinguists speak of "idiolect,"
one's own individual linguistic system (vocabulary, pronunciation,
sentence structure). Others talk of personal "style," one's own individual way of using language. In both, a child's talk conveys not only
content; it also conveys the child's own self. In their talking style
children convey a personality that is lighthearted, solemn, impulsive,
reflective, temperamental, and so on. And in their response to the talk
of others, children convey the unique people they are—accepting,
judgmental, competitive, appreciative, and so on. Why is it that, several months into a new school year when a teacher has gotten to know
her children, she can sit alone in a quiet place and hear each child's
distinctive talk in her "mind's ear"—a particular voice, particular
rhythms, favorite words, characteristic phrasing? She thinks of one
child and "hears" a complaint, she thinks of another and "hears" a joke
or an argument or a question or an explanation or an interminable
story of a recent event. In their talk, children reveal themselves; they
make their distinctive mark in their world, their "I-am-myself" in talk.

How does this talk fare in the classroom? In classrooms where
teachers see children as clay to be molded, the answer is that it does
not fare so well, for teaching-as-clay-molding tends to mold toward a
particular preferred shape. The children come to know that particular
ways with ideas and the talk that expresses them are approved; e.g.,
there are approved ways to interpret a story, to solve a problem, to be
humorous, etc. Insofar as they shape their ideas and talk to conform to
the limited set of behaviors that bears the teacher's seal of approval,
the children lose—or at least hide—their "I-am-myself" in talk.

But the child's development of language before coming to school
reveals a child who bears no resemblance to a clay lump and a process
that does not push and pound and pummel the child's expression into

particular forms. In fact, some child language acquisition research has focused on the ways in which the infant's and toddler's expressive behaviors shape the talk that adults (and others) use in interacting with the child.[8] Instead of being a clay lump, the child turns out to be one who creatively constructs language out of his or her ongoing experience in a language-filled world—people all around talking with one another and with the child, using talk to serve their many diverse social and cognitive purposes. Each child's experience of language is unique: unique both in the set of meanings expressed around and with the child and in the ways those meanings are expressed. Out of this absolutely unique experience comes the child's own talk—his or her own meanings and expression of them.

Graves speaks of the crucial importance of *voice* in writing:

> The writing process has a driving force called voice . . . it underlies every part of the process. To ignore voice is to present the [writing] process as a lifeless, mechanical act. . . . Teachers who attend to voice listen to the person in the [written] piece. . . . Voice is the imprint of ourselves in our writing. It is that part of the self that pushes the writing ahead, the dynamo in the process. (Graves 1983, 227)

Graves's "voice" in writing is analogous to the "I-am-myself" in talk—the person in the talk, the driving force, the imprint of the self. I hear five-year-old Erica's imprint in her rendition of *The Three Little Kittens*:

> You naughty kittens. You dirty kittens. My kids are dirty kittens. Then you shall have no pie. Aren't y'all embarrassed for me to be ironin' and washin' y'all's own clothes. Y'all should know how. You dirty kittens! Scrub on those mittens! Scrub on those mittens! And hang them out to dry. (Seawell 1985, 140; quoted in Lindfors 1987, 451)

And I hear Akemi's imprint in the story she dictates to her kindergarten teacher:

> Now I telling story, okay? Is Halloween story: One day four colors walking. But one witch sees four colors. Witch with four hands. Witch holds four colors. "Let go, let go!" Four colors running. Witch running. Four colors running home. Is Mother. Oh, good. (Paley 1981, 125)

But again the power of talk is double edged. Talk can conceal the self just as surely as it can reveal the self. Children's talk can convey a self that is not their own, not who they are but who they wish others to think they are. As teachers do we encourage this in children more than we realize? Do our constant "positive reinforcements" for behavior which is acceptable to us perhaps encourage children to attempt to project selves designed to please us, rather than to convey the selves they are and wish to be? Graves expresses concern about school experience threatening the self in the child's writing: "The school experience can . . . remove voice from the writing, and the person from the print, until there is no driving force left" (Graves 1983, 244). Just as surely, school experience can threaten the self in children's talk, encouraging them to present an "acceptable," conforming self, rather than the distinctive self that is theirs alone.

The Quiet Child

It is a fact that we humans evolved into creatures who have the capacity to speak. It is also a fact that some of us do it more than others. At long last, there are signs that we may be becoming more aware of quiet children, aware of them, that is, as beings who are not socially, emotionally, or intellectually impaired. First and second language acquisition research has begun to document the effectiveness of an "observer" or "comprehender" strategy in language development (Nelson 1973; Fillmore 1983). This research validates the quiet child's ways of developing and using language as an intellectual and social tool. Recent research gives this important message: A child who is relatively less talkative is not thereby handicapped in language or intellectual or social development—at least not unless we impose a handicap by valuing "talky" children more than others.

But whatever the message of this recent research, traditionally we have, as teachers, been quick to characterize quiet children as "painfully shy" (Is the quietness painful for the child or for us?), "retiring," "awkward," "unsociable," "unwilling to participate," "passive," "slow," "uncooperative." And we have, with the best of intentions, tried to encourage all children to be talkers. "Speak up so everybody can hear you," we say, or "We haven't heard from you yet, Stacy" or "I'm looking for more volunteers to tell us . . . ." I have mentioned already the heavy orientation in many classrooms toward talk as public performance (usually called "group discussion"). Such an orientation is not going to increase the likelihood of a quiet child talking more, of course. I think of Kingston:

> It was when I found out I had to talk that school became a misery
> . . . I did not speak and felt bad each time that I did not speak. I read

aloud in first grade, though, and heard the barest whisper with little squeaks come out of my throat. "Louder," said the teacher, who scared the voice away again. (Kingston 1975, 193)

Surely Kingston's teacher was well intentioned; just as surely, she was not helpful.

My experience with children whom adults designate as "quiet" is not that they are children who do not talk, but rather that they are children who are not inclined toward the public performance kind of talk that is valued in many classrooms. To be one who does not volunteer during whole group discussion or bring something for show-and-tell is not to be a nontalker. We would only hope that classroom opportunities are abundant for children to talk in whatever amounts and in whatever ways and situations they are comfortable talking. For some children this is quiet talk with a best friend on the playground or at lunch.

Why is it that as teachers we are so intent on getting less talkative children to talk more? I think it is because there is a general idea loose in the world that the *production* of talk—actually emitting verbal sounds—is empowering. But is it? Does the act of speaking itself necessarily give a child power and involvement? This is an important question because if true, then more talk is better for everyone and we could justify pressuring quieter children to talk more "for their own good."

I think that another look at evolution is in order here. Homo sapiens did indeed evolve into speaking creatures, but so did they evolve into speech-interpreting creatures. Speaking and interpreting are, after all, but two sides of a single coin. Biological mechanisms (anatomical and neurological) evolved in us no less for interpreting than for producing talk. And it may be that substantial empowerment for the quieter child lies in the capacity to interpret and respond to talk.

Quiet children, no less than any others, are actively engaged in connecting with others, understanding their world, and revealing themselves within it—making their mark. An important source of connecting with others for these children may be their response to the talk of others, for example, accepting another's invitation to play, or laughing at another's joke. The talk of others around these children may offer important ideas to help them increase their understanding of the world—new ideas to consider, reflect on, reject. And it may be in the quieter children's response to others' talk that they reveal themSELVES—as sympathetic people or sullen ones or as people who appreciate humor. Notice that all of these depend on the presence of talk in the quieter child's world—talk to interpret and to respond to. It is the *presence* of talk which is crucial: talk of the child, talk with the child, talk around the child.

Finally

The oral language "curriculum" is not a scope and sequence of behavioral objectives, not lists of skills to be mastered, not bits of knowledge to be attained. It is, rather, the ongoing process of inviting and sustaining children's talk and response in classrooms, as they carry out their deepest human urgings: to connect with others, to understand their world, and to reveal themselves within it. The classroom must be a community for speech-producing and speech-interpreting creatures. These are the creatures evolution built children to be. Every child we teach is just such a creature.

Now *that* is something to think about.

Notes

1. For some children, "talk" is carried out manually by signing.
2. For a fuller discussion, see Lindfors 1987, Chapter 12.
3. Last night I happened upon my report card from fifth grade. At the midpoint of the year the teacher had written this ominous comment: "Judy's constant chattering may affect future work." Times have not changed. I suspect that what she perceived as my "constant chattering" was my connecting talk with friends.
4. See Heath 1983 for a description of ways of developing and using language in three different communities, and the resulting difficulties that the children of these communities encountered when they came to school.
5. I am indebted to Carol Peterson for this example.
6. I am indebted to Mimi Miran for this example.
7. See Lindfors 1987, Chapter 10, for examples.
8. See the Motherese literature, well represented in Snow and Ferguson 1977.

Works Cited

Britton, J. 1973. *Language and Learning*. Harmondsworth, England: Pelican Books.
Bruner, J. 1986. *Actual Minds, Possible Worlds*. Cambridge, Mass.: Harvard University Press.

Chukovsky, K. 1968. *From Two to Five.* Translated and edited by Miriam Morton. Berkeley: University of California Press.

Donaldson, M. 1979. *Children's Minds.* New York: W. W. Norton & Company.

Dore, J. 1975. "Holophrases, Speech Acts and Language Universals." *Journal of Child Language* 2: 21–40.

Fillmore, L. 1983. "The Language Learner as an Individual: Implications of Research on Individual Differences for the ESL Teacher." In *On TESOL '82: Pacific Perspectives on Language Learning and Teaching*, edited by M. Clarke and J. Handscombe, 157–73. Washington, D.C.: Teachers of English to Speakers of Other Languages.

———. 1976. *The Second Time Around: Cognitive and Social Strategies in Second Language Acquisition.* Doctoral dissertation. Stanford University, Stanford, Calif.

Graves, D. 1983. *Writing: Teachers and Children at Work.* Portsmouth, N.H.: Heinemann Educational Books.

Halliday, M.A.K. 1977. *Learning How to Mean.* New York: Elsevier North-Holland, Inc.

Heath, S. B. 1983. *Ways with Words: Language, Life, and Work in Communities and Classrooms.* New York: Cambridge University Press.

Kingston, M. H. 1975. *The Woman Warrior: Memoirs of a Girlhood among Ghosts.* New York: Vintage Books.

Lindfors, J. W. 1987. *Children's Language and Learning.* 2nd ed. Englewood Cliffs, N.J.: Prentice-Hall, Inc.

Nelson, K. 1973. "Structure and Strategy in Learning to Talk." *Monographs of the Society for Research in Child Development* 38, nos. 1–2: serial 149.

Paley, V. G. 1981. *Wally's Stories.* Cambridge, Mass.: Harvard University Press.

Rosen, C., and H. Rosen. 1973. *The Language of Primary School Children.* London: Penguin Education for the Schools Council.

Seawell, R.P.M. 1985. *A Micro-Ethnographic Study of a Spanish/English Bilingual Kindergarten in Which Literature and Puppet Play Were Used as a Method of Enhancing Language Growth.* Doctoral dissertation. The University of Texas at Austin.

Slobin, D. I. 1979. *Psycholinguistics.* 2nd ed. Glenview, Ill.: Scott, Foresman and Company.

Smith, F. 1981. "Demonstrations, Engagement, and Sensitivity: A Revised Approach to Language Learning." *Language Arts* 58: 103–12.

Snow, C. E., and C. Ferguson, eds. 1977. *Talking to Children: Language Input and Acquisition.* London: Cambridge University Press.

Tough, J. 1974. *Focus on Meaning.* London: George Allen & Unwin Ltd.

Trevarthen, C. 1977. "Descriptive Analyses of Infant Communicative Behavior." In *Studies in Mother-Infant Interaction*, edited by H. R. Schaffer. London: Academic Press, Inc.

Urzúa, C. G. 1977. *A Sociolinguistic Analysis of the Requests of Mothers to Their Two-Year-Old Daughters.* Doctoral dissertation. The University of Texas at Austin.

3 Oral Language and Learning

Douglas Barnes
University of Leeds

Schools are funny places. We ask students to participate in achieving goals that they do not share, and we want them to be enthusiastic about it. It is no wonder that many classroom discussions are lackluster and consist mainly of single-word answers punctuating long-winded teacher questions. In the world outside of school, however, children set their own goals, and many youngsters who are monosyllabic within the confines of the school are articulate talkers when it comes to accomplishing those self-defined goals. Is it realistic to expect that students can draw upon their outside-world speaking skills as they deal with the institutional demands of school discourse?

When we speak of language in education we are often thinking of extending those skills and competences in speech and writing which are amongst the goals of teaching in elementary schools or in English classes in secondary schools. In this paper I shall direct attention instead towards language as a medium of learning, and for this reason I shall begin by considering the demands which school curricula place upon children's uses of language.

Typical Classroom Talk

Some typical patterns of classroom communication appeared in a geography lesson which one of my students recorded. At first glance it seems entirely normal: we are all so accustomed to lesson-talk that we find it difficult to see it afresh, to perceive what it makes possible and what it excludes. In this extract, the teacher is asking about the shape of sand dunes, while the students have in front of them a photograph of a desert scene:

> T: Sand dunes. They're usually in an unusual . . . a specific shape
> . . . a special shape. . . . Does anybody know what shape they are?
> Not in straight lines . . .

P: They're like hills.

T: Yes, they're like low hills.

P: They're all humpy up and down.

P: They're like waves.

T: Good, they're like waves.

P: They're like . . .

T: They're a special shape.

P: They're like boulders . . . sort of go up and down getting higher and higher.

T: I don't know about getting higher and higher.

P: Something like pyramids.

T: Mm . . . wouldn't call them pyramids, no.

P: They're in a semicircle.

T: Ah, that's getting a bit nearer. They're often in a semicircle and nearly always . . . we call them . . . well, it's part of a semicircle. . . . What do we call part of a semicircle? You think of the moon . . . perhaps you'll get the shape.

P: Water.

T: No, not shaped like water. . . . Yes?

P: An arc.

T: An arc . . . oh, we're getting ever so much nearer.

P: Crescent.

T: A crescent shape. Have you heard that expression . . . a crescent shape? I wonder if anybody could draw me a crescent shape on the board. Yes, they're nearly all that shape. . . .

This teacher is receptive and encouraging, for she is sensitive to her eleven-year-old students as people. Our task is not to criticize her but to understand some of the communicative constraints present in a typical classroom exchange. As usual, the teacher defines the topic and task, and the students must surmise what she is after. At first, they think she wants a description of the photograph, and therefore offer her phrases such as "bumpy up and down." They change their strategy only when she signals with "They're a special shape" that she wants a technical term, not a description. It is as if there were two language games: the students were playing the Describe-the-Picture game, whereas the teacher wanted the Hunt-the-Word game. Their task is to home in on what she wants, using clues such as "You think of the moon" to guide them, though the moon is quite irrelevant to understanding sand dunes. Some students fail to recognize the clues: most notable is the one who is still offering the descriptive "Water," having apparently missed the teacher's signal. The students can only reply to the teacher's initiatives, and their replies are designed neither to inform the teacher nor to restructure their own thoughts but only to show that they are taking part in the lesson. It has been suggested that the ability to "take part" in this sense plays a major role in determining whether a student is seen by the teacher as "intelligent" or not.

We should also note that what the students say is restricted to phrases and single words, so that they cannot develop or explore their responses to the lesson. (I shall say more later about "exploration.") In this episode, teacher and taught never recognize that they are talking about different matters; the students are looking at the photograph, but the teacher's "crescent" refers to a view from above. Because the exchange of ideas is so restricted and the students' perspectives given so little importance, classroom dialogue allows such misunderstandings to go unrecognized. Teaching a school subject, whether it be elementary math or economics in high school, is partly a matter of enabling students to adopt a pre-existing mode of discourse, and a good deal of teaching time and skill is devoted to that purpose (Edwards and Mercer 1987). (Of course, "discourse" here does not mean only the language but the ideas and ways of thinking that go with it.) I do not wish to question that purpose, but to suggest that it can be pursued too wholeheartedly, at the expense of the students' eventual ability to join in the thinking for themselves, which I see as the final goal of schooling.

There are three ways in which teaching of the familiar kind illustrated in the "sand dunes" passage may not match the teacher's intentions. First, it does not allow the students enough time to work on whatever new knowledge is being presented to them and make it their own. (This will be returned to later, as it is an essential step in my argument.) Second, it is a poor model for other kinds of learning which are more important outside school, since it excludes the opportunity for students to define their goals, to enquire and gather information and ideas for themselves, to construct and criticize, question and interpret. All these are crucial elements in the lives outside school for which students are being prepared. Third, it ignores what the students already know; this is a most important element in learning, since new knowledge is built upon the reconstruction of the old.

The Teacher's Dilemma

At the heart of teaching lies a dilemma for each teacher to resolve. Schools are institutions where young people are socialized into aspects of the culture they are to share: they are expected to assimilate pictures of the world, to learn ways of going about their activities, and to take over some of the values and skills which constitute the culture, or rather the diverse cultures which make up society. Moreover, they are required to take part in cultural activities and milieux which are quite different from those they have previously experienced in their everyday lives. They have to learn to respond appropriately to teachers' questions, to join in standard activities, to pick up clues from teachers' voices, at the same time as learning what constitutes an acceptable piece of mathematical work or an acceptable composition in English (Edwards and Mercer 1987). That is, they learn to operate within frames of reference and to accept purposes and ways of organizing their activities which claim validity irrespective of their immediate usefulness to the student. (The young student who replies to the teacher's "Wouldn't it be nice to do some counting now?" with the answer, "No!" quickly learns that his or her interest in the matter is being solicited only as a matter of form.) This contrasts with children's experiences outside school, where they learn skills and knowledge because they want to.

At the very same time as schooling requires pupils to pursue goals that they do not share, it also seeks to transcend itself, for in a few years' time each one of these tyros will be out in the world making his or her own choices. We want these new young adults to be able to look critically at the world about them; we want them to be able to consider evidence, to make moral and social judgments, to "think for themselves" and thus to play an active part in shaping their own lives. This goal implies that teachers should eventually attempt to make themselves unnecessary. How is it possible to introduce students to preexisting systems and at the same time enable them to make independent choices? That is the dilemma which I propose to consider in relation to spoken language in classrooms, for the interaction between teacher and student through talk must play a central role in the strategies by which teachers seek to reconcile the two horns of the dilemma. The examples are drawn from secondary schools, though very similar considerations apply to younger children (Tizard and Hughes 1984).

Students' Speech In and Out of School

What language demands does schooling lay upon young people? Some years ago some of my students transcribed tape recordings of lessons in various curricular subjects which were being taught to students during their first few weeks at secondary schools in England (Barnes, Britton, and Torbe 1987). What surprised us most was the young people's passivity; they asked no questions and made no suggestions. It was as if they had no curiosity. When we looked at what the teachers were saying and doing, the reason for this was clear: the students were never invited to contribute from their own experience. Almost the only questions asked by the teachers were what we came to call "pseudo-questions," since they were asked simply to test the students' recollection or understanding. ("What can you tell me about a Bunsen burner?" asked one teacher. To answer, the student had to select from what he or she had been told. An infinite array of possible answers, such as "You can burn paper in it," would have been true but unacceptable.)

The only questions asked by students were intended to confirm that they had grasped the teacher's wishes. They played no active part in the learning: they made no attempt to test whether they had understood, to raise contrary examples, or to make links with their out-of-school experience. I have since come to realize that what we saw was normal; many North American studies of classrooms have reported similar findings. The teachers were concerned to introduce their students to new frames of reference, new ways of thinking, new ways of going about schoolwork. Only one or two of the teachers had any wish to tap the boys' and girls' existing views of how the world is, or to find out how they understood the matter in hand. Yet this must be an essential part of developing, refining, or even correcting their existing understanding.

Moreover, the lessons which we observed made very narrow demands upon the students' uses of language. In general, they were required only to answer, and these answers required mainly recall of information and procedures already presented to them by the teacher. They were not encouraged to initiate exchanges, to inquire, question, persuade, expatiate, surmise, criticize. It is probable that there was a sharp contrast between the range of functions which language was playing in their everyday lives and the competences that were being called on in lessons. Indeed, teachers often underestimate their students' language skills because they meet only those which the students are able to display in the restricted milieu of the classroom.

Since my teacher-students and I were concerned to explore what opportunities for participation were offered to young students, we were surprised and even a little shocked at what we found. Yet those teachers whom we observed might well have retorted that they were carrying out their proper task. They were certainly presenting academic knowledge to their eleven-year-old students; we doubted, however, whether they were giving those students enough opportunity to make that knowledge their own.

It is commonplace that school students seem to be different people outside school. There they are already deeply engaged in lives of their own, trying to make sense of the environment they find themselves in. This is not merely a matter of developing social awareness and skills, but of explanations of how the physical world operates. All the time, they are talking, testing their ideas on their peers, on their parents, on older relatives and friends, talking their way into a dependable account of how things are. They want to understand—not in order to complete a school task or to get a grade—but to pursue a purpose of their own: their explanations of how balls bounce relate to the games they play; their accounts of why people do things relate to their own hopes and purposes. In the world outside school, people talk and write and make things for some purpose, at the very least for the fun of it; in schools we set exercises as ends in themselves. How can teachers bring into school something of the desire to understand and control that makes young people's out-of-school talk engage with real problems and purposes? If schooling is to strengthen the learner's eventual ability to take responsibility for himself or herself, then it is this purposeful talk that must be harnessed.

Teachers' Perceptions of Language and Learning

Some years ago I asked a sample of secondary school teachers why they set written work and what they took into account in doing so, and analyzed their replies according to whether they tended more towards "Transmission" or "Interpretation" (Barnes 1976). Teachers at the "Transmission" end of the scale taught as if their task was to transmit a pre-existing body of knowledge and practices, while the learner's task was to reproduce the teacher's performance. The other end of the scale was represented by what we called "Interpretation," because some teachers assumed that, in talking and writing, the learners were actually working upon what they had been taught, reinterpreting what they already knew, and relating it to the new ideas and experiences that had been presented to them in school. Transmission teachers saw language as a mere medium which did not affect the learner's grasp of knowledge; interpretation teachers believed that certain kinds of talking and writing played a valuable part in the learning.

Although this research referred to teachers' perceptions of the functions of written language, it seems very likely that similar perceptions direct their use of talk in the classroom.

The view taken by the Interpretation teachers is now called Constructivism by some psychologists. When we learn, we do not simply add to our store, but in a greater or lesser degree reshape and reinterpret our existing pictures of the world. Some new experiences, some information and ideas, fit comfortably into our view of the world; others require us in a greater or lesser degree to redraw the picture in order to take full account of them. An example may make this clearer. A science teacher passed a beaker full of cold water through a Bunsen flame, and when the class had seen that the bottom of the beaker had become misted with droplets of water he asked them where the water had come from. Most of the students tried to assimilate this to their existing ideas, suggesting that the water from the atmosphere had condensed on the glass, though this had not been the case before the beaker was passed through the flame. Other suggestions included the idea that the water had come from inside the beaker.

T: Wonder what you meant by "steamed up." What's steam? What is steam?

P1: Heat rising off the water.

T: Steam is . . . heat rising? (Yes) From?

P1: The water.

T: From the water. Which water?

P1: In the beaker.

T: So, you think this that appeared on the outside of the beaker . . . is heat rising on the inside of the beaker. So what, where, how's it got there? (Pause) Come on, follow through your idea. How did it get from there to there?

P1: It went over the top.

T: It went over the top. So you think that . . . something came from in there and went over the top to there. Fair enough. That's your idea. You've got another idea, apparently.

P2: This beaker is cold. And you put that under and it makes it steam 'cause hot touching cold straight away. You know.

T: All right. Now what's cold and what's hot?

P2: The water's cold that's in the beaker and all the beaker's going to be cold.

T: . . . The beaker is cold. Right?

P2: So when it touches the cold beaker, . . . because of the heat touching the cold it will just steam it up . . . with the water.

T: Right. So that it's something to do with the heat . . . meeting cold?

P2: Mm.

T: And that's causing a steaming up.

As the lesson continued it became clear that the class had to make a major adjustment in their thinking, since the water was a product of the burning of the gas. The idea of water in connection with burning was so unfamiliar that it required the students to make a radical change in their view of the nature of burning. In this case, it was not possible for the students simply to store the experience within their existing schemes for understanding the world: they had to alter the scheme itself to incorporate the idea that water and burning are not irreconcilable. Such shifts in the schemes through which we understand the world are often slow to take place: they may even be painful and resisted. The struggle to reconcile the old and the new sometimes takes place through writing or through silent thought, but for most of us it takes place most readily in conversation with others.

Talking as a Means of Learning

What then is the point of asking students to talk (or for that matter to write) about what they are learning? In order to understand how learning can be supported and advanced by the students' own talk, it is useful temporarily to remove the teacher from the discussion and to listen to groups of students working on tasks they have been given. In removing the teacher, however, I am not implying that his or her participation in learning is unimportant or unnecessary. The first example is taken from a lesson in social studies; a class of twelve-year-old students has been studying the Viking groups who invaded Britain in the seventh century, and the teacher has now asked the students to decide what a Viking group would do when they first arrived on the shores of an unfamiliar country, a task requiring them to use some of the information they had been given:

> Carol: When the boat lands the first thing they'd have to do . . . be . . . to find . . . 'em place where they can build a house, and probably later on have . . . fields of their . . . crops and . . . places . . .
>
> Carol: . . . to keep . . . em . . .
>
> Barbara: They'd probably look round first.
>
> Carol: . . . cattle and (inaudible) . . . pigs and things.

Teresa: But they'd have to be out of the way of swamps and things . . . so they wouldn't be in any danger.

Barbara: You could say that when they arrived there they wouldn't use the . . . em . . . Roman things . . . had had already been put there.

Teresa: They wouldn't go near them because they were scared of the old Roman religions.

Carol: And . . . th' . . . they would p-probably . . . keep away from the . . . Roman towns erm . . . the . . . temples and that w-were mysterious and frightening places to them . . .

Carol: And . . . they were em . . .

Teresa: Yes.

Barbara: Yes . . . probably they were . . . an . . .

Carol: And they've got to take . . .

Barbara: . . . undereducated. (Amused)

Carol: . . . and they've got to take care of all their animals and things because . . . if they . . . went too far from home they could die of exposure.

The recording from which this transcription was taken makes it very clear how tentative these three girls were; the frequent occurrence of hesitations and of "probably," you could say, and so on, make it apparent even in transcript. Carol in particular is thinking aloud, ordering her thought while she is talking. She begins by making the task requirements explicit. Then Teresa mentions information which the teacher had given them about the Vikings' attitudes toward the remnants of Romano-British civilization, and they discuss this, eventually reinterpreting it in modern terms by describing the Vikings as "undereducated." Then they turn back to practical matters, and the discussion continues. The three girls are collaborating in building up a joint hypothesis, each adding a new idea to what has gone before. They are not learning in the sense of adding new facts to their store, but rather they are exploring the interrelationships and significance of the information they have already acquired, rearranging it and considering its implications. One teacher, when talking about a similar discussion, described its purpose felicitously as "working on understanding." As we have seen, conventional class teaching gives students little opportunity for such working on understanding, though it is an essential part of any learning that seeks to go beyond the mechanical recall of information. This is not to say that the teacher should not, towards the end of the lesson, take the opportunity to institute a "report back" session in which the ideas of the groups can be made more explicit and underlined.

Two Functions of Speech in the Classroom

It is useful to consider the range of uses that can be made of speech in the classroom. Students' speech can perform either of two functions, presentational or exploratory. Exploratory talk often occurs when peers collaborate in a task, when they wish to talk it over in a tentative manner, considering and rearranging their ideas. The talk is often but not always hesitant, containing uncompleted or inexplicit utterances as the students try to formulate new understandings; exploratory talk enables students to represent to themselves what they currently understand and then if necessary to criticize and change it. Acceptance and support by other members of the group play an important part in this: a critical outsider may make such exploration impossible.

Presentational talk performs a different and more public role. When students are called on in class, when they feel to be under evaluation, they seldom risk exploration, but prefer to provide an acceptable performance, a "right" answer. Some of the effects of this can be seen in the latter part of the exchange about sand dunes, quoted on page 42: the students' contributions became clipped and restricted ("water"; "an arc") because their purpose was to satisfy the teacher that they could perform as required, not to explore the topic. To say more would increase the risks of being wrong, as well as seeming inappropriate to the setting. Presentational talk and writing plays a necessary role in education, but its purpose is as much evaluation as it is learning. The questions and answers of the traditional "recitation" session inform the teacher whether students can reproduce what has been given to them: they do not support the students' attempts to relate these new ideas to what they already "know." If we take seriously what constructivist theorists tell us about learning, we see that, if teachers rely too much upon presentational talk and writing, this leaves the students no time for "working on understanding." We should not expect them to arrive without having traveled.

The three girls who were discussing the landing of the Vikings were utilizing and developing information and ideas that had been presented to them by the teacher and textbook. In so doing they showed that they had an ability to collaborate and to interpret that would probably not have appeared in a discussion led by a teacher. My purpose in illustrating such talk is not, however, to recommend small group teaching methods: they have a place in every teacher's repertoire, but they are only one aspect of good teaching.

Talking as Responding to Literature

The discussion of Viking landings required rational analysis based on the students' (no doubt limited) knowledge. We may fairly ask whether the same considerations apply to learning in English literature, where the major aims are likely to be for the students to interpret a text and respond personally to it. Some useful illustrations of what can happen are provided by a teacher who some years ago bravely arranged for a group of his students to be recorded while discussing a poem in one room, while he was recorded in another room teaching the same poem to the remainder of the class. The pupils were thirteen years old and not of high academic ability, and the poem he chose was "Original Sin" by Robinson Jeffers. The small group of students was asked to read and discuss the poem but was given no other direction. To understand the way he taught the remainder of the class it is necessary to know that, in England, teachers of English literature had adopted a constructivist view of students' responses to literature long before that name for it existed. This teacher appears to have taken the view that it is for the reader to construct a meaning for a poem, and that, consequently, his role as teacher was to guide and encourage this by questioning. Questioning is not always the most appropriate way of helping learners to think, however. Since teachers do not have direct access to their students' thoughts, it is all too easy for them to ask questions which impede learning by directing attention away from the issues that the students need to clarify. This happened to the teacher in question. He began by asking:

T: What is this poem about?
P: About the evils and that of man.
T: Mm . . . mm . . . Can you go on to say more?
P: No, not really.
T: Can you be a bit more specific?
P: Stone Age man.
T: Yes?
P: Hunting.
P: They were uncivilized.
T: Yes?
P: Just taking what they want.
T: Mm . . . mm . . . And what did they do—anybody over there?
P: Kill for . . . kill for their living.

T: Yes? Are we different?

P: We don't have to kill, sir, we get the meat from the shop, sir.

T: Pardon?

P: We're civilized aren't we?

T: Yes?

P: Other people do our dirty work.

T: Are we any different?

The teacher's well-intended questions fall flat. The first reply sums up the whole poem in a brief phrase ("About the evils and that of man"), and this seems to leave him at a loss. Perhaps as a result, the students' later responses are not attempts at interpretation of the poem but rather bids at providing "right" answers. The prevailing presentational function of classroom language has taken over: the students are not trying to make sense of the poem but to satisfy the teacher. One response is more promising, the sardonic: "We're civilized, aren't we? . . . Other people do our dirty work." It is a very pertinent line of thought, but the teacher, his attention upon opening up those aspects of the poem that he thinks useful, does not respond to this until later in the lesson. It is not my intention to criticize this teacher, who later in the lesson does make better contact with his students' thinking, but to illustrate the way in which classroom dialogue, by its very nature, narrows the range of possible interactions. In this case the teacher's efforts to support the students' explorations unintentionally impeded them. This occurs frequently enough in teacher-led discussion to suggest that it should not be the only mode of interaction in a teacher's repertoire.

On this occasion the students who worked without the teacher made better progress, as he was the first to point out. Here is an extract from the group's discussion:

> *Trevor:* Reckon the person who wrote this must have felt a bit sorry for himself . . . don't know about anyone else.
>
> *James:* It's about the cruelty of our men who are always killing animals, and people.
>
> *Trevor:* Yeah, but to prehistoric man isn't it . . .
>
> *David:* Well, it says we're all vicious here, don't it.
>
> *Rose:* Yeah, he doesn't seem to believe that we're civilized.
>
> *David:* He sort of hopes for death when he'll be cleansed don't he . . . when all his viciousness and . . .
>
> *James:* Get out of the world.

Trevor: When it says sort of man-handed ground ape . . . sort of as though we were made by someone.

David: Yeah . . .

Trevor: "The yellow dancer" . . . This must be the fire.

As in the teacher-led discussion, the group begins not with a detail of the text but with a wider perception of the self-pity evident in the poem, a judgment which seems to me exceptionally penetrating. James then makes a more conventional generalization ("It's about the cruelty of our men . . . "), and this makes it possible for them to clarify that the poem refers to all human beings, not just to the prehistoric people mentioned in the text. Rose then makes another leap of understanding by pointing out that the poem implies that we, too, are primitive. David next chooses to highlight the poet's desire to be cleansed. He does not attempt to explicate it, or to make any links (for example, with the poet's self-pity), but merely refers to it. The procedure that the group has taken up is indeed interpretive, but not through the conventional methods of literary criticism. They are, rather, highlighting and rearranging the elements of the poem, and in so doing, interpreting a detail here and there. It may seem a rationalistic discussion, but they are gradually moving closer to the experience of the poem. Later in the discussion, after the end of the quoted passage, Trevor reads out the line which describes the men watching the dying mammoth, and comments, "I reckon that was . . . sort of meaning we enjoyed the pain." The "we" is highly significant: although the students are constructing an interpretation of the poem, they are, as it were, "trying it out" in their own imaginative experience, though they find such negative feelings finally unacceptable.

Of course, not all group discussions go as well as this; such progress in exploring literature depends upon the students' attitudes to the poem, their willingness to work together, and their acceptance that such exploration constitutes useful learning. In this case their talk is a testimonial to their teacher's previous success in showing them that exploring a poem is worthwhile. Few students can be left to teach themselves, yet those of quite moderate academic abilities nevertheless have considerable ability to make sense of those parts of experience that they find worthwhile, and in a supportive context can "work on understanding" for themselves.

This group's discussion can help us to define what would constitute successful teaching of a poem; it would be teaching that enabled the students to do as these did, to find their own way into a poem, to move between overall generalizations and highlighting of details, exploring the links with their own world at the same time as the connections between parts of the poem. As we have seen, even a skillful teacher, in attempting to predict the structure of their exploration, can ask unhelpful questions.

Supporting Students' Understanding

There is no simple solution to the dilemma with which this paper began. As teachers, we wish to place our cultural competencies at the disposal of our students in the hope that they, too, will find them useful. We must interact with them so that they can join in our thinking and, if they wish, use it for themselves. If we try to impose it on them we are in danger of impeding them. As active participants in their lives, they have already taken possession of complex ways of making sense of the world, though these are not always visible in lessons. It is no service to our students to appear to suggest to them that these modes of discourse—these ways of understanding and acting—are irrelevant and useless. As teachers, we should encourage them to make use of their ability to participate and understand, for the social and cognitive skills which they have developed in various contexts in and out of school provide their most valuable resources as learners. Our task is to enable them to use these abilities in classroom talk, so that when they approach the knowledge that is our stock-in-trade they make an active and critical attempt to relate it to their own concerns and understanding of the world.

Works Cited

Barnes, D. 1976. *From Communication to Curriculum*. Harmondsworth: Penguin Books.
Barnes, D., J. Britton, and M. Torbe. 1987. *Language, the Learner and the School*. 3rd ed. Harmondsworth, England: Penguin Books.
Edwards, D., and N. Mercer. 1987. *Common Knowledge: The Development of Understanding in the Classroom*. London and New York: Methuen.
Tizard, B., and M. Hughes. 1984. *Young Children Learning*. London: Fontana.

II Talk in the Learning Community

4 Negotiation, Language, and Inquiry: Building Knowledge Collaboratively in the Classroom

Cynthia Onore
City College, CUNY

Teachers are all the time teaching about talk. We can't avoid it, since talk is our medium of exchange. When teachers tightly control the flow and the topic of talk, students learn that talk—at least talk in institutions such as schools—is disembodied from the world of meaning. When teachers share control with students, students learn that talk is a means for constructing knowledge. The scary thing is that when students do learn about talk as a vehicle for choice and for negotiating what will be learned, then teachers discover that their classrooms are full of twenty or thirty other teachers. Then you have to rethink what it means to teach. That's the scary thing, and that's the exhilarating thing when you do a good job of teaching your students about talk.

Conversations reveal much more than they literally say. The nature of entire contexts can be exposed by the kinds of conversations that take place within them. Clues about the relative status of the participants, the nature of their relationships, and the purposes they have for talking with one another are revealed by the forms and functions of the conversational language. Read the dialogue below and see if you can determine what the context is and who the speakers are:

S1: Who are these two people?

S2: A woman and her maid.

S1: What kind of relationship do they have?

S3: Friendly.

S2: They get along.

S1: Is that all?

I would like to express my deep appreciation to Shirley Gillis for opening up her classroom and exploring with me insights about children's learning. Many thanks to Garth Boomer, of course, for his responses to a draft of this paper and for sharing his ever-deepening perspectives on curriculum negotiation with me.—C. O.

S3: Well, it seems like they're friends.

S1: Yes, but, do employers and employees usually have relationships like this? Are they usually so friendly?

S2: No.

S3: Yes.

S1: Well, we have two different answers here. Does anyone agree with Sandy? Terry, do you agree?

S4: No. I don't think they're friends.

S1: OK. Now, how does the Inspector treat the maid?

S3: He's OK.

S1: Really? What does he say to her?

S2: He wants to know why she wants to learn to drive.

S1: Does the Inspector treat the maid with respect?

S5: No.

I think you'll agree that the clues in this conversation point quite clearly in one direction: this is a class "discussion." I have reproduced here only a small portion of a seven-minute segment of this high school literature lesson during which the teacher posed twenty-two questions, all of which were rapid-fire and required only factual recall through short answers, or yes/no responses. All of the teacher's questions and her automatic evaluations of each student's response communicated that there was one right answer to every question. A few students dominated what interaction there was while the rest either whispered to one another or sat quietly, looking bored. All the while, the teacher worked very hard. She was animated, enthusiastic, and energetic.

I have shown a number of people this excerpt of classroom dialogue without identifying the context or the speakers and have asked them to tell me what they think the context is and how they know. And whether or not the guessing-game players are educators, they easily recognize this context as a classroom because it captures something very familiar to anyone who's ever been a student. The dominance of one person over all of the others through controlling the substance and form of the conversation, the not-so-subtle evaluations of each answer, the insistence on one particular point of view, and the attempt to force a consensus about the topic at hand all convey the essence of "schooling."

Certainly, this teacher could have been a more skillful discussion leader. She could have varied the kinds of questions she posed so that students might have been encouraged to interpret and analyze rather than simply recall information. She might have also used strategies for supporting students in posing questions of their own. But as long as the purposes the teacher had for this "discussion" remained to test the students' recall of the story, or to guide the students toward one way of seeing the story they had read, the amount and kinds of talk the students would engage in would resemble the dialogue I have reproduced. Such so-called class discussions may in fact do more to limit learning than they do to support it. And the better teachers are at orchestrating the manner in which students swallow the bitter pill of learning, the harder it is to get beneath the surface of classroom talk and examine the structure of knowledge in which students and teachers are participating together.

Without fundamentally altering the messages the students were receiving about who has the knowledge, who determines what kind of knowledge is legitimate, and how to go about getting knowledge if you do not have it, the teacher and her class would have been locked into a "discussion" which is really a thinly veiled lecture about the one valid meaning of the story, the teacher's meaning.

My point here is that the way the teacher conducted this discussion is only one aspect of how language is being used in this classroom. This class discussion, I believe, raises larger questions about language use in the classroom. From the perspective of the relationship between language and learning, and how language and learning connect to issues of knowledge and control, there are deeper issues for exploration. For example, what is the nature of school knowledge in this classroom? What kinds of messages about school knowledge are students receiving from the classroom talk? These are the questions I will attempt to explore in the remainder of this paper.

The Nature of School Knowledge

In the classroom discussion I have described, learning is a process of reproducing the contours of the teacher's thinking, knowledge is a commodity consisting of single, correct answers, and the teacher is the sole transmitter and evaluator of learning. In other words, knowledge is in the teacher's full and individual control. Such a knowledge structure will profoundly affect and ultimately control what and how students learn, not just what and how they will talk. That, at any rate, is the principal assertion of this paper.

Based on such a small sample of classroom talk, my conclusions about teaching and learning may seem unfair. But this is exactly the

composite picture of school knowledge that Michael Stubbs (1976), a
British sociolinguist, draws after reviewing numerous studies of classroom talk. Stubbs's conclusions are supported by the findings of
Goodlad (1984) and Sizer (1984), to name just two of the many recent
critics of public schooling here in the United States. Here is Stubbs's
description of knowledge in a typical classroom:

> Classroom knowledge consists of strings of short answers which
> can be individually evaluated. Classroom knowledge is therefore
> essentially closed, not open-ended. All questions have correct
> answers. Teacher-pupil talk is effectively a monologue with the
> pupil supplying short answers on demand to contribute to the
> teacher's train of thought. (99)

Stubbs is suggesting that teachers need to go beyond simply encouraging more language use in the classroom, though that would certainly help some. Classrooms must be forums for students to set and solve
meaningful problems if learning is to be open and not closed. Teachers
must reconceptualize the kinds of control they assert if students are to
be encouraged to negotiate and explore their own lines of reasoning.
Evaluation must be tied to the learner's purposes and intentions if
assessment is to support learning. All of this implies a thoroughgoing
redefinition of curriculum, a new way of defining what classroom
knowledge consists of, alternative concepts of power and authority,
and new roles for teachers and students.

That was what the British researchers who studied classroom language, and whose work was the spur behind the American "Language
Across the Curriculum" movement, intended. But, as Garth Boomer
(1988) has pointed out, when these researchers' ideas have been translated into classroom practice, they have become a way to develop
students' reading, writing, speaking, and listening abilities rather than
an approach to reformulating the nature of school knowledge. According to Boomer, rather than seeing language across the curriculum as a
way to improve students' literacy, the thrust should be, "Let's improve learning by looking at how language affects and shapes learning. This involves school and faculty policies focused on matters of
thinking and meaning and learning" (2).

Negotiating the Curriculum

There is classroom talk which can improve learning by addressing
"those matters of thinking and meaning and learning" which Boomer

argues ought to be the central concern of language across the curriculum. Boomer (1982) has, himself, developed such an approach to knowledge building which grows out of a classroom saturated with student talk directed toward joint meaning making and goal setting. This partnership between students and teachers is called "negotiating the curriculum."

I am going to take you inside a classroom where you will see students engaged in learning which is simultaneously open-ended and the joint responsibility of learners with their teacher. The goals and directions for learning will be collaboratively set in order to satisfy both individual and group concerns. What learners already know will be tapped and extended by building bridges between their old and new knowledge. This is learning which will depend on students' using their own language to learn.

In the course of negotiating the curriculum, the role of the teacher, the definition of curriculum, and the nature of knowledge will be radically transformed as well. You will not just see more language use by students. You will see a language-rich environment in which the teacher is a colearner, in which students collaborate with one another to build knowledge, and in which students will reflect on and assess what they have learned in order to complete the learning cycle. This classroom will look very different from the one we glimpsed earlier, the one that was so familiar and so easily recognized.

Principles Underlying Curriculum Negotiation

Before looking at a classroom, let me sketch the principles guiding curriculum negotiation as well as the four practical steps to follow in order to negotiate. Jon Cook (1982) and his Australian colleagues conducted hundreds of interviews with teachers and students of all ages and abilities in order to define how people learn best. They found that learners learn best when they are *engaged,* when they are supported through collaboration with peers and teachers to *explore,* and when they have the opportunity to *reflect* on their learning, to stand back from it and assess what and how they have learned. Engagement, exploration, and reflection form the basis for the negotiation process. In negotiating the curriculum, the purposes and intentions of the learners are of central importance, but they must be integrated with the constraints under which the teacher and the institution operate.

Negotiation is driven and organized by a community of learners addressing the following questions:

1. What do we already know, assume, or believe about the subject at hand?
2. What do we want or need to find out?
3. How will we go about finding out answers to our questions or solutions to our problems?
4. How will we assess what we have accomplished? How will we know what we have found, and with whom will we share our findings?

Negotiating the Curriculum: One Classroom in Action

Let's turn now to a classroom of second graders early one November. This heterogeneous group in a small suburban New York classroom is about to embark on a typical November topic—the Pilgrims. Mrs. Gillis, their teacher, assumes that Thanksgiving has been a topic for these students in their kindergarten and first-grade experiences, and so she anticipates that the children may respond with boredom and disinterest. Nonetheless, Mrs. Gillis feels an obligation to treat the topic. After all, every class in her school will be studying Thanksgiving as well as celebrating the holiday in some way. In order to stave off boredom, her own as well as the children's, and to give the students a chance to share whatever knowledge they already have, Mrs. Gillis decides to negotiate the curriculum with her students. Keep in mind that the topic of their inquiry is nonnegotiable. What the children choose to learn, how they will go about learning, and how they will share their learning is, however, open to negotiation.

What Learners Already Know
and What They Want to Find Out

Mrs. Gillis asks the students what they know about the Pilgrims. The class is divided into small groups and each group is asked to make a list of everything it knows about the Pilgrims. After about fifteen minutes of small group talk, the whole class convenes in front of a flip chart. Mrs. Gillis records on the chart what the students already know or think they know. This chart is entitled, "What We Know about the Pilgrims." In order to create their small group lists, the students had already engaged in a form of negotiation with one another, using oral language as the mode of negotiation. Some children knew things about the Pilgrims that other members of the group did not know, so that part of the seemingly straightforward process of compiling a list involved the knowers in becoming teachers of those children who did not know. The children switch roles as knowers and learners with one another quite naturally throughout the small group talk.

This process continues as each group shares its list with the whole class. Mrs. Gillis's role becomes that of teacher-as-facilitator. If one child reports on a piece of information that others are not familiar with, Mrs. Gillis asks for clarification or elaboration. If there is only one child who is aware of a particular piece of information, she asks that child to keep that item on a personal list of "Knowns." Once this part of the negotiation process was complete, the class generated this composite list:

What We Know about the Pilgrims

1. They made up Thanksgiving.
2. They made friends with the Indians.
3. They sailed on the Mayflower.
4. They were settlers.
5. When they landed, it was at the end of Cape Cod.
6. The Indians taught them how to plant corn.
7. The king wouldn't let them do what they wanted to, so they left.
8. They didn't have much food on the ship.
9. Some died on the ship.
10. They built houses on the coast.
11. Some got sick on the Mayflower.
12. They dug for salt.
13. The kids played games on the ship—leap frog, tug-of-war.
14. They taught each other a lot.

How Old Knowledge Can Lead to New Learning

During the whole group session, questions naturally emerged. Mrs. Gillis asked the children to write their questions in their journals as they came out. Then she sent them back to their groups and asked them to decide what they would like to learn about the Pilgrims. The children generated their own questions and shared their questions with one another. Like the knowledge the children had, some questions were individual and some were collective. Note how the questions grew quite naturally from the information they had generated and recorded. They were engaging in the process of inquiry by allowing what they already knew to lead them in new directions:

What We Want to Know about the Pilgrims

1. How long did it take to make the Mayflower?
2. How big was the Mayflower?
3. How many people died on the Mayflower?
4. How many people were on the Mayflower?
5. How long did it take to get from England to America?
6. What kind of food did they have on the Mayflower? How much?
7. Did they eat fish?
8. What was the captain's name?
9. What kind of houses did they have? Who built them? How did the rain stay out?
10. How long did the Pilgrims live?
11. How did they get off their boat?
12. How did they become Pilgrims? Why were they called Pilgrims?
13. How did they make their clothes?
14. Do they still have the real Mayflower?
15. Who discovered the land?
16. Who ruled them?
17. Was the Mayflower bigger than the Titanic?
18. Are there any Pilgrims living today?

Questions 1, 2, 3, 4, 5, and 8 center on the ship, the Mayflower, and the details of the journey, and so they appear to grow from the simple statement (#3) that "The Pilgrims sailed on the Mayflower." Questions 6 and 7, which center on food, are related to the statement, "They didn't have much food on the ship." (#8). Question 9, about housing, is a derivation of statement 10, which asserts that the Pilgrims built their own homes, and so on. Contrasted with the question-and-answer session which formed the opening of this paper, this field of inquiry is clearly framed, not by the contours of the teacher's thinking, but by the children's own knowledge, interest, and connection making. They are building on what they already know from inside as well as outside of school. In the context of negotiation, the source of knowledge is not as important as the act of connecting knowns with unknowns. And so the range of children's understandings, even those often deemed irrelevant, intrusive, or tangential, can come fully into play in the negotiation process. Additionally, there is a natural modulation between individual knowledge and collective knowledge and questions. The entire negotiation process sets up a dialectical relationship between individual and collective knowledge. If Mrs. Gillis does not dominate the knowledge-building process, neither does any single child.

You will see this process quite clearly operating in question #17, which compares the Mayflower to the Titanic. Here the students are bringing their out-of-school knowledge to bear on in-school learning. At the time that the children were studying the Pilgrims, the Titanic had just been located beneath the Atlantic Ocean, and quite a few of the children knew this. The process of collaborative curriculum building created a central place within the curriculum for something that was part of the students' out-of-school knowledge. It allowed them to make a potentially old topic, Thanksgiving, a new one. It guided them in their inquiry, invested them in learning, and simultaneously built upon what they already knew to make new knowledge. In this way, negotiating the curriculum is satisfying two of the principles of learning on which it is built: engagement and exploration.

Douglas Barnes (1986) would probably say that these children were on a "hot topic." What distinguishes a "hot topic" from a "cold" one is that a hot topic addresses the learner's purposes and intentions rather than only those of the teacher. Hot topics do not require that learners be externally motivated to learn. Hot topics are intrinsically satisfying to learners.

If we contrast Mrs. Gillis's classroom, which is enacting a negotiation model of teaching and learning, with traditional curriculum process and content, what Boomer (1982) designates the "motivation" model, we can see the advantages of negotiation for building school knowledge and for creating "hot topics." At the best of times, according to Boomer, in a motivation learning model, the teacher's and students' intentions for learning will overlap somewhat. More typically, however, there is little overlap in intentions, not just between teacher and student but among the students themselves, a factor limiting successful collaboration. The teacher must therefore spend a great deal of time and energy on motivational activities in the hopes of generating some co-intentions (1982, 128–29). But, even at its best, in the motivation model, "the children's learnings only approximate to the teacher's goals, so the curriculum may touch only a little of each child's key and associated interest" (128).

In addition, asking learners to state what they already know about a topic and what they would like to learn helped Mrs. Gillis avoid a typical pitfall of treating school knowledge as a commodity owned by the teacher: telling learners what they already know. John Dewey (1933) calls the process of informing learners about what they already know an "impertinent interference" (282). Dewey says, "To pry into the familiar, the usual, the automatic, simply for the sake of formulating it is both an impertinent interference and a source of boredom" (282). Dewey would find much to support in Boomer's model for negotiating the curriculum on this basis alone.

How the Children Learned

Let us return to Mrs. Gillis's class to see what and how the children used curriculum negotiation to learn. The students reviewed what was on their list and selected the question about the relative sizes of the Titanic and the Mayflower as their first investigation. Mrs. Gillis guided the class in planning how to go about finding an answer to this question. One child suggested, "We can read and ask people." Mrs. Gillis asked, "What do you think we should read?" Another child said, "Maybe the newspaper tells the size of the Titanic." Three children volunteered to go home that evening and see if they could locate the information in the newspaper. Someone else suggested reading a history book to find how large the Mayflower was. Mrs. Gillis noted on another chart who would be responsible for which tasks.

The next day, the class had the information they needed to compare the sizes of the two ships. Mrs. Gillis suggested marking the length of the two ships on the school playground. The children assembled outside and measured the proper number of feet and made chalk marks on the macadam surface. They were then able to see not only that the Titanic was larger, but by how much. Let me point out here that the children were learning about measurement simultaneously, even though this was not the focus of the investigation. Unlike traditional curriculum, where it is assumed that what is learned is equivalent to what is taught, in negotiation it is acknowledged that a great deal of learning is incidental, unplanned, and even unconscious. But it is learning, nonetheless.

The class also decided to go to the library together and select a number of books to help them with many of their questions. One ongoing activity was Mrs. Gillis's daily reading from a book on the Mayflower voyage. Whenever the children found an answer to one of their questions, they checked off the question on the chart.

One small group of children was particularly interested in finding out if anyone in their town was a descendant of the Pilgrims. Mrs. Gillis, a Mayflower descendant herself, volunteered to be interviewed by this group, which together generated the questions that would guide their interview, and selected one of their members to record Mrs. Gillis's answers. These children decided to share their information with the class through an oral report.

Throughout this process, Mrs. Gillis's role was that of collaborator, facilitator, and orchestrator rather than motivator. Classroom talk was not an end in itself but a means for building knowledge. Not only were the children developing their literacy abilities, they were also using language in all of its modes to learn, and they were learning how to learn.

Reflection as a Moment in Learning

The third principle of learning guiding, negotiating the curriculum, provides that learners learn best when they have the opportunity to reflect on what they have learned. Learners need both to produce knowledge for themselves and to contemplate what they have produced. This reflection on learning may involve self-assessment, sharing the products of learning with peers, and evaluation by the teacher.

I hope it is clear from my description of the learning process in this classroom that learning was not controlled by the teacher's preset curriculum. As a result, the children's learning was largely individual. At the same time, however, there was a core of common knowledge being built.

In a traditional setting, this lack of uniformity of input and output would present tremendous problems of assessment. While I do not wish to suggest that evaluation is not rendered more difficult by negotiating the curriculum, there are distinct advantages. One problem with the motivation model of learning is that when students follow the teacher's line of reasoning, whatever they might learn that does not fit in the prescribed curriculum cannot be reflected upon, and so learning is incomplete. Boomer (1982) has suggested that the motivation model "leaves a good deal of what has been learnt unexamined and unevaluated, because the teacher, or external examiner, tests only what is set on the curriculum" (128). By contrast, in the negotiation model, the teacher can get a sense of what students have learned while the students are allowed to reflect on their learning. The teacher does not assume that what is taught is exactly what is learned.

Mrs. Gillis discussed with the children when they would like to
share and assess their work and how the sharing and assessment
would take place. In order to help the children assess what they had
learned and to help herself evaluate what had gone on, Mrs. Gillis
suggested that each of the children write about what he or she had
learned about the Pilgrims. Here are three of the children reflecting on
what they have learned, or in Paulo Freire's (1987) terms, "knowing"
what they have learned.

Amanda wrote:

> Once there was some people thay are calld pilgrims thay wanted
> to have there own church. So, thay asked the king. The king said
> no! So the people went to Holend. But the peoples children were
> lerning Duch. So, the people went back to England on a boat calld
> the Spedwell. When thay got back to England thay packed tere
> things. and thay berded back on the Spedwell. but, on ther way
> tere was a stom and the spedwell berok. but luchalea there was a
> nuther boat cold the Mayflawer. So thay all borded on. the pil-
> grims sald for 66 days. there was a lote of stoms. and all of them
> brock a bem. but luhaley thay had a big bult that thay were going
> to use for bilding. So thay useed it to hold the bem up menweil
> Stephen Hopkins (illegible) . . . a log time after that the people got
> to America.

Amanda's interest centered on what happened on the voyage itself.
Mike, on the other hand, focused his inquiry, and therefore his learning, on what happened to the Pilgrims once they landed in America:

> The pulgrims saild on the Mayflour from Spayn to America. They
> met two Indins named Skwatow and Samaset. The Indins tautht
> the Pilgrumes haw to plant corn and furtilise the corn with fish.
> And once thay sind a pese tredy so the Indins codnot bring that bo
> and arow to the pilgrims vilige, the pilgrims cod not bring ther
> guns to the Indins vilige. Today we selabrate the day the Pilgrims
> had the first thanksgiving.

Kevin asserts, in a tone of complete ownership and authority, what he
has learned about:

> I know the Pilgrims journey. It all started at England when the
> pilgrims wanted to go to a place were there was freedom. They
> bought a boat, It was the Speedwell. They got half way and the
> speedwell started to leak. The Pilgrims had to go back and get a
> new boat. They rented the Mayflower. They got to where they
> wanted to go. They gave Thanks for making it There safecly.

Mrs. Gillis's assignment required the children to synthesize and organize what they had learned. Each student's ability to create a coher-

ent picture out of the bits and pieces of his or her learning was affected by a range of factors, including individual development. One child wrote only 30 words. Another wrote 350 words and attempted to discuss all of the following: the reasons the Pilgrims left England, what happened on the Mayflower, the landing at Cape Cod, the encounters with the Indians, and the first Thanksgiving. You will note, however, that even in the sample of three texts I have quoted, there is some knowledge which all of the students seem to have developed. Even taking individual differences into account, then, what and how the children learned represents both individual and collective concerns and interests. Assessment, then, is both individual and social, and contains both negotiable and nonnegotiable elements.

The Nature of the Language of Negotiation

The classroom language used to bring the children to the point of confidence and ownership which they exhibit in these culminating pieces of writing was exploratory, that is "hesitant, incomplete, hypo-thetical, directed not to make confident assertions but to explore the range of possible accounts" (Barnes 1986, 73). It is paradoxical that learning through exploratory language use, though this type of lan-guage is less controlled and controlling, has more power to generate confident assertions and make connections than does "presentation-al" language, which, by contrast, is focused on getting the right answers to teacher- or textbook-generated questions. Language in its presentational function is concerned with "satisfying the teacher's criteria. It is abbreviated, it serves the purpose of educational control and it brings pupils' statements into line with the teacher's frame of reference" (73). With its implicit goal of control over students' learning, presentational language supports learning which is short-circuited. School knowledge built through the presentational function, then, will tend to oversimplify issues, smooth over potential controversy, avoid obstacles, and exclude anything novel from being explored or disco-vered (Dewey 1933, 282).

In a recent study, Linda McNeil (1986) places the presentational function of language in a wider teaching context which she terms "defensive teaching." According to McNeil, defensive teaching is de-signed, above all, to control. Unfortunately, one of the consequences of control is that we sacrifice engagement, responsibility, and ownership over learning to create an illusion of harmony and order. That is the central contradiction of a motivation model of curriculum design. The

In her earlier life as a student, this teacher learned to be afraid of her own questions. She translated this fear into her own practices as a teacher. As a teacher, we saw her pedagogy enacting her belief in single rather than multiple perspectives. We observed her conveying to students that knowledge is a commodity which teachers alone possess. In her former life as a student, this teacher believed that teachers transmit learning to their students, and so when she began to teach, she was a transmitter, not a collaborator. She had learned to distrust her own voice, her own language, and her own questions as a learner, and so she tightly controlled how her students used language. She did not see language as a mode of negotiating meanings.

The reawakening of a natural and purposeful need to know and a desire to learn, and the rediscovery of her own meaning-making capacities was spurred on, developed, and dignified for this learner by negotiating the curriculum. These qualities of learning may be engendered in ordinary, day-to-day conversation in the classroom. Not only is genuine conversation a means to achieving learning, it is the result of negotiating the curriculum as well. When learners are given a voice in their own learning and opportunities to build knowledge collaboratively, their already-present potential for engagement in learning will be tapped. This is the real purpose for encouraging classroom talk.

Works Cited

Barnes, D. 1986. "Language in the Secondary Classroom." In *Language, the Learner and the School*, edited by D. Barnes, J. Britton, and M. Torbe, 11–87. 3rd ed. New York: Viking Penguin.

Boomer, G., ed. 1982. *Negotiating the Curriculum: A Teacher-Student Partnership.* Sydney, Australia: Ashton Scholastic.

Boomer, G. 1988. "Reading the Whole Curriculum." In *Metaphors and Meanings: Essays on English Teaching by Garth Boomer*, edited by B. Green. Hawthorn: Australian Association for the Teaching of English.

Cook, J. 1982. "Negotiating the Curriculum: Programming for Learning." In *Negotiating the Curriculum*, edited by G. Boomer, 133–49. Sydney, Australia: Ashton Scholastic.

Dewey, J. 1933. *How We Think.* Boston: D. C. Heath.

Goodlad, J. I. 1984. *A Place Called School.* New York: McGraw-Hill.

Sizer, T. R. 1984. *Horace's Compromise.* Boston: Houghton Mifflin.

Shor, I., and P. Freire. 1987. *A Pedagogy for Liberation.* South Hadley, Mass.: Bergin and Garvey.

Stubbs, M. 1976. *Language, Schools, and Classrooms.* London: Methuen.

5 Asking Questions about Questions

Theresa Rogers, Judith L. Green, and
Nancy Ryan Nussbaum
The Ohio State University

At least from the age of Socrates, the most prominent feature of teacher talk has been the question. But questioning implies that the person posing the question is ignorant, while the person answering the question can potentially relieve that ignorance. In much classroom questioning, however, the roles are completely reversed: the teacher knows the answer and the student is ignorant (ignorant, at least, of what the teacher will accept as the correct answer). So why do we continue the pretense of questioning our students in such circumstances? Are there alternative ways of conducting classroom discussions?

In this chapter, we will raise questions about questions. However, questions are only one form of interaction between teacher and students as they work together to build a lesson. Therefore, we must also ask questions about the relationship of questions to the actions and other forms of talk that occur in the lesson. In other words, to understand what a question "means" in a given lesson, we must also ask how questions function in classrooms, what students need to know in order to answer a question, and what getting "the" answer to a question tells the teacher about student knowledge and/or ability.

This view of questions and their relationship to talk and actions in classrooms assumes that lessons are not merely scripts to be followed by the actors but rather are constructed by the teacher and students as they interact, interpret each other's words and actions, and decide on ways to contribute to the lesson that is being constructed. Another way to think about the role of talk in classroom lessons is to view a lesson as a group writing project guided by the teacher. To contribute to the unfolding composition (e.g., the words, actions, and meaning of the lesson), both teacher and students must read, interpret, and at times revise what is being "composed" (Green, Weade, and Graham 1988). Lesson, therefore, is an evolving, dynamic event created through the talk, actions, and interactions of the teacher and students. Viewed in this way, what students learn within a lesson as well as how they participate depends on how they interpret the unfolding "social text" (e.g., who can talk, when, where, about what, to whom, for what purpose, in what ways) and "academic or content text" (e.g., topics and themes being developed).

Questions play a special role in the composition of the social and academic texts of the lesson. The content of questions provides students with clues about what is important to know about the topic under study, while the way in which questions are asked provides information about the social structure of the lesson and the type of lesson being constructed (e.g., recitation, discussion). For instance, if the teacher uses a lesson structure in which students are expected to listen to a teacher (or student) exposition and then respond to teacher questions at specific points in the lesson, the teacher and students are constructing what is generally referred to as a recitation lesson (Dillon 1984; Edwards and Furlong 1978). In contrast, if a teacher involves students in the construction of group knowledge in ways that build a general disposition to listen to, consider, and be responsive to what others are saying, then the teacher and students are constructing what is generally referred to as a discussion lesson (e.g., Bridges 1987).

Thus questions are not isolated forms of talk but rather are embedded in longer sequences of talk through which the social structure and academic topics and themes of the lesson are constructed. Therefore, in what follows, we will depart from the typical approach to the study of questions teachers ask which focuses on exploring questions separate from the way in which they are used in a lesson and where they occur in the lesson. Instead, we will focus on what questions "do" in actual lessons and how specific patterns of question-asking influence both the type of lesson constructed, and what students have an opportunity to learn through participating in these lessons.

Questions versus the Questioning Process

To explore what questions "do" in classroom lessons, we must first distinguish between the questions that are asked and the process of questioning during classroom lessons. A focus that considers only the questions that are asked ignores the context in which the question occurred, the social and academic purposes questions serve in the lesson, and factors that influence the ways in which students respond. In other words, a focus on individual questions isolates the question from its use in the lesson, and the question itself becomes the object of study. Questions, viewed in this way, are seen as being one type or another (e.g., factual, interpretive, predictive, text based). Underlying this focus is an assumption that the question itself exists at a particular level and has a reality separate from the context in which it was used as well as the way in which it was perceived and interpreted by the participants (Farrar 1985; Morine-Dershimer 1985; Weber 1988).

For example, consider the following question: Who is the most important person in the story? In isolation, this question might be considered an "inferential," "reader-based," or even "interpretive" question. Now consider the same question in the context in which it occurred. The question was asked during a third-grade reading lesson in which *Sidewalk Story* (Mathis 1970) was being discussed:

T: Who was the most important person in the story?

S: Lily and Tanya.

T: You think they were both important?

S: Lily, because she did most of the stuff.

T: OK.

It is only in view of what followed this question that we can see how the question functioned to produce a particular answer, and that the student came to understand this after hearing the teacher's second question. At that point, the student was able to provide the expected answer. The teacher confirmed that the student had understood the purpose of the question by evaluating the student's second response positively, and the lesson continued.

As this example illustrates, focus on the questioning process requires that we consider the ways in which questions are used in the ongoing talk between teacher and students in lessons, and that we understand how people use language to accomplish their goals and to participate in everyday classroom events. This way of exploring questions requires that we consider more than the question itself. It requires that we consider the complex nature of the questioning process:

• Who asked the question of whom

• When and where the question was asked in the lesson

• What purpose the question served in the lesson

• What information or knowledge was required to answer the question at the specific point in the lesson

• How participants' responses influenced the ways in which the interaction continued to develop

- What was accomplished by participating in the interactions

These questions are the same questions that we need to ask if we are to understand what is required to participate in and learn from everyday life in or out of classrooms.

Understanding Classroom Questions

To understand when and how questions are used in classroom lessons and how they are perceived, it is helpful to contrast them with questions that are asked in other settings. Mehan (1979) provides a clear illustration of the difference in questioning in and out of classrooms in the following examples:

> *Teacher:* What time is it, Denise?
> *Denise:* 2:30.
> *Teacher:* Very good, Denise.
>
> **and**
>
> *Teacher:* What time is it, Denise?
> *Denise:* 2:30.
> *Teacher:* Thank you.

He argues that the first question is one typically heard in classrooms, whereas the second is one that could be heard anywhere. What distinguishes these two questions is more than the type of response. These questions differ in intent, when they would be used, who would use them, and the demands placed on the responder. That is, the first questioning cycle above would appear odd or inappropriate to someone outside of the classroom setting since it involves an evaluation of the response to a question that was asked. In out-of-school settings, it would not generally be socially appropriate for someone to ask a question to which he or she already had an answer, nor would it be appropriate to evaluate the response.

While a "need to know" is a condition of questioning in the out-of-school setting, it is often not a condition in classroom lessons. Thus, Mehan argues that many of the questions teachers ask are seen as "pseudo" questions by students in that the teacher already knows the answer and does not really "need" the information.

Further support for Mehan's view of classroom questioning comes from a study of students' perceptions of questions in language arts lessons as compared with questioning on playgrounds and at home

(Morine-Dershimer 1985). Students reported that teachers asked questions "to tell," or "to teach," while mothers asked questions because "they wanted to know." In addition, students who perceived their teacher as asking "real questions" had higher reading achievement than those students who perceived their teacher as asking "pseudo questions" or who perceived questions as primarily seeking a particular answer. Thus, differences in teacher style and student perception of questioning influenced what was learned.

These examples raise questions about how questions function in a classroom, what is involved in responding to a question, and what answers to questions tell teachers and others about what students know. To explore these questions about questions, we must take a closer look at what occurs during questioning and how questions function in classroom lessons.

Questioning and Response in Classroom Lessons

Questions in classrooms serve a variety of functions beyond the ordinary one outside of classrooms of asking questions to obtain "needed" information. For instance, as part of an ongoing lesson, classroom questions often provide information to students about what the "right" or "preferred" response is (Dillon 1984; Heap 1978; Rogers 1988). The following example from a ninth-grade literature lesson illustrates how "the" answer can be "given" or provided in the question itself:

> The teacher and students are discussing the story, "The Open Window," by Saki (1930). The following exchange was observed at the beginning of an extended discussion of the story:
>
> *Teacher:* In terms of the plot, though, can you tell me briefly what happens in the story?
>
> *Georgia:* (Georgia raises hand and teacher nonverbally acknowledges her turn) Well, this guy, Framton Nuttel goes to this house . . . (cut off by teacher's next question)
>
> *Teacher:* OK, why does he visit them?
>
> *Georgia:* He is sort of shy and nervous and he needed people to help him . . . (cut off by teacher's next question)
>
> *Teacher:* OK, you said he was nervous. OK, to answer the question, why does he visit them? Was his sister embarked on some idea for him to cure his nervousness?
>
> *Georgia:* Yeah.
>
> *Teacher:* OK, because he was going to go . . . well . . . I'll keep asking.

In this example, the teacher did not receive the "preferred" answer to the first question, as indicated by both her interruption of the student's initial response and the posing of the second question, which is more limited or focused. This question indicates that what the student started to say was not on "target"; that is, the student was not providing the information the teacher wanted as the response to the question. Therefore, the teacher asked the second question, which provided more information about what was "preferred." Once again, the student begins to respond to this question and is interrupted before she can complete her answer. At this point, the teacher embeds the answer that was preferred from the outset in her next question: "Is the sister embarked on some idea for him to cure his nervousness?" She then receives a "yes" from the student. Her next response shows that she has still not received "the complete answer" she preferred and will continue to question students until she does receive the "exact" response she wants or provides it herself. Thus, she overtly sends signals to students (and to the observer) that there is "one" answer, that the student has not provided it, and that the questioning will continue until she obtains the "preferred" response.

The question of what the "preferred" response was can be seen when the remainder of the exchanges about plot are considered:

Paul: (Paul raises hand to respond to the teacher's statement: "I'll keep asking")

Teacher: Paul.

Paul: Well, I kinda got the idea that he's not mentally ill or anything, but sorta had a problem. I mean, more than the usual.

Teacher: Yeah. He's extremely nervous and anxious, and he's what? He's come to this country home, these retreats, at his sister's bidding, to visit these people. He wanted to go and stash himself in the corner and not have any contact with people. So she's given him this introduction to go to these people, supposedly to cure his nerves.

Dan: I thought it was his doctor.

Teacher: His doctor? His sister. (emphasis on sister) His sister gave him these letters of introduction. (paraphrases the sister's words) Go to these people. Don't hole yourself up in some retreated area. (continues talking) OK, so Georgia (the original student who responded to the initial question), you're going to continue. He's come to these people (said in a rising tone that indicates that the student is to continue)

Georgia: And the niece is there and the niece says something to him. Essentially on that date, she tells him that an uncle and a cousin a few years ago got stuck in a hole or something and they never found them and the aunt still thinks they will come back. So then she comes down, the aunt comes down … (teacher interrupts student)

Teacher: So let me stop you there. So the great tragedy of Mrs. Sappelton (said in a rising tone that indicates that the student is to continue)

Georgia: Is that her husband and nephew died.

Teacher: Right. OK, continue.

Georgia: Then the aunt comes down and says, "Oh, I'm sorry for making you wait." And so she's talking about how they are going to come back. And the guy is really horrified. And then they do come back and he runs away.

Teacher: And he runs away. OK, so in terms of plot, it's pretty straightforward . . . (omitted some talk about the similarity between the character's name and the name of a student in this class). Vera has told the story and frightened poor Mr. Nuttel and he dashes out in the end. OK, so the plot is pretty straightforward.

Teacher: Now, how would you describe Vera?

By examining all of the talk about plot, we can see how the teacher directs students to "her interpretation," not their interpretation of the story events. She does this in two ways. First, the teacher calls on a student (Paul) who has volunteered to continue to answer the original question. He responds and the teacher reinterprets his response and says, "YEAH, HE'S EXTREMELY NERVOUS AND ANXIOUS." She then asks a question which she answers herself. The answer elaborates the information presented before Paul volunteers to respond. Paul's response, then, can be seen as an interruption in the teacher's answer. She then returns to the answer she was building toward.

The next exchange with Dan clarifies the error in Dan's statement but also refocuses students on the teacher's turn and the preferred answer to her original question. That the teacher has provided sufficient information for students to continue the preferred direction is indicated by her calling once again on Georgia to continue the plot summary. What is interesting to note is that the teacher calls on Georgia directly and uses an intonation that is a "complete this sentence or story" intonation. She does not ask a new question. Georgia continues the story line until the teacher overtly interrupts her with a question that gets directly to the main point of the plot summary—that Vera has fabricated the story, which is referred to by the teacher as the "GREAT TRAGEDY OF MRS. SAPPELTON." The interruption, then, summarizes succinctly one of the major events of the story, a key to the story's outcome.

The "complete the sentence" pattern that occurred above is now used again. Georgia responds by providing the appropriate response to complete the sentence. She is then given permission to continue the plot summary. The teacher ends this exchange in two ways. First, she repeats, "AND HE RUNS AWAY." Her restatement serves to complete the story with Georgia, to accept Georgia's response, and to signal to others that she has regained the direction of the lesson. Second, she summarizes by indicating that she feels the plot is "STRAIGHTFORWARD."

In this segment of the lessons, the teacher has engaged the students in an elaborate "dance" in order to construct what she refers to as a "straightforward" summary of the plot or events of the story. However, what was straightforward to the teacher was not straightforward to the students, as indicated by their responses and by the ways in which she directed the "dance." To know what was expected of them, the students had to correctly interpret the teacher's moves from moment to moment since the information about what was expected was not explicit. For example, in this segment of the lesson, the teacher provided information about what was expected through her questions, by interrupting students' responses, by using a rising intonation to invite students to continue the response that she had begun, and by repeating students' phrases.

Lessons such as these raise questions such as these: What do students need to know in order to answer a question? What happens when the student's response is different from the response that is "preferred" by the teacher? And most important, whose knowledge is constructed or reconstructed during these conversations?

Student Interpretations versus the Preferred Response

That students see a difference between their interpretations and teacher's preferred interpretations can be seen in the following excerpts from interviews of students conducted during a study of response to literature (Rogers 1988). These interviews are with students in the class in which the above lesson was observed. Students were interviewed about their perceptions of the role of student and teacher in classroom literature lessons.

> *Gary:* There is usually a class theme. Everyone gets the same idea. They read the story and then the teacher will tell them what she interpreted and the class will say, Oh yeah, that's right. They [the students] don't really form the ideas.

> *Dora:* Well, if the teacher goes on one line of thought, then you will look at it more. And if you didn't look at it before, it will become your outlook even if you didn't realize it. I'd still keep mine, but I'd put hers down first on a test.

What is evident in these two statements is that Gary and Dora perceive a difference between their personal responses and the teacher's preferred responses. The students understand that they can have a personal response to the story but that this response may not be the one that is expected in the lesson or on the test. These examples indicate that they are also aware that the preferred response is not always overtly stated but must be extracted or inferred from the teacher's talk and actions.

Preference: A Closer Look

The question of preference may be more complex than was illustrated in the above example. For instance, as indicated below, some questions may have many "candidate" responses to communicate the same information. However, what "counts" as the preferred answer is limited in the context of the lesson (Heap 1978). Thus, as we explore talk between teachers and students, we need to ask the following questions if we are to understand how such talk functions to signal information about what is appropriate and expected of students: Is there more than one "candidate" for the answer? Does one answer "count" and another not in the particular situation? What cues are available to help a responder select the "preferred" or expected response?

The following exchanges occurred in a second-grade reading lesson in which the students and teacher were talking about the story *Rumpelstiltskin*, which they had recently read:

> *Teacher:* No. Who helped her [the woodsman's daughter] Mineen?
>
> *Child:* Rumpelstiltskin.
>
> *Teacher:* Yeah, the little man. We don't know his name is Rumpelstiltskin yet, do we? The little man. OK, what was the first thing the prince said—sorry, that the girl gave to Rumpelstiltskin, to the little man? We better call him the little man because we don't know really he's Rumpelstiltskin yet.

Heap (1978) argues that this example demonstrates a "breakdown" in the lesson as indicated by the teacher's response to the student's answer and by the information she gives in her own response. What is interesting in this example is the teacher's own answer. She, too, calls the little man Rumpelstiltskin and then has to correct herself. Thus, her response to the student: "We don't know his name is Rumpelstiltskin yet, do we?" and her response to her own use of Rumpelstiltskin: "We better call him the little man because we don't know really he's Rumpelstiltskin yet," provide information that there is only one preferred response to this question at this particular point in the lesson, regardless of whether the answer that the student, and subsequently the teacher, gave is correct.

The existence of multiple possible responses is common since there are many ways to communicate the same information, yet as Heap argues, only one may be preferred in certain circumstances:

> First note the commonplace that one thing or person can be called by many different names. That is, there are multiple identifiers that can stand as correct answers to "Who?" questions. In this case there could be "a man", "the antagonist", "the dwarf", "the elf", "the funny old midget", "the bearded gentleman", "the guy with the funny hat", as well as "the little man" and "Rumpelstiltskin". All of these identifiers could be used in some circumstances to refer to the person who helped the Woodman's daughter spin straw into gold. They are all correct in some (general) sense. Yet in some circumstances and for some purposes some identifiers are preferable over others. So while all are correct not all will (always) be preferred as answers to "Who?" questions. (1978, 2–3)

What this teacher signaled in her response was that, although Mineen's answer was correct, it was not preferred since they were discussing only the "just-read-part-of-the-story" at this particular point in the lesson. Therefore, it is not enough for students to know the correct response; they must know what the preferred response is at the particular point of the particular lesson they are engaged in.

These two examples, "The Open Window" and *Rumpelstiltskin* lessons, show that preference is not usually overtly stated in lessons, but can be inferred from what is observed during the interactions between teachers and students. In order to determine the preferred answers, students (and observers) must learn to "read" the teacher's intent from his or her actions and responses during the lessons.

The result of these lessons, in which the teacher's preference takes precedence over student responses, is that it is the text and/or the teacher's knowledge that is reproduced (Bloome 1986). However, if building the students' knowledge is the desired end of lessons, then asking questions in order to get the appropriate or preferred answer is not fruitful. In the next section we will explore alternative ways of questioning that may help to avoid the pitfalls of asking "pseudo" questions or questions that narrow rather than expand student responses.

Toward Questioning and Discussion in Classroom Lessons

We have attempted to illustrate that, while it is assumed that questions function in classrooms to build student knowledge, it is often the case that they actually limit students' opportunities to build their own knowledge. The asking of known-answer or pseudo questions has the effect of signaling the teacher's authority over the students (Beynon 1985). In the remainder of this paper, we would like to explore alternatives to questioning and alternative ways to question students that allow students to build and share their own knowledge.

In the examples above, the pattern of talk is characterized by recurring sequences of teacher questions and student responses in which the students come to know that the teacher has a preferred response in mind. These patterns of interactions in lessons can be characterized as recitation sequences rather than discussions (Dillon 1984). In contrast, discussions involve students and teachers in an exchange of information in order to construct group knowledge. For instance, Bridges (1987) has outlined three major characteristics of discussions: (a) discussions involve members of the group contributing from their different perspectives, opinions, or understandings; (b) discussions involve a general disposition on behalf of members of the group to listen to, consider, and be responsive to what others are saying; and (c) discussions are guided by the central purpose of developing the group's knowledge, understanding, and/ or judgment on the matter under discussion.

Some differences between recitation and discussion are illustrated in the following examples of two eighth-grade literature lessons. In the study in which these lessons were observed (Rogers 1987), a single eighth-grade class was divided into two groups of equal ability. With one group, the regular classroom teacher conducted a lesson using the recitation technique, and with the other group a teacher-researcher used discussion techniques. In the recitation group the teacher prepared a list of questions to ask the students before the class. In the discussion group the teacher collected written responses that the students prepared after reading the story the previous day. In the excerpts that follow, both groups are talking about instances of caring or sympathy in the story, *Flowers for Algernon*, by Keyes (1966).

At the start of this lesson excerpt the students are referring to a scene in which Charlie, now intelligent, defends a retarded bus boy in a restaurant:

Teacher: OK, Karl? (The teacher is responding to Karl's bid to speak.)

Karl: Well, he [Charlie] jumped up and he made a scene and said, "Leave him alone." He tried to defend the boy and then ran out of the restaurant.

Teacher: What characteristics would you attach to this scene—in terms of Charlie? If you had one word that you had to pick that reflects the way Charlie reacted to the situation, what would that word be?

Karl: Sympathetic.

Teacher: OK, do you think there is a theme of sympathy in this story?

Karl: Well in that particular scene.

Teacher: Or do you think there is a sympathetic theme that runs through the story? Do you think people react with a sense of caring toward other people in the story?

Karl: Well, that's not the main theme I got out of the story.

Teacher: Well, do you think it could be a theme? Not necessarily the main theme.

Karl: Well, it could be, but there are other themes.

Teacher: You don't think it is a theme at all in this story?

Karl: Well, it is a theme. I don't think it is a main theme.

Teacher: OK, what do you think is the main theme?

Karl: I think that people like you for what you are, not how smart you are. I got that from quite a few examples.

Teacher: OK, give me an example.

Karl: Like, he was not happier when he was intelligent and his friends were starting to leave him.

Teacher: Do you think that was because he was smart?

Karl: Well his friends were so used to treating him like an inferior being, so used to laughing at him and now he is smarter than they are and they're kind of afraid of him.

Teacher: OK, Anne?

Anne: Like when they say, "Oh, don't you know what time it is?" or whatever.

Teacher: Do you think they are laughing at him when they say that, Anne?

Anne: No. He just—now he thinks that when he was mentally retarded, he thought everyone was really smart.

Teacher: Uh-huh. OK, Tony?

This excerpt begins with Karl raising his hand and being acknowledged by the teacher. Karl then begins to describe a scene from the story. The teacher asks him to characterize the scene with one word. The student responds by saying "sympathetic." The teacher then asks if there is a theme of sympathy in the story. Karl responds by saying there is a theme of sympathy in that scene. This is apparently not the preferred answer as indicated by the teacher's rephrasing of the question: "OR DO YOU THINK THERE IS A SYMPATHETIC THEME THAT RUNS THROUGH THIS STORY?" Karl responds by saying that this is not what he got from the story. Once again the teacher rephrases the question: "WELL, DO YOU THINK IT COULD BE A THEME? NOT NECESSARILY THE MAIN THEME." This time Karl responds by saying that it could be. At this point the teacher gives her final rephrasing of the question: "YOU DON'T THINK IT IS A THEME AT ALL IN THIS STORY?" Karl finally provides an acceptable response: "Well it is a theme. But I don't think it's a main theme." The teacher then gives him permission to say what he thinks the main theme is and a new topic is introduced.

What happens in this section shows that the teacher and student are negotiating the answer. The student has his own personal interpretation that does not match the preferred response. The student "struggles" throughout this segment to maintain his own voice without breaking the flow of the lesson. He does this by partially agreeing with the teacher's interpretation and by restating his own interpretation in a modified form. What is interesting to note is that the teacher engages actively in the negotiation and ultimately accepts the fact that Karl has an interpretation that was not the one that she preferred. This occurs only after Karl accepts her interpretation in some way.

In other words, this segment shows a teacher who is trying to persuade a student that there is a particular theme in the story that is central to understanding the story. The student has a different interpretation and tries to "protect" his own interpretation. In this series of exchanges, the teacher never explicitly states her interpretation but rather indicates what she prefers through her questions. The questions, therefore, serve to signal what is preferred and thus what students need to know about this story. In addition, when the total lesson is considered, what becomes evident is that the issue of sympathy in the story is not addressed in any substantial way, nor is it reintroduced with other students.

However, once Karl is given an opportunity to describe his own interpretation, other students contribute to the lesson, and the tone of the exchanges begins to sound more like a discussion. The teacher ends the segment by calling on another student rather than continuing the dialogue that is developing. This action allows the teacher to "retake the floor" and direct the rest of the lesson.

When Karl was asked one year later about the role of teachers and students in lessons such as these, he made the following comments:

> In the first grade, they teach you, they ask you, "How did you like this story?" and then you tell them and you don't have to give them evidence so from second grade on they say, "I want you to give hard evidence and support your ideas," and before you know it you're writing five-paragraph essays and they say, "Well, don't use your opinions in your thesis, now." And gradually they allow you to use less and less of your emotions until it's not allowed. That's where we are now. I don't get any emotional reaction out of my reading anymore. All teachers want you to do is tell them how this relates to the theme they've given you. What the tests essentially say is, "This is the theme, give me evidence." It's like, OK, that was fun. Instead of saying, "How did you feel about the story? Give examples in your answer."

This comment confirms the description of the lesson provided above. What is remarkable about this comment is that it retraces a shifting pattern of expectations for students participating in reading or literature lessons over the course of schooling. That is, this student saw the expectations of schooling as shifting from grade to grade in terms of whose "voice" is heard.

This excerpt and the student's comments above raise questions about how the interactions between teachers and students influence what students learn about interpreting stories and what students need to "do" in order to get the "preferred" answer. It also raises questions about whose authority "counts" in interpreting stories and what role students' interpretations play in reading/literature lessons. In other words, as Searle (1984) asks: "Who's building whose building?"

In the next excerpt, the teacher-researcher sought to develop an approach to interpretation that contrasted with the approach of the regular teacher. The teacher in this segment attempted to construct a lesson about the same story that supported student interpretation over the teacher's own interpretation. Thus, what was "preferred" in this lesson differed from what was preferred in the other lesson. In both lessons, however, the teachers had a particular goal in mind and a preferred way of interacting with students and interpreting stories. In the second teacher's lesson the teacher "preferred" dialogue among students that enabled them to see that multiple responses to and interpretations of the story were possible.

At the start of this lesson the teacher is asking students to elaborate on their written responses to the story *Flowers for Algernon*:

> *Teacher:* OK, Cindy, you said this story reminded you of other stories about cruelty but, Alice, you said this was a caring story.
>
> *Alice:* Yes, because Miss Kinnian cared a lot for Charlie. She wanted him to become smarter.
>
> *Teacher:* So you thought this was a caring element?
>
> *Alice:* Yes.
>
> *Bob:* I think in a way what Alice said is right. You always want people who are disadvantaged to do better and do as well as anyone else. But in the story what is reflected is once they become better, you're not exactly sure what to do. You don't know whether to be happy for them or whether you resent them for being more intelligent than you are. Or if they should thank you for helping them or what. You don't know what to feel because originally you want them to do better but if they become better it really creates a problem.
>
> *Cindy:* Well, I think it is about cruelty because, well, I think it is caring, too, because Miss Kinnian cared and she was friends with Charlie and all that, but it was cruelty because the doctors knew something could go wrong—a lot could go wrong. When Algernon died, Charlie figured out that he was going to die, too. Miss Kinnian seemed like she was sorry and I knew she must have meant it. But she must have known before the experiment that there was a chance Charlie would die.
>
> *Teacher:* So how do you think she felt at the end?
>
> *Cindy:* Guilty.
>
> *Teacher:* OK, let's talk about Joe and Frank.

This segment begins with the teacher referring to Cindy's and Alice's comments written the day before. Cindy had commented in her written response that the story reminded her of stories of cruelty and Alice said that she thought it was a caring story. The teacher begins the dialogue and invites Cindy and Alice to share their interpretations, interpretations that she knows are contrasting. What is interesting to note is that the teacher does not appear to elicit much dialogue with her direct statements or questions. Alice confirms the teacher's statement. The dialogue does not really begin until Bob responds to Alice's comment and extends her interpretation with his own.

Cindy then joins the conversation. Her contribution is interesting since she begins by disagreeing, but then also supports the caring theme. She then disagrees once more. Like the teacher and student in the first excerpt, Cindy agrees to agree with the theme as stated by her peers but then proceeds to restate her own interpretation. This action serves to support the flow of conversation but permits her to insert her own "voice." The teacher's next action builds on Cindy's response and asks her to extend the response by suggesting how Miss Kinnian felt at the end of the story. Cindy responds with "guilty." Her response completes the interactions and the teacher and students then discuss another point in which students had contrasting interpretations.

These students were also interviewed about the second teacher's approach to responding to literature. The student's responses indicated that this particular approach was not usual or expected in schools but that it provided ways for them to share their knowledge, examine how others interpreted stories, and clarify their thoughts by hearing other interpretations.

> *Susan:* It was a lot better, because I wasn't being graded on the teacher's interpretation because you didn't give one. We were kind of mad at you for not giving us one, but it may be better for us because it gives us a chance to interpret the way we want.
>
> *Bob:* Well, in this unit you had us write the essay and draw on our own conclusions so it became the students explaining it to other students instead of the teacher. . . . I thought it was good because a lot of the students have different outlooks, different points of view.

These examples show that students can develop ways of discussing interpretations of stories. However, as one student indicated, this was not expected and they did not know what the "preferred" response was for the test. Thus, simply changing the strategies did not ensure that students would see the new approach as "counting" in school.

Questioning Questions

The examples of classroom lessons presented in this paper were not intended to suggest one approach was "good" and the other "bad" but rather to raise questions about the ways in which teachers interact with students. That is, we are not arguing that teachers should not ask questions but rather that the question of questioning is a larger issue.

What we are arguing is that we must begin to explore what questions "do" in classroom lessons: what they signal to students about the information in the text and the lesson; how chains of questioning send signals to students about the "preferred" responses or ways of knowing; and whose "voice" counts in lessons. Questions themselves are not good or bad; patterns of questioning do, however, influence what will occur, with whom, in what ways, for what purposes, when, where, under what conditions, and with what short-term and long-term consequences.

Underlying this discussion has been the assumption that the ways in which teachers interact with students send messages or signals to students about what to know, how to display this knowledge, and what to do in a lesson. Participation in lessons, therefore, becomes patterned. Expectations are generated both within and across lessons that are similar about what "counts" as important. The two excerpts in the latter part of this paper showed two approaches to interacting with students about text that have different outcomes for students. What teachers do in the face of student responses and what they do to elicit student participation influence the nature of the lesson that unfolds. These interactions, in turn, influence what students can and do learn from participating in the construction of the lesson.

Finally, student comments from interviews showed that the patterns of action and interaction in classrooms are perceived by students as information about what to know. Thus, students learn to "read" the expectations and preferences of teachers. The questions that must be raised then are: What are students learning? And what do we know when we hear or see a preferred response? The challenge for teachers concerned with building student knowledge is one of learning to see beneath the "procedural display" (Bloome 1986) of students and finding ways of exploring and extending student knowledge as well as finding ways of helping students explore and extend their own knowledge. One place to begin is to ask yourself questions about the questions you ask.

One way to begin examining what questions "do" in classrooms, how they function, is to analyze your questions in the context of your classroom lessons. In order to do this, it is necessary to look at the questions and responses in naturally occurring interaction sequences. For instance, you could tape-record actual lessons and then ask the following questions based on an examination of the question-response sequences:

Who is allowed to ask questions of whom in my classroom lessons?

Do my questions narrow or expand the range of possible responses?

What do my questions signal to students about what is important to know or learn from the text or the lesson? Do my questions match the goals of the lesson (e.g., to review, assess, interpret, problem-solve, etc.)? Whose knowledge is being constructed through the interactions in my lessons?

Works Cited

Beynon, W. J. 1985. *Initial Encounters in a Comprehensive School.* Barcombe, England: Falmer.

Bloome, D. 1986. "Building Literacy and the Classroom Community." *Theory Into Practice* 25, no. 2: F1–F6.

Bridges, D. 1987. "Discussion and Questioning." *Questioning Exchanges: A Multidisciplinary Review* 1, no. 1: 34–37.

Dillon, J. T. 1984. "Research on Questioning and Discussion."*Educational Leadership* 42, no. 3: 50–56.

Edwards, A. D., and V. J. Furlong. 1978. *The Language of Teaching.* London: Heinemann Educational Books, Ltd.

Farrar, M. T. 1985. "Teacher Questions: The Complexity of the Cognitively Simple." Unpublished manuscript.

Heap, J. 1978. "Rumpelstiltskin: The Organization of Preference in a Reading Lesson." Paper presented at the annual meeting of the Sociology and Anthropology Association, London, Ontario, June 10–13.

Keyes, D. 1966. "Flowers for Algernon." In *Points of View: An Anthology of Short Stories,* edited by J. Moffett and K. R. McElheny. New York: New American Library.

Mathis, S. B. 1970. *Sidewalk Story.* New York: Viking.

Mehan, H. 1979. "'What Time Is It, Denise?': Asking Known Information Questions in Classroom Discourse." *Theory Into Practice* 28, no. 4: 285–94.

Morine-Dershimer, G. 1985. *Talking, Listening, and Learning in Elementary Classrooms.* New York: Longman.

Rogers, T. 1987. "Exploring a Sociocognitive Perspective on the Interpretive Processes of Junior High School Students." *English Quarterly* 20, no. 3: 218–30.

———. 1988. "Students as Literary Critics: The Interpretive Theories, Processes, and Experiences of Ninth-grade Students." Dissertation. University of Illinois at Urbana-Champaign. Saki (Munro, H. H.). 1930. "The Open Window." *The Complete Short Stories of Saki.* New York and London: The Viking Press.

Searle, D. 1984. "Scaffolding: Who's Building Whose Building?" *Language Arts* 61, no. 5: 480–83.

Weber, R. M. "The Questioning Routine in Reading Lessons." Unpublished manuscript. State University of New York at Albany.

6 Play Talk, School Talk, and Emergent Literacy

Lee Galda and A. D. Pellegrini
The University of Georgia

For young children, talking is fun. There's nothing more natural to a child than play, and play is mainly a verbal construction. But that play talk is far from idle. Some serious learning results from children's practice in creating imaginative play worlds through talk. Not surprisingly, some kinds of play talk are particularly important as precursors to the kind of literate-based language that schools especially value and cultivate.

Children's oral language is important. It is important for its own sake and because certain forms of talk are parts of school, generally, and literacy events, specifically. In this chapter we will discuss some of the ways in which a specific type of preschool children's talk, talk during make-believe play, relates to subsequent use of school talk and early literacy.

An assumption of our work and this chapter is that the function of a piece of talk serves to affect the form of that talk. Take, for example, the following:

> *Anna:* Once there was a girl whose name was Boozu and she lived in a little house. And then she got a little brother. And she needed a big house. And then she asked her mommy to buy her a bigger house because her brother had so many toys. And her mother did.

When Anna tells a story (the functional dimension), as in the above excerpt, that language is usually characterized by temporal conjunctions (the formal dimension) such as "and," and "and then" (see Halliday 1967; Pellegrini, Galda, and Rubin 1984 for a discussion of the form/function issue). When her intention is other than storytelling, her language changes. For example, if she is trying to persuade someone to

The authors acknowledge the comments of Susan Cox. The work reported in the chapter was partially supported by a grant from the NCTE Research Foundation to the second author. Correspondence regarding the chapter should be addressed to either author at: Aderhold Hall, University of Georgia, Athens, Georgia, 30602.

give her something, she might use causal conjunctions such as "be-cause." She alters the form of her language according to its function. What this means for education is that teachers can structure children's sociolinguistic experiences in the classroom to serve specific functions (for example, to persuade, to give directions, or to make-believe). The result is that specific forms of language will be elicited by these experiences. So, rather than use direct instruction techniques to facilitate children's use of a specific register, or language variant used in a specific situation, we recommend putting children in contexts which will elicit those forms.

In this chapter we will talk about the ways in which a specific context, preschool children's make-believe play, elicits the forms of language which typify the school register, that is, language which children are expected to use with teachers and peers when talking in school settings about school subjects. Further, these forms of oral language also seem to be important for children's emergent literacy, that is, their growing ability to encode and decode print.

The general idea that forms of language follow their functions and, more specifically, that language serving an imaginative, or make-believe, function, relates to school language and literacy has been most persuasively argued by M.A.K. Halliday (1967). Halliday argues that fantasy, because there is little reliance on what is physically present, relies on language to convey meaning, to redefine roles, props, and situations. For example, a glass of soapy water becomes transformed into an ice cream soda when Chloe asks, "Would you like this delicious ice cream soda?"

Experience and careful observation and research with preschool children show that the fantasy mode elicits elaborated, cohesive language and metalinguistic verbs, language which reflects the properties valued in school talk. These are the forms of language children use to make object transformations (changing the identity of an object such as transforming a block into a truck, "*Brmmm*") and ideational transformations (changing the identity of roles, situations, and nonexistent objects, "You be the Daddy"). The following excerpt from two preschool boys playing with blocks will illustrate:

> *Turn 1. Jack:* I wanna play fireman. [Ideational transformation: role]
>
> *Turn 2. Mick:* OK. We can drive our big, old, red fire engines. [Object transformation: using blocks for trucks]
>
> *Turn 3. Jack:* Why'd ya say old. They're new because they have to be shiny and fast.

language appropriate for them. Similarly, in the Mick/Jack dialogue excerpted above, Jack, in turn 3, used the verb *say* to clarify, in this case, an object transformation. Generally, children use metalinguistic terms for clarification. We have found that younger preschool children (3 ½ years of age) used metalinguistic verbs while engaging in make-believe play with their peers, while older preschoolers (4 ½ years of age) used them during realistic, *not* fantasy, discourse with their peers. This probably means that the younger children learned and practiced using metalinguistic verbs during fantasy and transferred this skill to other, realistic peer discourse situations, just as they will transfer it to those situations requiring school language.

Why is the use of metalinguistic verbs important? David Olson (1983; Torrance and Olson 1984) suggests that children's use of meta-linguistic verbs is a necessary step in the process of becoming literate. Use of metalinguistic verbs, according to Olson, indicates that children are consciously aware of the process by which meaning is linguistically conveyed. Further, knowledge of these terms enables children to participate in school literacy events which involve these terms. Thus children will understand the instructional register ("Find the *word* that begins with "b.") that they encounter in school. Olson further argues that children's use of metalinguistic verbs, and simultaneous metalinguistic awareness, occurs during the *primary* school period as children encounter print. We suggest, as noted above, that *preschool* children use these verbs during play and peer discourse to clarify roles and transformations. Consequently, make-believe play seems to be an excellent context in which to develop this skill.

Play, Language, and Emergent Literacy

Play and the language of play predict children's emergent literacy. Writing, reading, and play are symbolic activities; that is, they all involve representing something else with language. As such, early measures of representational facility, in the form of make-believe play, should predict other representational forms, like emergent literacy; particularly early writing. This idea, which is outlined in the theory of L. S. Vygotsky (1978), views symbolic play as the avenue by which preschool children develop the ability to manipulate symbols. These manipulations, initially, are tied to specific objects and, as such, are object transformations. For example, Jason gives his toy doll animate qualities when he asks it, "Hurt?" after administering a pretend injection. He uses an object (a doll) to symbolize a real baby.

With all children's play, manipulations become less tied to objects; that is, they become ideational transformations. For example, 5-year-old Niki cradles her imaginary and invisible baby and asks, "Is that better now?" Her symbol for the baby is not an object and thus her symbolic transformation is more abstract than Jason's. The ability to use these abstract transformations is a good indicator of children's emergent writer status (Galda, Pellegrini, and Cox, in press) to the extent that, in both early writing and make-believe play, children are using abstract symbol systems to make and convey meaning.

Where symbolic transformations in play are linked to early writing ability, use of metalinguistic verbs is linked to emergent reading status. Children's facility with metalinguistic verbs, which they earlier learn and practice during make-believe play, indicates the broader competence with the language of literacy events, such as letter names and sounds, which is so important to early reading (Walsh, Price, and Gillingham 1988). Facility with these metalinguistic terms seems to be particularly important in reading contexts which stress reading as a skill, with linguistic components that must be labeled. In order to discuss letters, words, sounds, blends, etc., children must use metalinguistic language.

It is important to note that we have found children's emergent reading and writing status to be unrelated. That is, when IQ is equalized, children who do well in emergent reading situations may not do well in writing situations (Galda, Pellegrini, and Cox, in press). Further, some children may not be reading or writing, but the language which will help them do so is incipient in their make-believe play. Teachers should be aware of children's "multiple literacies" (Wolf et al. 1988), so that they can construct meaningful experiences for children in different domains.

How to Stimulate Children's Make-Believe

Make-believe is an important facilitator of school language and literacy for preschool and kindergarten children. The skills learned and practiced here develop into more traditional school-based skills. To facilitate this make-believe, we recommend, first, the construction of classroom interest centers which will elicit different functions of language, including the imaginative function (Pellegrini 1985). More specifically, doll and housekeeping centers tend to elicit fantasy from girls, and blocks elicit fantasy from boys; children seem unwilling to actively participate in centers that they see as sex-role inappropriate (Pellegrini and Perlmutter 1989).

Second, the role of the adult is to put out materials and then leave. We have found that adult presence actually inhibits children's fantasy and language uses. Children should be provided with numerous themes to enact. Besides everyday "scripts," children should be shown films and read books. Besides the inherent joy of these media, they provide stimuli with which to play.

Last, we think, and theory concurs (e.g., Pellegrini 1985; Piaget 1970), that make-believe is important for preschool and kindergarten children as a learning medium. As they engage in make-believe play, they learn and practice cognitive (perspective taking) linguistic (conveying meaning through language), and social (cooperation) skills.

Works Cited

Cook-Gumperz, J. 1977. "Situated Instructions: Language Socialization of School-age Children." In *Child Discourse*, edited by S. Ervin-Tripp and K. Mitchell-Karnan, 103–24. New York: Academic.

Galda, L., A. D. Pellegrini, and S. Cox. (In press). *Emergent Literacy and Play*. Paper presented at 1989 American Educational Research Association meeting, San Francisco.

Halliday, M. 1967. "Notes on Transitivity and Theme in English, Part 2." *Journal of Linguistics* 3: 177–274.

Olson, D. 1983. "'See! Jump!' Some Oral Language Antecedents of Literacy." In *Awakening to Literacy*, edited by H. Goelman, A. Oberg, and F. Smith, 185–92. Exeter, N.H.: Heinemann.

Pellegrini, A. 1985. "Explorations in Preschoolers' Construction of Cohesive Text in Two Play Contexts." In *Discourse Processes* 5: 101–108.

Pellegrini, A. D., L. Galda, and D. Rubin. 1984. "Context in Text: The Development of Oral and Written Language in Two Genres." *Child Development* 55: 1549–55.

Pellegrini, A. D., and J. C. Perlmutter. 1989. "Classroom Contextual Effects on Children's Play." *Developmental Psychology* 25: 289–96.

Piaget, J. 1970. *Structuralism*. New York: Basic Books.

Torrance, N., and D. Olson. 1984. "Oral Language Competence and the Acquisition of Literacy." In *The Development of Oral and Written Language in Social Contexts*, edited by A. Pellegrini and T. Yawkey, 167–82. Norwood, N.J.: Ablex.

Vygotsky, L. 1978. *Mind in Society*. Cambridge, Mass.: Harvard University Press.

Walsh, D., G. Price, and M. Gillingham. 1988. "The Critical but Transitory Importance of Letter Naming." *Reading Research Quarterly* 23: 108–22.

Wolf, D., L. Davidson, M. Davis, J. Walters, M. Hodges, and L. Scripp. 1988. "Beyond A, B, and C: A Broader and Deeper View of Literacy." In *Psychological Bases of Early Education*, edited by A. Pellegrini, 122–51. Chichester, England: Wiley.

7 Talking Up a Writing Community: The Role of Talk in Learning to Write

Anne Haas Dyson
University of California, Berkeley

As teachers, we sometimes overestimate our importance to our students. In their eyes, we are not the most significant figures in the classroom. To the contrary, teachers are sometimes regarded as mere peripheral beings that impose themselves as nuisances into the really important affairs of peer interaction. That world of peer interaction, that child collective, can provide instruction every bit as effective as the teacher's direct instruction. This oral environment is especially supportive as a medium for nurturing writing development. But we "peripheral" teachers need to be wise enough to know how to set up a climate in which students can take the initiative to talk up their writing.

Talk. The very word brings to mind images of at least two people who are not only sharing information but also building or maintaining a relationship, a social connection. Each past conversation helps shape the context for future ones as, through talk, we build a network of human relationships, a social world.

In literate communities, writing may figure into this social world and the ongoing talk that energizes it. Listen, for example, to first graders Julia and Regina, as Julia's talk about her writing reverberates through her classroom:

> Regina is hard at work in her journal when Julia hurries
> over to her table and interrupts her:
>
> *Julia:* Regina! Guess what I wrote in my journal. "I love Bill [a teacher of the older children]."

Support for this work was provided in part by the Office of Educational Research and Improvement/Department of Education (OERI/ED), through the Center for the Study of Writing. However, the opinions expressed herein do not necessarily reflect the position or policy of the OERI/ED, and no official endorsement by the OERI/ED should be inferred.—A.H.D.

Regina: Let me see.

And as Regina pauses to read Julia's text, Luan, another classmate,
gasps and then runs from table to table, whispering in girls' ears
about Julia's bold text.

Regina and Julia were special friends, having talked and played together for almost two years. In the above conversation, writing figured
in a functional way into their relationship—and, indeed, into the social
life of their classroom. The children were brought both literally and
figuratively close together, as they shared the conspiratorial feeling
that comes with being a little bit shocking.

In this chapter, I take a close look at Julia's and Regina's classroom
community. I examine talk's role in helping children become literate
members of this community; that is, I focus on how, through *talk*,
writing becomes "relevant to life" in this community (Vygotsky 1978,
118).

I stress three interrelated aspects of talk's dynamic role in writing
growth. First, talk provides the *social energy* that brings writing into the
nurturing network of human relationships. Through talk during
shared activities, children establish a network of relationships—they
become classmates and, often, friends. Talk about the shared activity
of writing brings that writing into this network. Second, talk serves
individual children as an *analytic tool*. Young children use talk to help
them plan and monitor many kinds of constructive tasks, including
drawing and block building. But during writing tasks, talk helps children analyze and manipulate language itself. Finally, talk does not
only support writing—it is supported by writing. That is, talk is a *social
consequence* of writing in a literate community, as in the social talk that
flowed from Julia's writing.

While my focus here is on young children, for authors of all ages, talk
contributes to and is enriched by writing. Indeed, in whole societies,
literacy finds a prominent niche if and when the information conveyed
through symbols (through written language) becomes part of the social network—when people talk about written materials and when
those materials can affect their views of themselves and their participation in the world (Heath 1986). I thus examine here, in a small community, a global phenomenon—the blossoming and maintaining of
literacy through talk.

This small community was located in an urban magnet school
where I observed extensively. (For further details, see Dyson 1989.)
One teacher, Margaret, was responsible for language arts instruction
for the school's three classes of primary-grade students: the kinder-

gartners, the first/second graders, and the second/third graders. All of the children worked regularly in journals, as they sat together drawing, writing, and talking. While the children worked, Margaret circulated, talking to them about their ideas and the mechanics of production and, in the kindergarten, acting as scribe for their dictations.

In the following pages, I discuss the powerful role of talk in learning to write, illustrating that role through excerpts from the daily dramas in Margaret's classroom.

Talk as Social Energy: Weaving Writing into the Network of Human Relationships

A basic function of written language is to allow people to communicate across great distances of time and place. And yet, young children are introduced to written language within the familiar activities of everyday life: People who matter to the young child use written language to accomplish ends that matter. Talk is interwoven in these literacy activities. For the learning child, it is talk that invests a text with meaning and, at the same time, that weaves a social web linking family members to each other and to the text.

Consider, for example, a grocery list at the center of family menu planning, an illegible phone message or returned check surrounded by a family argument, a letter to Grandma evolving amidst parent-child planning, or an "I love you" note that elicits an oral response and a hug. In such ways, talk reveals to the child the printed graphic's propositional meaning and social significance—its capacity to affect how people behave toward each other.

Children entering formal schooling will have had varied degrees and kinds of literacy experiences. School will offer some children their first opportunities to engage with extended written language. And school will demand of all children increasing evidence of their prowess at written language use. Writing and reading gain new social significance: they become marks of academic competence or incompetence.

This aspect of school literacy—its use as an indicator of required academic competence—is potentially problematic. Writing may no longer be—nor have the opportunity to become—an avenue for social participation. Rather, it may be only a performative skill to be mastered and displayed for teachers and parents. Thus, children may write sentences with periods, but they may not organize those sentences to serve varied pragmatic purposes or to give voice to their daily concerns.

Classrooms, though, have a powerful resource that can potentially provide an antidote to writing as competency performance—that resource is the children themselves. Their relationships with each other, forged through talk, can provide a nurturing context for writing as social participation. Within the peer group itself, the children may view writing as an important competency—an important skill. But, in time, the peer talk interwoven with the children's activity may invest writing with more powerful meanings: written messages may begin to figure into children's reactions to and relationships with each other.

An Illustration of the Child Collective

In group settings, children attend to other children. This lively peer interest has been commented upon by skilled teachers and researchers working with children from a variety of backgrounds, including Sylvia Ashton-Warner (1963), who worked with Maori children, Vivian Paley (1986), with middle-class U.S. children, and Susan Philips (1983), with Native American children.

Students in Margaret's classroom showed intense interest in what their peers were doing. Margaret did not specifically ask the children to talk with each other about academic or other tasks, but she expected them to share experiences, ideas, and, at times, possessions (e.g., extra hangers and plant pots for class projects). During journal time, she accepted their chatter as the normal by-product of children together, and she gave them opportunities to formally share their work. Margaret thus established a classroom structure that allowed children's relationships to grow through the talk surrounding their academic tasks, including their writing.

Sometimes the children's talk reflected their growing solidarity. Listen, for example, to the following journal-time conversation in which the children playfully acknowledge the importance of the journal activity in the adult world and their own capacity as "kids" to act in opposition to that world:

> *Jake:* Wanna put some cotton in here after every paper and make it a fat book and make it look like it's finished?
>
> *Manuel:* Yeah.
>
> *Jake:* And stick some cotton in it, and then we'll be finished with our thing. And make our mom and dad think we did lots of pages.
>
> *Hawkeye:* And then your mom and dad will say, "Hey! You skipped pages, you little kid."

Mostly, though, the children's talk reflected their interest in each other's activity and their desire for others to be interested in their own work. As individuals, they aimed to be viewed as socially competent but unique individuals, special members of the group. Within each class, the children displayed and acknowledged competence and specialness ("I know my phone number." "That's good, Manuel."), and pointed out shortcoming ("Where's the castle? That's a castle?!?!") (Dyson 1988). Through it all, they enjoyed one another, sharing past experiences and playfully creating new ones.

Initially, children's talk with each other about the content of their journals tended to focus on their drawings. The children called attention to their own efforts, and they admired those of others. The first and second graders, especially, were critical of drawn figures that did not look sensible to them. They listened to the oral stories some children told during drawing, and they responded to those stories, laughing at amusing ones, objecting to illogical ones, and sometimes joining in on the unfolding drama.

In the following example, Regina's peer, Jake, overhears her self-directed talk as she draws and tells a story about a little girl. Regina refers to the girl, who is dressed in a pink shirt and a brown jumper, as a Brownie. Jake first teases Regina and then critiques her drawing. But, in the end, he becomes quite interested in the real-world experiences behind Regina's efforts:

Jake: [teasing] You're a Brownie! You're a Brownie! [Jake, who enjoys language play and who is himself of mixed Black/Anglo ethnicity, seems to be teasing Regina about her skin color. But she does not understand and responds quite indignantly.]

Regina: No, I'm a Girl Scout.

Jake: You're a Brownie [still teasing]. Brownies do not wear um pink [seriously]. Brownies deliver cookies.

Regina: So do Girl Scouts.

Jake: You delivered any cookies? . . . [omitted data]

Regina: [talking to herself again] She's [the drawn girl] wearing a pink shirt with stripes. They have to [all the Brownies have to] wear the same thing.

Jake: They can't wear pink shirts.

Regina: They can wear pink shirts with stripes. I was 4 and I always wore this stuff. We sold popcorn.

Jake: OOOOh. Popcorn is yummy.

Regina: We had cheese and ice cream.

Jake: OOOOOh.

Regina: Chocolate fudge and we had chicken. I had french fries.
[And on Regina goes, telling Jake about the pleasures of being a
Brownie.]

Through the above interaction, Regina's symbolic world supported
and was supported by the social world. Jake was interested in his peers
and their activity, and so he was interested in Regina's activity. The
interaction led to a sharing of experiences and joint pleasures—popcorn, cheese, and ice cream—and an exchange of opinions about the
logic of Regina's efforts. That is, talk about Regina's symbolic world led
the children to reflect about experiences in the wider world of people,
places, and things. Through talk in the social world they shared, Regina's private symbolic world gained real-world relevance for both
children.

The interaction that enveloped Regina's talking and drawing foreshadowed the talk that eventually brought the children's written texts
into the ongoing social life of the classroom. Initially, however, the
content of writing was not a central part of the children's social life in
the way that the content of their talking and drawing was. The meaning of the written graphics themselves (the black-and-white squiggles) was not as accessible to peers as was the meaning of drawn
pictures. And much of the talk during writing focused on the mechanics of production, for talk was a major tool for gaining control of the
complex writing act. In the next section, I examine this aspect of talk's
role in writing.

**Talk as Analytic Tool:
Controlling the Complex Writing Act**

As noted in the previous section, children learn about written language through the oral medium—through participating in literacy
activities with other people who talk about and thus make apparent
the functions and meanings of particular texts. But children who understand, for example, that a string of letters represents a message do
not necessarily understand precisely how black-and-white squiggles
on paper mediate between them and other people. Children may not
initially view print as representing language; rather, they may view
print as directly representing meaning, analogous to how a picture
represents meaning (Dyson 1983; Ferreiro and Teberosky 1982; Vygotsky 1978).

In classroom settings, adults and more expert peers help children
ask a "key question" about print: "'How does something I can say look

in print?' or, vice versa, 'What does that print say'" (Torrey 1969, 556)? That is, they help children grasp "that print is a form of language like what you speak and hear" (Torrey 1979, 141). Adults might act as scribes for a child's dictations; in this role they pay close attention to the child's language—repeating the child's words exactly, monitoring their writing by pronouncing those words out loud, rereading those words, asking if what they have written is correct, maybe then correcting, or editing, the written words (McNamee, McLane, Cooper, and Kerwin 1985). That is, they use language as a tool (through repeating, rereading, questioning) to analyze language as a written message.

Adults or other children might act as analytical responders to a child's independent writing; in this role they also pay close attention to the child's language. They might ask the child to read the text, repeat the child's words to verify their understanding, or break down the child's message, asking about the correspondence between parts of the text and parts of the message ("Oh. Where does it say 'father'?"). Again, people who are interested in children's efforts help children use language as an object of attention and as a tool through which it is analyzed.

When child writers grasp this essential insight—that print is related in precise ways to formal characteristics of speech—they themselves begin to use talk as both a source of written meaning and as a means for getting that meaning into print.

An Illustration of Talk as Tool

The children in Margaret's classroom struggled with the connection between print and speech. As they wrote, they tended to talk to themselves, rereading already-written text, slowly pronouncing words they were attempting to encode, and then rereading again. However, the children's very vocal struggle with encoding often elicited the attention of their peers, who could then offer advice. Listen, for example, to Jake and his peers in the following example; they illustrate talk's helpfulness as a tool for managing the unwieldy writing act:

> Jake has finished drawing and has been working hard on his text. He ekes out "There is a"—a variation of the common picture-labeling opening, "This is a." He next writes "three" and then rereads, "There are three." He self-corrects, though, to the more accurate (if less grammatical) "There is a three." He proceeds and eventually writes:
> There is a three designs in the sky and the.
> He backs up a couple of words, rereads, and attempts to sound out the next word:

Jake: "And the buh"

Jake figures out the *b* and then asks for the spelling of *big*. Next, he backs up and rereads once again:

Jake: "The big one, the big one is, ih, ih" [*one* is not written]

Jake spells *is*, and then, again, he rereads, perhaps to figure out what the next word should be:

Jake: "This [there] is a—this is a three designs in the sky and the big one—"

Jake realizes that he has not written *one*. He adds the word and once again rereads:

Jake: "There is a three—"

Hawkeye: "There is three."

Jake: "There is a three—"

Hawkeye: "There is three ⌈ designs in the sky"

Jake: ⌊ "designs in the sky
and the big one is—"

Hawkeye: "There is three designs in the sky." Erase that *a*.

Jake: Why?

Hawkeye: Because "There is A three designs—"

Johnny: There IS three designs [Johnny's subsequent comment suggests that he is pointing out to Hawkeye that, indeed, Jake does have three designs on his paper and therefore should not be corrected.]

Hawkeye: "There is—" Listen: "There is a ⌈ three designs"

Johnny: ⌊ "three designs"

Jake: ⌊ "three designs
in the sky."

Hawkeye: That doesn't make sense.

Johnny: Yes it does. You don't know nothing. Jake, however, erases the *a*.

To encode his message, Jake used speech to focus on written language—repeating, rereading, reconsidering. His peers overheard his struggle and offered their own advice.

As the above excerpt suggests, spoken and read text gradually became a legitimate object of attention within the peer group; like a labeled or otherwise explained drawing, it could be the focus of intense discussion.

Talk as Social Consequence: Weaving New
Social Networks through Talk about Writing

The preceding sections of this chapter have portrayed talk as writing's nurturing force. Talk carves out its social niche, tames its awkward first steps. But talk's relationship with writing is not unidirectional. For writing, in turn, nurtures talk and thus the social relationships talk supports. Just as talk brings writing into the network of human relationships, writing can channel talk in new ways, bringing about new kinds of human networks, networks woven through talk about text. Avid readers, for example, might ask each other, "Have you read . . . ?" "What do you think of her books?" "Did you see the review of . . . ?" Indeed, authors can thus become invisible members of social groups.

Talk about authors and their texts is important to groups for reasons both social and intellectual. Through such talk, group members link themselves together, establishing common values and expectations for written language—perhaps even acquiring a special vocabulary for talking about and analyzing texts (Heath 1986).

In classrooms in which young children draw and write about their ideas, spontaneous group talk may initially focus on drawing rather than writing. In time, however, writing's content may assume center stage. Indeed, in the structured peer response groups of older middle and secondary school students, spontaneous peer talk seems to focus on content (Freedman 1987). This attention to content can be powerfully influenced by the talk about writing modeled by the teacher (Sowers 1985). But it is also influenced by the children's own interest in each other's activity. Written messages can become the center of spontaneous social interactions and intellectual debates, which talk can feed back into individual writers' efforts (Dyson 1987).

Illustrations of Talk as Social Consequence

In Margaret's classroom, writing gradually became more important as the children progressed from kindergarten to third grade. The children began spontaneously to call attention to their written texts rather than only to their drawings (e.g., "Listen to this" occurred along with "Look at this"). Children became known among the peer group for certain journal themes; for example, during his second-grade year, Jake was known for his bubble car stories. Choosing to write a particular kind of story could be a way of proclaiming one's solidarity with—or desire to be accepted by—a particular child or group of children.

Through written messages, children could not only gain peers' attention but also engage their intellectual energy as the children debated a text's logic or truthfulness—or the author's knowledge and goodness (if, for example, someone wrote a "lie"). Moreover, they could bring their peers into their written texts, making them characters in their stories; in this way, they developed a new way of playing together. Children were thus learning that written language does not just represent meaning—it figures in a very active, formative way into the life of a community.

In the following example, Jake uses his *written entry* to engage his friend Manuel in a lively and *oral* drama:

Jake and Manuel are sitting together working on their journals:

> *Jake:* Now I'm gonna write a story about Manuel. This time he's gonna be alone [i.e., unlike other stories I have written about Manuel, this time I will not be in the story with him]. It's gonna be an adventure story.
> [to Manuel] You're going back in time.

Jake begins writing, stopping to reread his story and, as he does so, both Manuel and Maggie voice an objection:

> *Jake:* [rereading] "Once there was a jet and Manuel is going to fly the jet and Manuel is going to shoot them—"
> *Maggie:* Who's the *them*?
> *Jake:* The *them* is the bad guys.
> *Manuel:* The bad guys?
> *Jake:* Yeah.
> *Manuel:* The *them* is the bad guys? Who's the bad guys?
> *Jake:* The *them*.

Jake's reasoning here may be a bit circular, but he is being forced by his friends to consider the ability of his audience to understand his message. He seems to remember their concern, as, later, he refers to the "real bad guys."

> *Jake:* Uh, Manuel, you get to see Buck Rogers.
> *Manuel:* What?
> *Jake:* Buck Rogers.
> *Manuel:* Oh, oh, you mean in your story. [Note how Manuel is distinguishing between the imaginative text world and the social world in which that text is read and talked about.]
> *Jake:* Yeah. Buck Rogers, twenty-first-century person. . . This guy's [Manuel's] going to get blown to pieces if he doesn't do what Buck Rogers says. 'Cause they're going to go against the real bad guys.

Jake's text soon reads as follows:

> Once there was a jet and Manuel is going to fly the jet and Manuel is going to shoot them but then Manuel is going in time and when he does he is going to the twenty-first century. Manuel is going to see Buck Rogers. Buck is going to teach Manuel how to get the bad guys and they are to find the real bad guys.
>
> *Jake:* And now he's [Manuel's] going to get blown to pieces, and we'll never see him again.
>
> *Manuel:* What? I'm going to get blown to pieces?
>
> *Jesse:* Yup. [giggles]
>
> *Manuel:* What an idea for the story to have. [Manuel again distinguishes between the story and social world, and his brother, Marcos, picks up on Manuel's point with a story-like comment:]
>
> *Marcos:* And Manuel got blown into nothing. The end. [Manuel laughs.]

Manuel objects to this possible turn of events, pointing out that he is "just a little kid." Surely Buck would have some sympathy for him. And Jake agrees:

> *Jake:* You might get your butt saved by Buck Rogers. You want your butt saved by Buck Rogers?
>
> *Manuel:* What I want is my body saved. I don't wanna die. . . .
>
> *Jake:* You gonna be glidin', boy. You're gonna have some fun, boy. You're gonna be scared to death.
>
> *Manuel:* Well, can I have fun with you? [Manuel is trying to reason through the story with Jake at this point.] Because if you're right where I am you can't blow me up because you don't want to blow up.

In the "Buck Rogers" event, Jake's writing served as a focal point for peer engagement. In Margaret's classroom, such spontaneous talk about writing foreshadowed individual children's voiced concerns about how their peers might respond to their writing (Dyson 1987). Children thus appeared to help each other learn that their written texts figured into their social worlds— that peers might, for example, question, laugh, or empathize as they heard or read those texts.

The Role of Talk in Learning to Write: Developing the Dialectic between the Individual and the Community

In the preceding sections of this chapter, I have discussed the interrelated aspects of talk's role in learning to write. To give life to this presentation, I have drawn upon observations made in Margaret's classroom. In the community of children she guided, talk enveloped each child's writing, bringing it into the ongoing social life of the classroom—and, as the children gained control of writing, it, in turn, gradually came to shape talk and, through talk, the children's shared lives. Thus, in time, talk set in motion a dialectical relationship, not only between itself and writing, but, more important, between the individual writer and the social group within which that individual's writing figured.

This is precisely the sort of social dialectic that the Russian psychologist Vygotsky (1978) viewed as critical to learning. Throughout our lives, the responses others give to our behaviors enlarges our appreciation both of the social world within which we live and of the power of our own individual behavior. In this section of the chapter, then, I aim to highlight this developing dialectic.

In the opening anecdote, Regina, a first grader, interrupted her journal activity to attend to Julia and her giggle-inducing text. At this early point in Regina's growth as a writer, the classroom social life surrounded but did not imbue her writing. Regina's talk suggested that, like most of her first-grade peers, she concentrated during writing on analyzing and spelling her message; she abandoned her own journal work to attend socially to others.

In time, the social life of the classroom no longer surrounded but began to infuse the children's writing. Their joint talk during writing seemed to shape their individual reflections. While writing, they no longer used speech primarily to analyze and spell planned messages; they began to analyze the content of those messages. They were coming to understand that the ongoing actions of writers were interactions with others: Words are chosen, written, and considered for their capacity not merely to represent messages but to mediate between writers and readers.

Listen, for example, to Manuel reread his written text, not only to see if he has written the words he intended to write, but to see if his words will convey his intentions to others—his analysis of his text is directed beyond encoding and toward his anticipated interactions:

Manuel is in the midst of a long involved story about a snowman. He is working on the page in which the snowman goes in back of a house to look at a thermometer. The previous day a peer had had difficulty reading this page:

> *Manuel:* I think this page is a little bit hard, how he went into the house. [rereading] "Went into the house"— I mean, "went *by* the

house." I think people can tell just by the picture that um [laughs]—but I hope they can 'cause I don't know how I'm gonna write it so that this is . . . [Manuel's voice trails off, as he worries about whether or not his readers—his peers—will understand that the snowman went in back of the house.]

By their third-grade year, the children's social lives together were not only infusing but being shaped by writing. They were, in some ways, a literary collective, one whose memories of the past included the stories they shared. A year after he had written his snowman story, Sonia remembered it well:

> *Sonia:* Manuel?
>
> *Manuel:* Yeah?
>
> *Sonia:* Are you doing—Are you doing a story like you did um and you—you know, um, in your other um journal?
>
> *Manuel:* Last year?
>
> *Sonia:* With the snow. The whole journal was about snow.
>
> *Manuel:* Yeah, well it's maybe not the whole journal this time.
>
> *Sonia:* OK. 'Cause I just wanted to know, 'cause I thought that was sorta neat.

Moreover, writing was, for many of the children, a part of their friendship—a social activity, similar to going to the movies or playing chase. It was a legitimate child activity, not merely a school assignment. Indeed, the last day I visited the school, Regina, now a third grader, and her friend Marissa demonstrated how intertwined literacy was with their relationship:

Regina has just told me about her story called "I'm Coming to Get You":

> *Marissa:* It's a good story.
>
> *Regina:* I got the story from her because she had a book.
>
> *Marissa:* It was called "The Baby Sitter," but she changed it.

Marissa then tells me about the "funny poem" she has just written in her journal. It is a poem that Regina's grandfather had taught Regina, and Regina, in turn, had taught Marissa—a poem about monkeys and wine, geese and fiddles, and sweet potato vines.

Conclusion: Valuing Children's Talk about Text

The perspective on talk and writing presented here suggests that, as teachers, we must be concerned about both individuals' writing efforts and the classroom "functional system"—the classroom community within which individuals' writing matters. A strong system cannot depend only on talk between teacher and child. The social energy that is generated among the children themselves—their own desires for individual expression and social communication—may infuse writing itself.

Many kinds of child talk contribute to the health of a community of writers—even talk that may seem only tangentially related to the writing task itself. Through their talk about their symbolic worlds, including those drawn as well as those written, children may come to view such worlds as tools for reflecting on their own experiences and for jointly exploring common experiences. In this sense, discussions of Brownies and Buck Rogers can be at least as important as talk about periods and paragraphs for helping children realize the social significance of writing. For, from the Vygotskian perspective guiding this chapter, writing's social significance must be experienced through the external processes of groups if it is to be realized in the internal processes of group members. Eventually, individual children may begin to anticipate and perhaps even manipulate peer responses to the content of their worlds, just as Jake worked for Manuel's interest and playful alarm.

We might, therefore, judge the success of our teaching efforts, not only by how they seem to affect children's texts, but also by how they seem to affect children's talk. Our arranging of children in pairs or groups, our modeling of writing processes and audience response, and our discussing and informing about the physical and social world may influence whether or not children talk, how they talk, and what they talk about.

It was important, for example, that Margaret allowed children formal opportunities to share their work and that she both appreciated their efforts and was genuinely curious when she did not understand their sense. And it was good too that she encouraged the children, during these formal sharing times, to respond appreciatively to teach each other. But Margaret was the teacher, the expert, the one who set down the rules for journal time, who told their parents how they were doing. The children, being intelligent, knew that Margaret evaluated their competence (see Dyson 1988). They could not easily learn from Margaret their most critical lesson—that, for the writer, interaction does not happen *after* the writing is done; it happens *as* writing is done. It was the talk that Margaret influenced but did not control that made writing a social act—the children's spontaneous "Look what I wrote!"; "What does that mean?"; and "You're gonna be in my story!" Thus, writing that is a part of the children's world, not just the teacher's world, may better take root and grow with them into their adult lives. In the end, then, our most important teaching tool may not be any one teaching strategy or instructional material. Rather, it may well be the sort of stance toward children that we adopt. The most helpful stance would seem to include an appreciation of children, not simply as budding writers, but more important, as interesting people with experiences, opinions, and ideas to share with us and, just as important, with each other. And then, the literacy tools that schools value may be embedded within relationships that the child values. Text, like talk, may thus further the child's sense of belonging, that feeling of community that makes our school lives together both personally satisfying and socially meaningful.

Works Cited

Ashton-Warner, S. 1963. *Teacher.* New York: Simon & Schuster.

Dyson, A. Haas. 1983. "The Role of Oral Language in Early Writing Processes." *Research in the Teaching of English* 17: 1–30.

———. 1987. "The Value of 'Time Off Task': Young Children's Spontaneous Talk and Deliberate Text." *Harvard Educational Review* 57: 396–420.

———. 1988. "Unintentional Helping in the Primary Grades: Writing in the Children's World. In *The Social Construction of Written Communication,* edited by B. A. Rafoth and D. L. Rubin. Norwood, N.J.: Ablex.

———. 1989. *The Multiple Worlds of Child Writers: Friends Learning to Write.* New York: Teachers College Press.

Ferreiro, E., and A. Teberosky. 1982. *Literacy before Schooling.* Exeter, N.H.: Heinemann.

Freedman, S. 1987. *Peer Response Groups in Two Ninth-grade Classrooms.* Technical Report No. 12. Berkeley: University of California, Center for the Study of Writing.

Heath, S. Brice. 1986. "Critical Factors in Literacy Development." In *Literacy, Society, and Schooling: A Reader,* edited by S. deCastell, A. Luke, and K. Egan, 209–29. Cambridge, England: Cambridge University Press.

McNamee, G. D., J. McLane, P. A. Cooper, and S. M. Kerwin. 1985. "Cognition and Affect in Early Literacy Development." *Early Child Development and Care* 20: 229–44.

Paley, V. 1986. *Mollie Is Three: Growing Up in School.* Chicago: University of Chicago Press.

Philips, S. U. 1983. *The Invisible Culture: Communication in Classroom and Community.* New York: Longman.

Sowers, S. 1985. "Learning to Write in a Workshop: A Study in Grades One through Four." In *Advances in Writing Research: Children's Early Writing Development: Vol. 1,* edited by M. Farr. Norwood, N.J.: Ablex.

Torrey, J. W. 1969. "Learning to Read without a Teacher: A Case Study." *Elementary English* 46: 550–56, 658.

_____. 1979. "Reading That Comes Naturally: The Early Reader." In *Reading Research: Advances in Theory and Practice: Vol. 1*, edited by T. G. Waller and G. E. MacKinnon, 115–44. New York: Academic Press.

Vygotsky, L. S. 1978. *Mind in Society*. Cambridge, Mass.: Harvard University Press.

8 Talking in Writing Groups

Anne Ruggles Gere
University of Michigan

A traditional view of writing portrays writing as a solitary activity. Locked away in some garret with a sheaf of paper and a supply of ink, the writer labors in uninterrupted concentration. Not so for many real-world writers. In law offices, advertising agencies, engineering firms, and government agencies, the mode of writing is collaborative. Writing episodes are likewise social episodes. Thus approaches to teaching writing which make use of peer writing groups provide quite realistic preparation for writing tasks outside of school. But some educators are skeptical that peer writing groups can stay on task, or that they can provide useful advice for developing writers. To the contrary, students learn a lot about writing when they function in the reciprocal roles of writer and responder. But successful peer writing groups do not happen spontaneously. Teachers must help students learn how to function constructively in such groups.

"You'd better not come to observe my class tomorrow because the kids will be meeting in their writing groups." Many of us have said or have heard someone else say a sentence like this one. Several levels of meaning, packed together like layers of an onion, lie behind sentences like this one. One of the first layers contains the idea that organizing and encouraging writing groups is not "really" teaching. Teaching is an active endeavor, one that requires the instructor or "sage on the stage" to take a central role, and individuals who stand on the sidelines listening to students talk to one another cannot be described as teachers.

Another layer of meaning deals with the fixed nature of knowledge. In this view knowledge is a given—the information students need is not subject to question. Accordingly, the transmission of knowledge from those who know (teachers) to those who do not know (students) constitutes education. Still another layer of meaning deals with how talk works. If one assumes that a teacher should take a dominant role in the classroom in order to impart knowledge to students, and if talk—in the form of lecture or teacher-directed discussion—is the primary means for imparting knowledge, then one sees talk as a conduit. Talk, seen in these terms, can be analogized to an electrical cord as it carries knowledge from the teacher's mind to that of the student who will assimilate the knowledge.

These views of teaching as performing, of knowledge as fixed, and of talk as a conduit underlie statements that describe classroom use of writing groups as "not teaching," but alternative perceptions of teaching, of knowledge, and of talk exist. An alternative view of teaching emphasizes a facilitative role, describing the teacher as one who creates situations in which students learn. Correspondingly, knowledge can be described as created rather than fixed or given, and talk as the instrument by which meanings are negotiated and created.

Thinking of teaching as facilitative, of knowledge as socially constructed, and of talk as creating rather than simply conveying meaning eliminates sentences such as "You'd better not come to observe my class tomorrow because the kids will be meeting in writing groups" from teachers' conversations. This chapter explores the implications of these alternative views of teaching, knowledge, and talk by looking closely at how talk in writing groups supports learning.

Writing groups or peer response groups or teacherless writing classes or helping circles—these groups carry multiple names—have been employed in this country's classrooms for over a hundred years. Published accounts indicate that teachers have been asking students to read and talk about one another's writing since at least 1880 (Lord). Until the 1960s, writing groups did not receive a great deal of attention from teachers, from researchers, from publishers. But their endurance across decades of marginality suggests their inherent value: Writing groups aid learning. They aid learning by allowing students to talk about their work, and this talk helps students learn about writing.

Two teachers work in adjacent classrooms. Both give considerable attention to writing, but their methods differ significantly. The first arranges student desks in orderly rows and keeps classroom talk at a minimum so that writers will not be distracted. After students have developed ideas, they write first drafts to which the teacher responds in writing. Then they revise their work and hand in finished writing for the teacher to grade. The class next door is not nearly so orderly. Desks are frequently pushed into small circles while students meet in small groups to discuss their ideas for writing or to read and respond to passages from work-in-progress. Sometimes the noise level gets so high that students in the room next door complain, and the principal who walks by is prompted to ask, "What kind of learning is going on here?"

The answer is that at least two types of learning occur in classrooms which employ writing groups. The first, and most obvious, concerns the task at hand. Research indicates that students who participate in writing groups produce better writing than those who do not (Bouton and Tutty 1975; O'Donnell et al. 1985). Students in writing groups produce better writing because talk helps them identify and solve problems at many levels—word, sentence, paragraph, and whole piece of writing—and solving these problems leads to a better piece of writing. The second type of learning that occurs in writing groups extends beyond the task at hand. Students who participate in writing groups learn about the nature of writing. They develop a language to describe what they and others do to write, they learn about audience needs and expectations, and they develop criteria by which to evaluate writing. This second type of learning extends into the student writer's future.

Just as more than one type of learning occurs in writing groups, so writing groups take more than one form—two or more students may work together to produce a single piece of writing; students may respond orally or in writing to one another's drafts; students may develop criteria and evaluate one another's finished pieces of writing. And there are multiple variations of each of these approaches. Students may meet once to discuss a piece of writing in progress, or they may meet several times during the development of a single piece of writing. They may discuss proposed topics as part of generating ideas for writing, they may comment on the effectiveness of drafts, or they may offer suggestions for editing and mechanical correctness. In all their manifestations, writing groups foster collaboration among students—a collaboration enabled by talk.

Multiple-Author Groups

Although not a staple of all classrooms, the multiple-author writing task enables students to learn a great deal. When several students work together to produce a single piece of writing, they need to examine the task completely. If, for example, they are working on a project that requires research, they will often begin by deciding what information they need to gather. A class of junior English, for example, was divided into groups of three, and each group was charged with writing a report about an American writer whose work was being studied by the class. One of these small groups selected Emily Dickinson, and participated in this conversation during one of their first days together:

S1: Let's see, what do we need to find out?

S2: Well, we need to get some more information about Amherst during the nineteenth century. What was going on outside the house where Emily lived?

S3: I wonder if it matters since she hardly went out anyway.

S2: I think we should have some idea about what was going on— there was the Civil War and all that stuff.

S1: It's OK with me if we get more information about history, but I think we should also find out more about Emily's family. What kind of people were they?

S3: Yeah, we probably should. I think we should also check into other writers of her time. Who would she have read, anyway?

S2: This is all fine, but don't forget we need to look at her poetry, too.

S1: OK, I've got it. Why don't you do the history stuff, you do the other writers of the time and I'll do the family. Then we can all do the poetry and compare our ideas.

This division of labor does more than enable students to get the job done. It helps them understand more fully what the task requires. In the process of recognizing that historical, social, and familial background are necessary to a consideration of Emily Dickinson's poetry, the students who participate in this group are learning about the multiple perspectives necessary to their project. Identifying information necessary to the task and dividing the labor develop students' analytical skills. As they talk about their common project they see its various aspects and create ways to reduce each into a piece of work to be handled by a single individual. The process of talking about what a task requires enhances students' analytical skills because talk makes the division into parts more explicit than it would be for any student writing alone.

To be sure, students do not always move so smoothly or so quickly to analyze a task and divide it into individual parts, but the central strategy remains the same. Even when they initially fail to see how to begin or share the task, the process of talking about their work eventually leads them to a solution. Along the way they learn a great deal about how to work cooperatively with others. Research on the language of writing groups reveals that a significant portion of talk in writing groups deals with group procedures (Gere and Abbott 1985). Students make decisions about how the group should operate, give one another directives, and ask questions about how the group is working. Their conversations include lines such as this one, from a group in a sophomore class:

S1: Tomorrow we should talk about how to pull that draft together.

S2: You go first, Andy. Read your first paragraph.

S3: We're running out of time. What if we all make comments on that section and leave the rest for tomorrow?

These comments appear unremarkable until we consider the kind of language dominant in most classrooms. Research indicates that directives such as those above are rarely available to students (Sinclair and Coulthard 1975). Teachers are usually the only ones who make statements about allocation of time, solicit a response, or suggest the next activity. Students' classroom language is usually limited to making responses or asking occasional questions in response to teacher directives. By giving students access to a greater range of language, writing groups provide opportunities for linguistic growth as well as social maturation. Students learn to use a wide range of linguistic functions. They solicit information from one another, assign one another tasks, make observations about group processes and products, and decide how to allocate time. Talking in writing groups increases students' skills with a wide range of language functions.

Not all groups, of course, proceed the same way. Instead of dividing a writing task into portions to be completed by individuals, groups may decide to work more closely, involving the whole group in gathering ideas for and composing each part of the eventual paper. Small groups may even use a single pen and pad, producing work in which no single individual's sentences can be identified. If this sounds implausible, recall that professional writers such as Sandra Gilbert and Susan Gubar report that they write exactly this way, sharing a single yellow pad and losing track of which sentences are generated by whom. No matter what method they employ, group members talk about writing, and in the process, learn both strategies for improving the current project and skills that transfer to other writing.

A similar form of analysis occurs as students decide how to combine their efforts. If they have written separate parts, they will sometimes identify one individual as the general editor of the project. During this process of combining individual parts, students learn a great deal about synthesis. Their conversations focus on identifying redundancies, on developing ways to combine various ideas and information, on shaping transitions. These are, of course, processes familiar to writers who work alone, but by talking with others, students generate alternative strategies, become more self-conscious about decisions made, and develop a language to describe what they do. Here, for example, is an excerpt from a group discussion in a freshman class writing multiple-author papers about local history:

> *S1:* There's one place where it doesn't fit. I think the thing about the river needs to be repeated.
>
> *S2:* Do you mean the line about the bridge? Maybe we could move it to page two.
>
> *S1:* Yeah, that might do it, and then we could make a transition to the present.

Phrases such as "needs to be repeated," "make a transition," and "move that to page one" demonstrate students' growing ability to look at their own work analytically.

Response Groups

School writing does not often assign multiple authors to produce a single text. But the more common configuration of each individual producing a separate text likewise encourages learning through talk at the same time that it leads students to produce better writing. Talk about individual drafts fosters learning because the language of writing groups focuses on specific details in the text. General comments such as "awkward phrasing" or "good organization" or "sentences need variety"—the sorts of comments that can be transferred from one piece of writing to another—occur rarely in student writing groups. Instead, students attend to the language of the text, offering specific responses. Here, for example, is an excerpt from the conversation of a senior class response group talking about a draft read aloud by one of its members:

> *S1:* I think you should leave out the "I will" because that's saying you haven't done it yet. It stuck out to me there, and it stuck out at the end. I don't know why. I'm trying to think of what makes it awkward. I think what it is, um ... you're saying ... you're trying to describe the reactions, and why you're doing it ... when you should just say that you've done it. Not that you're going to do it, but that you, you look at it instead of from the present, from the past. Describe it in the past tense.
>
> *S2:* How about "So I'll proceed toward him ..." and I'll cut, I'll cut out "I feel ... slowly make my way."

The essence of what the first student expresses could be captured in a marginal "awk," but this student's process of exploring the problem of shifting tenses makes the issue much more explicit for the author. The author begins to think along with the responder, to see how the text is read by another because the attention of the group focuses directly on the language rather than dismissing it with a more generalized comment.

Students also develop a language to describe their own writing processes when they critique one another's drafts. Some writing groups listen to members read their drafts aloud and offer oral response while others read drafts silently and then discuss their responses. Either way, a conversation about writing evolves. Students discuss what they have done and what they plan to do in their writing. Their language contains exchanges such as:

> S1: What are you going to do next?
>
> S2: I usually write everything and then I cut it down. Now it's time to cut.

In saying aloud what she plans to do next, the second student in this exchange affirms her understanding of her own process of writing:

> S1: It needs more detail in that part about the garden.
>
> S2: Yeah, I guess I should develop that part, describe the flowers and everything.

Thanks to the observation of the first speaker, the second student in this exchange comes to a new understanding of what the word "develop" can mean to writers:

> S1: Shouldn't it be "The agent gave the ticket to my friend and me, not my friend and I"?
>
> S2: I think you're right. I just don't pay much attention to that kind of stuff when I'm writing a draft.

At the same time that it reinforces a point of usage, this exchange enables one student to understand how another proceeds while writing.

As they explain what they do as they write, students clarify their own processes for themselves, and at the same time, listening to the accounts of others reinforces the idea that there is no one "right" way to write. Comments such as the one above about the need for more detail can lead students to new activities in writing such as developing description in a second draft. In addition to talking about their processes or *how* they write, students in writing groups discuss formal aspects of writing. Their discussions include exchanges such as:

> S1: What about the introduction?

> *S2:* I can't write the beginning until I've decided what the main part will say.

Familiar terms such as "introduction" take on new meaning when students use them to talk about their own work.

> *S1:* I think that bit about Saturday night needs to be included.
>
> *S2:* Yeah, I need to make a transition between the first meeting and Saturday night.

Here the suggestion about a need for more information leads the second speaker to an elaborated understanding of how transitions clarify meanings in writing.

> *S1:* It seems awkward when you describe the reactions and why you're doing it . . . when you should just say that you've done it. You know, look at it from the past instead of the present. That's it, use the past tense here.

Use terms such as "past tense" as well as "introduction" and "transition" indicate students' developing vocabulary about writing. Intermingled with comments about processes and forms of writing are statements that demonstrate students' growing ability to make connections between their reading and their writing, to see how their work contributes to an ongoing intertextual conversation. Here, for example, are some excerpts from an eleventh-grade writing group:

> *S1:* It's got to show something like cracker boxes for furniture. I mean it's obviously not a very romantic life. You know, something like the way Dickens describes that house.
>
> *S2:* The sentences seem very choppy to me. But maybe it's OK. Hemingway uses short sentences like that.

By drawing on features of other texts to describe their own, students develop new ways of looking at their work. In particular, they become more sensitive to stylistic features in their own and others' writing. At the same time, they decrease the distance between their own writing and that of famous (capital A) Authors. They recognize that their own writing has something in common with what they read in books written by others, and in so doing, they begin to think of themselves as writers rather than drudges fulfilling a teacher's requirement.

This language about writing, whether it deals with processes, forms, or intertextual issues, plays an important part in students' learning. Not only do they learn about how other writers proceed and broaden their repertoires for thinking about writing, they develop language about writing. Psychologists describe language about language as *me-*

talanguage and claim that it contributes significantly to *metacognition*, or the ability to plan, monitor, and evaluate one's information processing (Sternberg 1984). Metacognition is often cited as a major contributor to general intelligence. As students reflect on what they do as they write (with phrases such as "time to cut" or "when I'm writing a draft"), consider possibilities in forms (using terms such as "introduction" or "transition"), or make comparisons across pieces of writing (as when they compare their sentences with Hemingway's), they are not only learning more about writing, they are exercising their metacognitive capacities.

The immediacy of writing groups also fosters students' audience awareness. They learn that what is clear to them is not necessarily clear to an audience, and as a result, they learn to take audience needs into account as they write. Here, for example, is an excerpt from a writing group in a fifth-grade class:

> *S1:* I like that part where you said that you remembered it so well.
>
> *S2:* When you said the town seemed smaller? They're adding on and stuff so it would be bigger if there's a train station there now.
>
> *S3:* What I meant was, with the fog it seems smaller.
>
> *S2:* OK, if you meant that, why didn't you put in because of the fog?
>
> *S3:* Maybe I should change it.
>
> *S4:* Why do you wish it was like it was before? You should put, you know, what you did before to make it real fun and stuff.

In this conversation the author (S3) is confronted by her audience directly and learns that the meaning she intended is not the meaning her audience inferred. To the audience the word "smaller" seemed inappropriate for describing a town where new buildings had been constructed. The perceptual distortions caused by the fog—although completely clear to the author—simply could not be grasped by the audience without more explanation. A student who hears her peers say that they do not understand is much more likely to want to revise her work than the student who has been admonished by the teacher to polish a draft. Writing groups draw upon the power of peer pressure to motivate revision. At the same time, writing groups foster audience awareness, enabling student writers to move away from their own perspectives and consider what information their readers will need. Hearing another student say that something is unclear helps them see their own writing from the perspective of an audience, and perspective-taking is an important part of writing. The immediacy of response possible in writing groups likewise contributes to its effect. Rather than receiving written comments on writing produced some time ago, students in writing groups receive responses as soon as they have finished reading their work aloud or as soon as their peers have read their work silently.

Many students claim that they internalize the voices of individuals in their writing groups so that, when they are writing, they imagine what a given person might say about the piece. This internalization of audience moves students one step closer to being effective critics of their own writing. One group of sophomores reflecting on the preceding year's experience in writing groups made these statements about the effect of working together:

> *S1:* Sometimes when I was writing I could just hear Tom saying, "I need to know what your topic is," and I would start writing an explanation for Tom.
>
> *S2:* Yeah, the same kind of thing happened for me. When I started using lots of "is" and "was" I could hear Susan saying, "I want stronger verbs."

By imagining what a writing group member might say in response to a selection of writing, students broaden their critical capacities and develop a better ear for their own writing.

Evaluative Groups

Perhaps the most effective means of encouraging students' self-criticism is to use writing groups to evaluate finished pieces of writing as well as to respond to drafts in progress. The challenge for the instructor is to make clear the differences between groups that respond to drafts and groups that evaluate finished selections. Writing groups that deal with work in progress generally do best to concentrate on issues such as general impression created, persuasiveness of argument or point being made, and effectiveness of phrasing, thereby avoiding premature consideration of mechanical correctness in writing. Insisting that students listen to drafts read aloud rather than reading one another's work silently can prevent students from becoming overly concerned with issues of usage in drafts.

Alternatively, groups dealing with finished pieces of writing find it much more productive to have copies of the whole paper so they can consider mechanical correctness as well as larger features of discourse. Taking different approaches—listening to drafts read orally and reading finished work silently—enables students to distinguish between revising and editing and, thereby, to understand the processes of writing more fully.

The task of writing groups charged with evaluating a finished piece of writing centers on developing criteria for evaluation. Prefacing a writing assignment with an examination of models enables students to develop evaluative criteria, to determine what makes "a good one." If, for example, the upcoming assignment emphasizes description, the instructor can provide an example of a good description, written by either a published writer or a good student writer. The class then reads the model piece very closely, paying attention to the ways the author achieves certain effects. The process of noting the features they like and figuring out how they were achieved leads students to develop a list of criteria for evaluating descriptive writing. This reference to an actual piece of writing makes criteria such as "use of detail," "coherence between paragraphs," or "development of ideas" come alive for students. Close readings of models—reading like writers—help students decide what to expect of finished writing by their peers.

Students in writing groups charged with evaluation of finished writing (as opposed to responding to work in progress) need to feel that their assessment matters. Assuming responsibility for assigning grades gives students a clear sense of the importance of their evaluations. Charging each group member with assigning a grade as well as making detailed evaluative comments not only reduces the teacher's paper load, but it also underlines the significance of student evaluation. Multiple copies of one group's writing are distributed to another group so that each member of the receiving group reads and evaluates the writing of another group. Teachers serve as arbiters if students feel their work has not received fair treatment and then the average of the several grades given by students in a writing group is recorded in the grade book.

Preparing Students for Groups

Successful writing groups, whether for responding or evaluating, do not emerge spontaneously in classrooms. They require special preparation, and it is this preparation that constitutes "real" teaching. Instructors who claim, "Oh, I've tried writing groups. They didn't work," usually go on to reveal that they did little to prepare students to participate in these groups. Preparation begins with creating an accepting climate in the classroom. Sharing one's writing with others is always a somewhat threatening experience—even for experienced writers—and teachers can make it clear that classrooms are "safe" places where cruelty and ridicule will not be tolerated. Putting a high priority on helping students get to know one another is one way teachers can signal safety in the classroom. Using get-acquainted exercises and encouraging students to share journal entries or personal anecdotes helps students appreciate and value one another. And it is particularly helpful if the teacher shares along with students.

Just as a climate conducive to successful writing groups must be developed and nurtured, so students cannot be assumed to have the skills necessary to successful participation in writing groups. As Hilgers (1986) notes, students do not know inherently how to work together; they must be taught. One of the first things instructors can do is to model responses to writing. A writing group of the whole, where the entire class considers the same paper, provides opportunities for demonstrating effective comments and for encouraging students to broaden their repertoires of response. The teacher can ask students to identify comments that would be most helpful to a writer faced with revising the piece under consideration. It does not take long before students recognize how little help is provided by comments such as "It flows so well" or "I liked the whole thing."

Groups can be constituted in a variety of ways. Instructors can simply allow students to group themselves, elaborate sociograms of the class can be constructed so that groups will contain at least some members who would like to work together, or arbitrary methods such as counting off groups of five can be employed. Perhaps more important than the method for establishing groups is monitoring and shifting once groups have begun working together. Teachers can rely on their own observations or comments from students to identify group problems, and rearranging students will usually solve difficulties. Once groups have been established, the question of procedures arises. The purpose for the group—whether to work collaboratively on a single piece of writing or to respond to drafts or to evaluate finished pieces—determines much of the procedure, but decisions still remain. In response groups, for example, teachers need to decide whether author or text should serve as the focus. That is, texts can be read with no explanation from the author, or the author can pose questions or problems to which the group responds. Another issue in writing group procedures is that of leadership. In most groups a leader will emerge without prompting, but the teacher needs to decide whether the leader should be institutionalized by being given duties such as taking attendance or recording responses.

When students have been prepared for both the form and content of their work, they can participate very effectively in writing groups. Research indicates that they stay on task and that their responses are largely useful (Gere and Abbott 1985). In response groups the majority of student comments deal with ideas developed in the writing, and students offer one another suggestions and ask questions designed to help improve writing. Even when writing groups digress to conversations about weekend activities and current happenings, these conversations usually contribute to the cohesiveness and supportiveness of the group. In fact, some of the most effective groups allow time for catching up with one another's lives before considering the writing.

When they are not talking about the ideas discussed in writing, students tend to talk about their own processes of writing. They share their insights and experiences, thereby gaining a broader perspective on the nature of writing. A small amount of the writing group's time is usually devoted to conversations about group procedures, deciding whose work to consider first, making sure everyone gets a hearing, and interpreting the guidelines established by the teacher. One indication of good preparation by the teacher is that these conversations typically do not last long. Students have a good idea what is expected and do not spend a great deal of time debating about what to do.

Indeed, the way students behave in a writing group provides a great deal of evidence about the quality of teaching that has gone before. When students proceed purposefully, demonstrating that they know what and why they are doing, they demonstrate that the teacher has made both purpose and expectation clear. As Harvey Wiener (1986) has noted, when writing groups meet, the good teacher is the most idle person in the room because students are well-prepared to do their work. From this perspective then, it is time to change the oft-heard sentence to: "You should come to observe my class tomorrow because the kids will be in writing groups."

Works Cited

Bouton, K., and G. Tutty. 1975. "The Effects of Peer-Evaluated Compositions on Writing Improvement." *The English Record* 26: 64–67.

Gere, A. R. 1987. *Writing Groups: History, Theory, and Implications.* Carbondale: Southern Illinois University Press.

Gere, A. R., and R. D. Abbott. 1985. "Talking about Writing: The Language of Writing Groups." *Research in the Teaching of English* 19: 362–86.

Gere, A. R., and R. Stevens. 1985. "The Language of Writing Groups: How Oral Response Shapes Revision." In *The Acquisition of Written Language: Response and Revision,* edited by S. W. Freedman, 85–105. Norwood, N.J.: Ablex.

Hilgers, T. 1986. "On Learning the Skills of Collaborative Writing." CCCC Convention, New Orleans, April.

Lord, A. A. 1880. "The Social Club." *New England Journal of Education* 11: 178–86.

O'Donnell, A., D. Danserau, T. Rocklin, J. Lambiotte, V. Hytherker, and C. Larson. 1985. "Cooperative Writing: Direct Effects and Transfer." *Written Communication* 2: 307–15.

Sinclair, J. McH., and R. M. Coulthard. 1975. *Towards an Analysis of Discourse: The English Used by Teachers and Pupils.* Oxford University Press.

Sternberg, R. J. 1984. "What Should Intelligence Tests Test? Implications of a Triarchic Theory of Intelligence for Intelligence Testing." *Educational Researcher* 13: 5–15.

Wiener, H. 1986. "Collaborative Learning in the Classroom: A Guide to Evaluation." *College English* 48: 52–61.

9 Reading and Response to Literature: Transactionalizing Instruction

Stanley B. Straw
University of Manitoba

The notion of "the reading group" is familiar, at least, in elementary schools. In many classes, reading groups are ways of tracking students by ability levels. Children are acutely aware of who is among the elite Bluebirds and which laggards are, in contrast, relegated to the low-achieving Sparrows. But small groups can function very differently in reading and in literature classes. Recent views of reading portray readers as transacting with texts, and we enrich the quality of reading by extending that transaction to encompass other readers. Students in cooperative and collaborative reading groups become more effective readers because they are encouraged to articulate their inferences and responses to others.

An Example of Reading:
Transmission, Interaction, or Transaction?

A few years ago, I was observing a group of high school students and their instructor as the students were preparing the oral reading of poetry for a language arts festival. Generally, oral readings were accompanied by an introduction on the meaning of the poem with some emphasis on the metaphors presented in the poem. The poet they were working on was Robert Frost; the poem, "Mending Wall." They were aware that Frost was an American and that he had dedicated a poem to John F. Kennedy at his inauguration as president of the United States in 1961. Shortly before their discussion of the meaning of this particular poem, there had been news reports on television about

I would like to thank Pat Sadowy for her insightful reading and response to this paper, as well as Susan Hynds and Don Rubin for their helpful editing of it. I would particularly like to thank Raymond Lavery for discussing his teaching experience with me in regards to the examples used in this paper and for his rich classroom experience from which he graciously allowed me to draw.—S.B.S.

attempted escapes from East Berlin to the West, as well as a short documentary about the Berlin crisis early in Kennedy's administration as president. Based on this background, they began a lively and cogent discussion of the poem "Mending Wall" as a metaphor for the Berlin Wall, characterizing the narrator of the poem as a symbol of the West and the neighbor, "like an old-stone savage armed" who "moves in darkness," as a symbol of the Eastern bloc.

Now, was this interpretation of the poem to be praised for its freshness and renewed application, or was it the teacher's responsibility to correct the students' reading as anachronistic? Based on my own conceptualization of the nature of reading, I saw the interpretation as a legitimate reading of the poem based, not on Frost's attempt to create a comparison with a major world development which took place half a century after he wrote the poem, but rather as a creation on the part of the students of a real meaning of the poem, a meaning they could relate to and understand on a personal level.

Unfortunately, before the students had the opportunity to present the poem, their instructor pointed out the impossibility of the interpretation, an action obviously informed by a view that, since Frost could not have known about the Berlin Wall, he could not have intended that the poem refer to the Berlin Wall; therefore a reading of the poem using the wall as a metaphor for the circumstances in Germany was both incorrect and not possible. The students subsequently abandoned the use of the poem and felt that their reading was "wrong." They chose instead "Take Something Like a Star" as their presentation poem, a little-known Frost poem that was so dense for them that they lost much of the energy and passion that had been associated with their reading of "Mending Wall."

The instructor, in this example, succeeded in doing at least three things by pointing out to students the "anachronism" of their interpretation: first, he privileged the intention of the author (or at least his ascription of the intention to the author) as the "best," if not the only meaning; second, he closed the text for the students, suggesting that some interpretations of the poem were simply not possible; third, he devalued the background and experience of students in their reading of the text. The instructor in this example clearly viewed reading as a *transmission* process, a transmission of meaning generated wholly by the author and communicated to the reader, unchanged, through the vehicle of the text.

How could this situation have been handled differently and what would a different handling imply about both the nature of reading and the nature of instruction?

Proponents of *interactive* models of reading would suggest that these readers were employing background experience and background knowledge in order to make sense of the poem—that is, they were calling up their rich internal schema and applying it to the text in order to understand it. On the other hand, reading-response critics such as Rosenblatt (1978)—the *transactionalists*—would suggest that these students, through their "transactions" with the poem, were constructing their own meaning within the range of possibilities provided by the text of the poem itself. Rosenblatt discusses this "new construct," this new meaning, as the real process of coming to know the meaning of any piece of literature. She characterizes this transaction as a conversation between reader and text—a negotiation between what the reader knows and what the text presents.

Instruction, Interaction, and Transaction

New conceptualizations of reading and literature as *interaction* and *transaction* can have profound impact on the ways we as teachers conceptualize our role in instruction. The move from a notion of determinant, text-based meaning—*meaning-getting*—to a conceptualization of reading as *meaning-making* in the presence of text suggests that many of our traditional vehicles for teaching literature may be in conflict with mature reading. That is, if reading is really interactional and transactional, then transmission methods—methods that assume the transmission of knowledge from author/text (and by proxy, from the teacher) to reader, that deny the unique constructions of meaning on the part of students—are at odds with the goals of our reading programs, which are to foster mature readings of texts (Bleich 1980; Tompkins 1980). Implicit in these new notions of reading is the idea of the social construction of knowledge and the role of talk in creating and consolidating meaning. Building the negotiation between reader and text is never done in isolation of the social circumstances in which learning and reading take place and are always the result of an oral exchange (talking) or the creation of hypothesized talk. One of the most powerful arguments for the reconceptualization of reading as interaction and transaction comes, it seems to me, from "social pragmatists" (Hunt 1990) who suggest that the procedures for meaning-making are learned through the oral exchanges and the social interactions that readers have, especially when they are exploring texts in groups.

One of the ways in which teachers are attempting to deal with this realization about the communal pursuit of knowledge in reading is through cooperative and collaborative learning methods. Roughly, the rationale for the use of cooperative and collaborative learning in classrooms runs something like this.

If the mature, independent reader is involved in active construction of text, in active negotiations of meaning, and if those negotiation strategies are primarily learned through students' use of talk both with us as teachers and with other students, then we cannot encourage mature, independent reading by *telling* our students what particular texts mean. We cannot even achieve this by asking questions of students that lead them to infer a particular meaning. We cannot assume that "meaning" will ultimately be the same for every reader. If all readers came to the negotiating table of reading with exactly the same background experiences, the same talk experience, the same social experiences, the same understanding strategies, then we might be able to teach the "skills" of reading in a particular order so that each reader could construct the same unvarying meaning in the face of any particular text. But that, clearly, is not the case. Each individual comes to the act of reading with significantly different experiences and, more importantly, different value systems derived from social experience. The imposition of meaning on the text by the teacher, rather than the allowance for negotiation with the text on the part of student readers, is not teaching literature, but is, rather, teaching dogma, the positive assertion of opinion, in this case the teacher's opinion, even though the teacher may equate his or her opinion with the dogma of the author. Meaning in literature is, ultimately, opinion, and interactive and transactional theorists suggest that the opinion is arrived at through the negotiation. If our purposes for teaching were to transmit dogma—or even to transmit knowledge—we would not use the actual literary text itself as reading material, at least not initially; we would, instead, use commentaries or "notes" (such as Cliffs Notes or Coles Notes) as our "real" texts and then show students how and why the meanings we have assigned to the literary text are valid. In fact, in a transmission model of teaching literature, this is often what happens: teachers present the meaning first and then show students how that meaning is explicated in or derived from the literary text; the literature is then used as an example of a particular meaning, rather than as a stimulus for thinking and the construction of meaning. The text serves as validation for the teacher-assigned meaning (See Bogdan and Straw 1990, for an elaborated argument on changing conceptualizations of reading).

The alternative becomes clearer as we view reading as a *meaning-making* process rather than a *meaning-getting* process. Instructionally, what we really want to do as teachers, it seems to me, is to teach students to become active negotiators in the act of creating meaning during and after reading—to help students become part of the conversation that is reading: the conversation between reader and text, between text and community, and among readers. This argues for socially-based, talk-based classrooms, classrooms that lead students to meaning-making rather than meaning-getting.

In an attempt to do this, we as teachers have searched for means of achieving the combined goals of helping students use talk to learn and to negotiate meaning with text within communities of readers. A group of instructional procedures referred to under the general rubric of cooperative-collaborative learning methods has emerged from this search. These methods range from highly teacher-directed activities, such as group practice and peer tutoring, to very open-ended, transactional activities such as Co-op Co-op. What differentiates these methods from each other is the amount of student and teacher input into the goals, roles, methods, procedures, and content used within the general group process.

The results of a huge amount of research across a wide range of grade and ability levels and across nearly every conceivable subject area suggest that, under certain circumstances, work in group settings is generally superior to teacher-determined knowledge passed on through transmission methods. Learning situations that require students to work in groups, to negotiate the processes of learning through talk (with us and with each other) appear to result in superior performance on a wide variety of measures, from academic performance to interracial tolerance, when compared with transmission methods. It would appear that, as students assemble knowledge, as they construct it for themselves, they become more adept learners. The process of articulating ideas through talk appears to aid students in assimilating, accommodating, and building knowledge.

The research and study on meaning-constructing group work comes out of two different "histories." The rationale for the first, usually referred to as "cooperative learning," is related to an attempt to help students become more cooperative and supportive of each other in classroom settings, especially in multicultural, multi-ethnic, and mainstreamed classrooms. These methods are often teacher-directed and teacher-structured. On the other hand, "collaborative learning" methods have come out of a history of a search for more meaningful transactions among students in classrooms and with the materials they are learning. The differences between cooperative and collaborative learning environments are, I think, similar to the differences between interactive and transactional models of reading. They both seem to be reasonable and workable alternatives to transmission education and appear to encourage not only greater cooperation on the part of students, but greater achievement as well.

While admitting their similarities, I am generally going to differentiate, for the purpose of discussion only, between what I am calling *interactive approaches* (those procedures usually associated with the cooperative learning movement) and *transactional approaches*, while admitting that different approaches may be more or less effective for any particular learning goal or circumstance (Fig. 1). *Interactive approaches* are approaches that leave most of the decision making and responsibility for instruction in the hands of the teacher. They are procedures that involve substantial scaffolding on the part of the teacher (that is, the building of the basic structures of instruction) and leave much of the process of learning to students. *Transactional approaches*, on the other hand, are procedures that transfer much of the responsibility for all aspects of learning to the students and allow for a much greater amount of student input, student decision making, and student control of learning. In transaction, the teacher, rather than being an architect who lays out the scaffold for learning for the students (as in the interactive approaches), becomes another builder of knowledge, an-

	INTERACTIVE APPROACHES (Teacher as Architect)	TRANSACTIONAL APPROACHES (Teacher as Fellow Builder)
Goals	Teacher generated	Collaboratively generated between students and teacher
Roles	Teacher assigned	Student negotiated
Methods	Teacher modeled	Student constructed (negotiated with teacher)
Procedures	Teacher modeled	Student constructed
Content	Teacher assigned	Student and teacher negotiated

Fig. 1. Possible differences between interactive and transactional approaches to group learning.

other constructor of knowledge, right alongside the students. As a colleague of mine says, "The teacher becomes just another voice among all the other voices in the classroom."

The two approaches can be differentiated in terms of five concepts: Goals of learning, roles in learning, methods of learning, procedures in group functioning, and content for learning. The figure attempts to diagram the basic differences in the approaches under these five concepts.

The figure may make interactive methods appear to be highly teacher dominated, and in some cases, they are; however, it is important to understand that this figure is an attempt to discriminate between interactive and transactional approaches to group-centered environments and to demonstrate that both approaches differ significantly from the assumptions underlying transmission models of teacher-active/student-passive education. The essential difference between interactive and transactional models is the role of the teacher as architect in one (interactive) and the role of the teacher as participant in the other (transactional).

Interactive Methods and Cooperative Learning Strategies

The research on interactive group approaches has come out of a number of areas. In this section, I will attempt to summarize that large and substantial body of evidence supporting the use of interactive group approaches in teaching in general, and in teaching reading and literature specifically.

Peer Tutoring

The oldest work in interactive group activity is probably the work in peer tutoring. Cohen and Kulik (1981) reported a metanalysis of the studies done in peer tutoring. They reviewed over 500 studies and chose the 65 strongest ones for further analysis from those studies done in real classrooms. They studied a number of factors that might affect differences between peer tutoring classrooms and transmission classrooms, including the amount of teacher-supplied structure present in the tutoring situations, the relative age of the partners, whether instruction was a supplement to teacher instruction rather than a substitute, and whether tutors were given any preprogram training in tutoring. The analysis was carried out in a variety of subject areas. They found that overall, in all subject areas, the effect of peer tutoring on both the tutors (the students who administered instruction) and the tutees (the students who received instruction) was approximately 10 percent higher than the effect of regular, transmission instruction. Although all tutoring situations appeared to help the tutees, *structured tutoring* seemed to be about twice as effective for them as *unstructured tutoring*, whereas there appeared to be little difference in the effect of structured over unstructured situations for tutors. *Cross-age tutoring* seemed to be more effective for tutees than *same-age tutoring*, whereas the effect of cross-age versus same-age tutoring seemed to be about the same for tutors. For both tutors and tutees, instruction that was a *substitute for teacher instruction* was about twice as effective as instruction that was a *supplement to teacher instruction*. Finally, *training tutors*, that is, whether tutors were trained or not, did not seem to make a significant difference for either the tutors or the tutees.

My personal experience and my observations in classrooms would suggest that peer tutoring is most effective when material is concrete and when the purpose of instruction is to teach skills or strategies. In the reading classroom, for example, a teacher might wish to use peer tutoring when teaching students how to use underlining to summarize material or to look for specific symbols or imagery in literature. I recently observed a junior-high classroom in which the teacher had presented the concept of metaphor, hyperbole, and the characteristics of the ballad, and had given the students a list of "critical questions" to use in recognizing these. She initially taught the lesson to a group of students who had finished reading three short poems earlier than other students: "The Highwayman" by Alfred Noyes and "The Shooting of Dan McGrew" and "The Cremation of Sam McGee" by Robert Service. She then used these students as tutors when other students finished reading the material in class. In this example, the teacher was able to work with a group of students having difficulty with the literature they were reading, while other students taught the recognition of the literary devices to their peers. She was able to accomplish so much more during class period, while all of the students were able to pass the mastery test given at the end of the unit.

Peer tutoring, as this example shows, is a fairly restricted form of group instruction. However, students appear to be effective at taking on instructional roles; this is particularly true when the peer tutoring students are clear about expectations and when more able students act as the tutors. It is also true when the content or skills to be learned are concrete and the goals for success are clear. When these requirements are met, it appears that students can be more effective teachers and explainers of information than many teachers themselves.

Cooperative Learning Strategies

Johnson and Johnson (1985) have carried out extensive research comparing cooperative learning situations with what they call "competitive" and "individualistic" learning situations. Competitive situations are those in which students compete with each other in achieving success; individualistic situations are those in which an individual student's success or failure is unrelated to those of his or her peers. Johnson and Johnson have reviewed hundreds of studies on cooperative learning and have completed a number of metanalyses on these studies. In the area of achievement, they report that cooperative learning was superior to both competitive and individualistic learning circumstances, such that students engaged in cooperative learning achieved approximately 30 percent above students in a transmission setting, particularly when high-level thinking strategies were involved.

In response to questions about subject matter and ability of students, Slavin (1985) states from his review on cooperative learning: "The positive effects of cooperative learning methods on students' achievement appear just as frequently in elementary and secondary schools; in urban, suburban, and rural schools; and in [diverse] subjects. . . . Most studies show that high, average, and low achievers gain equally from the cooperative experiences" (10–11). Johnson and Johnson (1985) make a similar observation from their own research: "High-, medium-, and low-ability students were mixed within the cooperative learning groups. Clearly the high-ability students did not suffer from working with medium- and low-ability students. In the studies that measured the achievement of gifted students separately, three found that they achieved higher when collaborating with medium- and low-ability students, and one found no difference in achievement [over transmission]" (105–6).

These interaction methods of cooperative instruction include a rather wide variety of methods. Some of these are described below:

Student team learning/learning together is a set of methods in which a teacher presents a lesson, cooperative groups work to master the content of the lesson, a quiz or tournament (group competition) is given on the material, and recognition is given to successful teams. This set of methods is especially useful for activities that require mastery over particular content or skills. Recently, I observed a teacher using this procedure with the structure of essays. He had taught his tenth-grade students to recognize the structure of an essay and then to apply it to a comparison of Emerson's "Nature" and an essay from the current issue of *Time*. They later worked together in order to write their own essays on topics of importance to them in their own lives. Members of each group became committed to making sure that the other members of their team became knowledgeable about the essay form and could both recognize it in literature and write it on their own.

Jigsaw II is a method in which students meet in "expert groups" to learn material, each expert group within the class having different material. After the expert groups have worked together so that each member of the group is, in fact, an "expert" in the material, the classroom is rearranged so that new groups are created so that one student from each expert group is in each of the newly created "home" groups. The task of each member of these home groups is to teach what she or he has learned in the expert group to the other members. Many literature teachers have found this procedure useful in that the expert groups study different pieces of literature, all related to the same theme, and then return to the home groups to teach their pieces to the other members of the group. I worked recently with a teacher who was developing a unit on race and the effect of prejudice in literature. Using the Jigsaw II procedure, she asked students to read one of four short stories ("After You, My Dear Alphonse" by Shirley Jackson, "The Enemy" by Pearl S. Buck, "D. P." by Kurt Vonnegut, and "One, Two, Three Little Indians" by Hugh MacLennan). Students were assigned to particular short story groups on the basis of their ability to read the stories, although all of the stories centered on a similar theme. They worked out their interpretations of the stories in expert groups, then returned to their home groups to teach their story to their peers and then to discuss how the themes derived from each of the stories were alike and different. Each student then had to write a "mini-essay" on one of the central issues identified in all four short stories.

Reciprocal teaching and interactive teaching (Palincsar and Brown 1986) are procedures that begin with teacher modeling and explanation of reading strategies to students. Groups of students then meet to discuss a procedure, and each student within the group then takes a turn at "being the teacher," demonstrating and explaining the process to other students. The group discusses the teaching experience each time, questions the "student/teacher" and gives feedback to him or her. This procedure is repeated until each person has had an opportunity to demonstrate the process to the other students, teach the process to peers, and receive feedback. The students are then assessed individually on their ability to use the procedures in actual reading circumstances. Literature teachers have found this procedure particularly helpful in teaching students how to integrate and use background experiences in understanding the literature they read. Recently I worked with a teacher who wanted to develop his students' comparison/contrast abilities. Initially, he asked students to write about receiving a gift as a child, using a set of prepared questions such as "How did the gift make you feel?", "Who did you show the gift to?", "Why was it important to you?", and "Why did you want to share the gift with someone else?" He then asked students to read Katherine Mansfield's "The Doll's House," asking the same questions about the three girls in the story. Then students, in groups, were asked to teach each other how to draw analogies between their own experience and the experiences of the characters in the story. They taught each other to develop comparison/contrast charts in order to talk about and, ultimately, write about how their own experiences were alike or different from those of the characters in the stories.

Peer-response groups is a procedure in which students within a group individually complete an assignment (such as reading and then writing about a piece of literature). The group then reads each student's assignment and discusses how it could be improved, expanded, focused, elaborated, or so on. Individuals respond to the group's assessment by further clarification, questioning, discussion, and, finally, by reworking the assignment. Students are encouraged to work together in pairs or small groups as they encounter problems in completing their final assignments. These procedures have proven to be especially effective in the teaching of composition skills, although they can easily be applied to reading and response to literature. I observed a teacher as he used peer-response groups in teaching students to write character sketches in response to Daniel Keyes's novel, *Flowers for Algernon*. Students were asked to write about the characters of either Alice or Charlie and then to comment on how they themselves related to either of these characters. In writing about both the characters in the novel and themselves, students learned to reflect on character, on their response to character, as well as to help each other develop articulate responses.

Transactional Methods and Collaborative Learning Strategies

Collaborative learning strategies are very similar to many of the cooperative learning strategies described above, except that the amount of student decision making in the groups is much greater in collaborative learning. The teacher releases much of the control, in terms of goals (what is to be learned), the roles of students within groups (the leader, if there are leaders, is chosen by the group), methods of learning, and the procedures within the group. Some collaborative methods, in addition, leave the choice of material or content to be learned to the students (for example, they are allowed to choose which piece of literature they wish to study). Collaborative learning is not as well researched as either peer tutoring or cooperative learning, and the results are much less generalizable to a broad range of instructional situations. However, much of the work in collaborative learning has been done with students reading and responding to literature. For example, Dias (1985) found that high school students who studied in collaboration with peers performed significantly better on measures of interpretation than students exposed to a more traditional, transmission approach. The research my colleagues and I have been doing suggest that students at grades 1, 3, 8, 10, and 12 have more mature responses to literature when exposed to collaborative learning situations.

Collaborative learning is a fairly unstructured situation in which students are asked to read and discuss pieces of literature and then respond to the literature either in small groups or in a journal-like format. They are subsequently asked to respond to the responses of their fellow students, discuss the literature further, and then to write or present a semiformal response to the piece. For example, Kagen (1985) reports a collaborative method he calls Co-op Co-op. In this method, students meet in groups, decide on the goals for their own study, assign roles to certain members of the group, and complete a class project. His results indicate that not only do students achieve better under these circumstances, but they also have more positive attitudes toward class and the materials. Similar results are reported in a series of studies by Dias (1979), Bryant (1984), and me (Straw 1989).

A pair of teachers recently employed collaborative learning/group investigation procedures in a grade 12 novel study on important social issues of the twentieth century. The novels they used were: *Ordinary People* by Judith Guest, *The Grapes of Wrath* by John Steinbeck, *Brave New*

World by Aldous Huxley, *In Search of April Raintree* by Beatrice Culleton, *Obasan* by Joy Kogawa, *Cry, the Beloved Country* by Alan Paton, *Two Solitudes* by Hugh MacLennan, and *One Flew Over the Cuckoo's Nest* by Ken Kesey. Every student was asked to read at least four of the novels and to create a group around the novel that they would most like to work on in-depth. After reading and briefly discussing each novel they had read, the students joined an in-depth group and worked for four to five days on preparing a way to present their novel to their peers (e.g., audio presentation, radio play, role-playing, TV script, talk-show format). They made their presentation to their peers and devised a number of ways in which the students might respond to the novel. Subsequent to the presentation, they had to write a paper generating a theme taken from at least three of the novels. Although they were expected to do their paper individually, they were expected to use their peers as resources, particularly in discussing any technical aspects of the novels. This in-depth study led most students to read all of the novels and to attempt to incorporate their responses to more than three novels into the paper they wrote.

In many ways, collaborative learning procedures and other transactional methods may be a goal for teachers to strive for rather than a starting point of instruction. In working with teachers, I have found that they often feel insecure about releasing the goals, roles, methods, procedures, and (especially) content of their classes to the discretion of their students, particularly students they may perceive as young or immature. In many ways, this is a valid concern, but at times one that is severely overstated. Students can often, with very little training, operate effectively and successfully on their own if the teacher adequately structures the classroom and prepares the students for the experience (as evidenced by the research in peer tutoring and my own research in grades 1 and 3). One of the ways of preparing students, other than making sure that they have the materials and alternatives available to them, is to begin group learning activities with an interactive method such as peer tutoring or one of the cooperative learning strategies. When both students and teachers are comfortable with these methods, then it may be appropriate to move to activities that are more transactional in nature. If the nature of the reading process is transactional (as I believe it is), then the goal of our instructional procedures should be that our classrooms be organized as transactionally as possible, employing procedures that give students a wide variety of choice in how to negotiate and achieve their own learning.

Why Do Cooperative and Collaborative
Learning Strategies Work?

When working with teachers, I often discuss with them why cooperative and collaborative learning strategies appear to be so powerful, especially in learning literature. The first reason, obviously, is that these methods more nearly approximate the actual act of reading. Reading is constructive, socially mediated, and independently motivated, and so is this range of methods for classroom organization. Second, oral language and talk lead to the use of higher-level learning and knowledge strategies. Johnson and Johnson(1985) conclude that "the discussion process in cooperative groups promotes the discovery and the development of high quality cognitive strategies for learning . . ." (155). Third, the occurrence of disagreement among group members leads to a higher quality and quantity of learning. Johnson and Johnson (1982) refer to this as *cognitive controversy*. When managed constructively, cognitive controversy promotes curiosity and uncertainty about the correctness of one's views, and, consequently, an active search for more information, and higher achievement and retention of material. It promotes the "search for truth" by encouraging active negotiations, both with other students and with texts. Fourth, cooperative and collaborative learning procedures can increase the time on task, that is, the amount of time students spend in profitable learning. When students are involved in whole group discussions led by the teacher (transmission), the opportunity for "tuning out" and spending less time in active learning is greater. And, as Berliner (1981) points out, higher engaged learning time leads to higher achievement.

Fifth, cooperative learning gives students opportunities orally to rehearse material, ideas, and to explore possibilities more fully. It gives students the opportunities to "try out" more possibilities than in whole group, teacher-directed circumstances. Sixth, cooperative and collaborative learning, again managed correctly, gives students immediate and meaningful regulation and feedback. High positive and corrective feedback gives students much more support and encouragement in learning reading, and results in higher comprehension and response (Tierney and Cunningham 1984). Seventh, cooperative and collaborative learning gets students actively involved in their own learning (rather than passively involved in listening to the teacher) and thus can significantly raise the students' commitment to learning. Eighth, the talk and feedback that takes place in groups, as well as the teaching that happens between students, can aid in developing individual metacognitive monitoring systems. As members of the group monitor another member's performance, students can develop personal monitoring systems by modeling the group's critiques. As students monitor a peer's learning and performance, they learn to monitor their own also, and as Baker and Brown (1984) point out, this metacognitive monitoring is significantly related to increased performance and learning.

Finally, it makes students aware of the processes they use in learning, asks them to articulate those processes, and, in the role of teacher, allows them to explain and refine the procedures they use when reading and responding to literature.

Some Cautions about Group Learning Technique

As teachers go about attempting to "transactionalize" their classrooms, a number of cautions should be pointed out. Most of these cautions come from a combination of efforts on the part of cooperative learning researchers, researchers in learning and metacognition, and researchers in teacher and school effectiveness. I have chosen the ones I feel are most important for teachers to guard against when implementing cooperative and collaborative learning strategies in their reading and literature classroom:

1. Cognitive controversy does not imply dissonance. The work by Johnson and Johnson (1982) suggests that cognitive controversy is helped when it is "constructive conflict" (230). They suggest that controversy can be constructive when the conflicts encourage the groups to become more aware of problems, when controversy encourages change rather than rigidity, when it energizes students and increases motivation, when it stimulates creativity, when it encourages cohesiveness in group interactions, and when the controversy is based on trust.

2. Materials (i.e., literature) used in cooperative-collaborative settings, like materials used in other successful teaching settings, should be within the reach of students; as Tierney and Cunningham (1984) point out, "teachers should have students read easy materials and perform comprehension tasks they can complete with high success" (638). Perhaps this is more important in cooperative and collaborative learning circumstances since groups work somewhat autonomously, and groups that experience frustration in completing tasks assigned to them have a tendency to break down (Johnson and Johnson 1982). Related to

this point is that cooperative and collaborative learning classrooms should give students opportunities to cover more material rather than less material. Rosenshine and Stevens (1984)
suggest that there is a positive relationship between the amount
of material covered and achievement on the part of students.
Barr (reported in Rosenshine and Stevens 1984) found that
groups helped teachers cover more content than when they
worked with a class as a whole group.

3. Students must be actively engaged a large percentage of time
   with academic materials and activities. Berliner (1981) and Stal-
   lings (reported in Rosenshine and Stevens 1984) have pointed
   out that engaged learning time is directly related to achievement
   and success. If cooperative and collaborative learning circumstances create situations in which students spend less time in
   academic pursuits than in traditional classrooms, then the activities are not likely to succeed. However, cooperative and collaborative learning classrooms can give students an opportunity
   to be engaged more than in traditional classrooms—as long as
   they keep on topic and on task.

4. Teachers, when using cooperative and collaborative learning
   strategies, need to maintain a high academic emphasis. The use
   of group learning should not suggest a relaxation of the emphasis on academic excellence. Rosenshine and Stevens (1984) suggest that the most successful school reading programs are those
   that maintain a high emphasis on achievement and are task
   oriented.

5. The use of cooperative and collaborative learning strategies
   should not suggest a decrease in the expectations of performance. In fact, it should result in an increase in expectations. Weber (reported in Samuels 1981) has suggested that one of the
   characteristics of exemplary reading programs is their consistently high expectations for student performance. In the same
   vein, valuable teaching and learning practices, such as the assignment of homework and the expectation that it should be
   done, should not be affected by the use of cooperative and collaborative learning strategies in class.

6. Cooperative and collaborative learning groups should be organized in such a way that allows for effective feedback to students
   on their ideas and their work. Feedback needs to be generally
   positive (Tierney and Cunningham 1984, suggest about 80 percent of the time), and help—either from other students or direct-

ly from the teacher—should be given when feedback is negative. This requires the teacher to develop a positive, risk-taking environment in the classroom, often demonstrating how feedback should be given, and to provide students with procedures for helping other students in their cooperative groups.

7. Interactive and transactional instructional models appear to be most effective with heterogeneously grouped students—heterogeneously grouped by ability, background, experience, school success, and so on. The research suggests that diverse groups appear to be more effective, both for more able and less able students, where there is a diversity of individuals. Experiences in heterogeneous groups seem to build the confidence of both strong and weak students and to help students value the diverse backgrounds and abilities of their peers.

With respect to cautions about interactive and transactional classroom practices, it should be made clear that the use of cooperative and collaborative learning strategies in class should not compete with other activities that appear associated with students' success in learning about and responding to literature. The teacher who finds response journals, for example, an effective way of working with literature should not discontinue that activity in order to establish response groups in the classroom.

Conclusions

In this paper, I have attempted to outline a transformation that I see taking place in our conceptualizations about the acts of reading and, especially, of reading literature. I have discussed this in detail elsewhere (Bogdan and Straw 1990), but, in general, I perceive a movement from a conceptualization of reading as a *transmission* process to a conceptualization of reading as a *transactional* process, with a conceptualization of reading as an *interactive* process and a step along the way toward transaction. As our conceptualizations of reading have and are changing, so are our conceptualizations about teaching. Although change in teaching seems to lag substantially behind our concepts of reading, teaching practices are now being investigated that are more interactive and transactional. A major group of those methods can be classified under the rubric of cooperative and collaborative learning strategies or, as I have termed them above, *interactive and transactional* situations. I have attempted to review the research on the effectiveness of these methods, to suggest what some of the strategies are, and to suggest why they seem to be an effective means of getting students to learn about and respond to literature. Finally, I have suggested that the use of interactive and transactional classroom methods should not obviate the use of instructional methods that are effective, such as increased engaged learning time, amount of material covered, and high expectations.

Many of us who are working in the field of reading and literature feel that we are on the brink of a new era in our conceptualizations of the reading process. I also feel that this brink is being reached in methods for dealing with reading and literature in classrooms. Instituting interactive and transactional teaching procedures in our classrooms may, in some ways, be very foreign to us; but if we believe our own rhetoric about the interactive and transactional nature of reading, then we need to reexamine our teaching strategies and adjust them to correspond to our new conceptualizations of reading.

Works Cited

Baker, L., and A. L. Brown. 1984. "Metacognitive Skills and Reading." In *Handbook of Reading Research*, edited by P. D. Pearson. New York: Longman.

Berliner, D. C. 1981. "Academic Learning Time and Reading Achievement." In *Comprehension and Teaching: Research Reviews*, edited by J. Guthrie. Newark, Del.: International Reading Association.

Bogdan, D., and S. B. Straw, eds. 1990. *Beyond Communication: Reading Comprehension and Criticism*. Portsmouth, N.H.: Boynton/Cook-Heinemann.

Cohen, P. A., and J. A. Kulik. 1981. "Synthesis of Research on the Effects of Tutoring." *Educational Leadership* 39, no. 3: 227–29.

Dias, P. 1985. "Researching Response to Poetry: Part I: A Case for Responding Aloud Protocols." *English Quarterly* 18: 104–18.

Hunt, R. A. 1990. "The Parallel Socialization of Reading and Literature." In *Beyond Communication: Reading Comprehension and Criticism*, edited by D. Bogdan and S. B. Straw. Portsmouth, N.H.: Boynton/Cook-Heinemann.

Johnson, D. W., and F. P. Johnson. 1982. *Joining Together: Group Theory and Group Skills*. Englewood Cliffs, N.J.: Prentice-Hall.

Johnson, D. W., and R. T. Johnson. 1985. "The Internal Dynamics of Cooperative Learning Groups." In *Learning to Cooperate, Cooperating to Learn*, edited by R. Slavin, S. Sharan, S. Kagen, R. H. Lazarowitz, C. Webb, and R. Schmuck. New York: Plenum Press.

Kagen, S. 1985. "Co-op Co-op: A Flexible Cooperative Learning Technique." In *Learning to Cooperate, Cooperating to Learn*, edited by R. Slavin, S. Sharan, S. Kagen, R. H. Lazarowitz, C. Webb, and R. Schmuck. New York: Plenum Press.

Palincsar, A. S., and A. L. Brown. 1986. "Interactive Teaching to Promote Independent Learning from Text." *Reading Teacher* 39: 771–77.

Rosenblatt, L. M. 1978. *The Reader, the Text, the Poem: The Transactional Theory of the Literary Work.* Carbondale: Southern Illinois University Press.

Rosenshine, B., and R. Stevens. 1984. "Classroom Instruction in Reading." In *Handbook of Reading Research*, edited by P. D. Pearson. New York: Longman.

Samuels, S. J. 1981. "Characteristics of Exemplary Reading Programs." In *Comprehension and Teaching: Research Reviews*, edited by J. Guthrie. Newark, Del.: International Reading Association.

Slavin, R. 1985. "An Introduction to Cooperative Learning Research." In *Learning to Cooperate, Cooperating to Learn*, edited by R. Slavin, S. Sharan, S. Kagen, R. H. Lazarowitz, C. Webb, and R. Schmuck. New York: Plenum Press.

Tierney, R. J., and J. W. Cunningham. 1984. "Research on Teaching Reading Comprehension." In *Handbook of Reading Research*, edited by P. D. Pearson. New York: Longman.

Tompkins, J. P. 1980. *Reader-Response Criticism: From Formalism to Poststructuralism.* Baltimore: The Johns Hopkins University Press.

Recommended Readings

Buck, P. S. 1968. "The Enemy." In *America Reads* series, edited by R. C. Pooley, E. Daniel, E. J. Farrell, A. H. Grommon, and O. S. Niles. Glenlawn, Ill.: Scott Foresman.

Culleton, B. 1983. *In Search of April Raintree.* Winnipeg, Man.: Pemmican Press.

Emerson, R. W. 1985. "Nature." In *Macmillan Literature Series.* New York: Macmillan.

Frost, R. 1985. "Mending Wall." In *Macmillan Literature Series.* New York: Macmillan.

———. 1985. "Take Something Like a Star." In *Macmillan Literature Series.* New York: Macmillan.

Garner, H. 1974. "One—Two—Three Little Indians." In *The Canadian Experience: A Brief Survey of English-Canadian Prose.* Toronto: Gage.

Guest, J. 1982. *Ordinary People.* New York: Penguin.

Huxley, A. 1979. *Brave New World.* New York: Harper & Row.

Jackson, S. 1984. "After You, My Dear Alphonse." In *Inquiry into Literature I*, edited by B. Fillion and J. Henderson. Toronto: Collier Macmillan.

Kesey, K. 1977. *One Flew Over the Cuckoo's Nest.* New York: Penguin.

Keyes, D. 1970. *Flowers for Algernon.* New York: Bantam.

Kogawa, J. 1983. *Obasan.* Toronto: Penguin.

Mansfield, K. 1975. "The Doll's House." In *Experiences*, edited by J. B. Bell and E. W. Buxton. Toronto: Wiley.

MacLennan, H. 1986. *Two Solitudes.* Toronto: Macmillan.

Noyes, A. 1985. "The Highwayman." In *Macmillan Literature Series.* New York: Macmillan.

Paton, A. 1987. *Cry, the Beloved Country.* Toronto: Collier-Macmillan.
Service, R. 1970. "The Cremation of Sam McGee." In *Quest,* edited by W. Eckersley. Toronto: J. M. Dent (Canada).
———. 1981. "The Shooting of Dan McGrew." In *Exits and Entrances,* edited by B. King, P. LeDrew, and G. Porter. Toronto: Academic Press.
Steinbeck, J. 1976. *The Grapes of Wrath.* New York: Penguin.

10 Teacher/Student Talk: The Collaborative Conference

Muriel Harris
Purdue University

As trained readers and responders, teachers often feel comfortable knowing what to tell students about the quality of their final written drafts. For better or for worse, we do know how to give summative evaluations of compositions. But as writing teachers become equally interested in helping students learn about the processes of composing, opportunities for student-teacher interaction come at many points, not just when the deed is done. What kinds of student-teacher interaction—and at what junctures—are most likely to promote growth in writing?

One of the more encouraging recent trends in writing instruction has been the recognition of the social nature of writing. Thus, we now talk about writing for others in a world of words, an emphasis which involves being aware of that audience of readers as well as providing the context, structure, and information readers will need. The act of entering that world of words is in itself a socializing process as the writer becomes conscious of stepping into the public forum and joining the conversation. And that recognition of the social—and socializing— nature of writing has yet another benefit: it leads to greater recognition of the social environment needed as writers develop. Putting writers in peer groups for discussion, review, or evaluation of drafts is one way to provide the social context that is needed. Yet another way, the teacher/student conference, creates opportunities for the kind of talk which is a true collaborative dialogue between teacher and student, as we see in this brief excerpt:

> *Kim:* I think that paragraph about how I set up the tent—it needs something. But what? I'm . . . it's not strong. It . . . what I want to say about getting the tent up is it's so complicated.
>
> *Mrs. Annan:* Complicated. That's a good word to think about. Here, in this sentence, you used the word "complicated," but I didn't know what you really meant. What's complicated about putting up a tent?

Kim: For one thing, my dad had to show me how to lay it flat on the ground. When you start—and you unfold the tent—you have to lay it really flat. And the rain flaps go in a certain way. Then, the pegs need to be set so you—so the tent is tight when it goes up.

Mrs. Annan: Oh. I didn't know that. How about putting those details in the paragraph? Here … right here, what about right after this sentence?

Kim: Would that make the paragraph stronger?

Mrs. Annan: Sure. If you could show us how you had to struggle with all that, your readers can begin to feel a little of what you were going through. Especially since you said it was so hot. Can you write it so we can see what you went through to get that tent up? That's the kind of specific detail that will make that paragraph come alive. What *do* you have to do with the rain flaps?

This kind of one-to-one conversation, the collaborative dialogue between teacher and student, can be so helpful that we should also recognize it as a necessity for the developing writer, as necessary as providing multiple opportunities to write. Because teacher/student talk can be so productive for writers as they generate drafts of writing and as we offer instructional guidance and respond to their writing, talk may come to replace the traditional practice of written response by the teacher/reader. Indeed, those walls of squiggles, phrases, and endnotes we leave behind on student papers are, with increasing frequency, seen as an archaic, time-consuming, and not very productive procedure. In fact, it is somewhat akin to relaying our messages via smoke signals when we could be using teleconferences. Fortunately, though, no hardware, software, or other forms of technology are needed for student/teacher collaborative talk. What is needed is both a rationale for such talk so that we recognize its purpose, and also some strategies for carrying on productive dialogues with our students.[1]

But, before launching into a discussion of the *why* and *how* of student/teacher talk, I suspect that it is useful to define the kind of dialogue I am referring to. Teacher/student talk, as I use the term here, does not refer to those short bursts of conversation among the welter of voices in a class discussion. Nor is such talk the one-way communication of a teacher lecturing (however well-intentioned that lecture is)

---

[1] I do not mean to imply here that there are no problems associated with teacher/student talk. Finding time, learning to work with various types of students, and keeping the conversation on track are merely some of the many problems that have to be considered. I offer a discussion of these problems in *Teaching One-to-One: The Writing Conference*, and Donald Graves's *Writing: Teachers and Children at Work* is a highly useful book on this and many other aspects of teaching writing.

to a listening student in a so-called "conference." (Students know exactly what lies ahead when the teacher says, "See me after class"— not a conference but a teacher monologue.) Instead, the truly useful kind of talk is the dialogue of real conversation, the give-and-take interaction of two speakers, asking, answering, discussing, trying out, and exploring together, with neither monopolizing the conversation. Such talk goes on at various times as students write. It can be as brief as a few short spontaneous exchanges during a writing session in class or as extended as a scheduled time together before or after class hours.

The Roles of Teacher/Student Talk

While it is difficult (and dangerous) to categorize the different kinds of talk that can occur, there are some broad distinctions that are useful to keep in mind. One way to think about teacher/student talk is to lump some of it into that which assists writers in generating and developing a piece of writing. Other teacher/student talk is focused less on a particular piece of writing and more on mastering writing skills in general. Finally, another large chunk of teacher/student talk provides feedback on writing that has been produced. Often, all of this goes on in the same conversation. But for the purposes of this discussion, I shall tease out each of these kinds of talk as if they occur separately. First, we will look more closely at teacher/student talk which occurs when writers generate material, then at talk which goes on when writers are acquiring information and strategies, and finally, at talk in which teachers offer responses to the writing that is produced.

Generating Content through Talk

Conversations with writers as they explore, generate, and develop ideas for their writing—the production aspect of composing—can be so fruitful that "talk" ought to be at the top of any list of invention heuristics we offer students. Having writers respond to various questions such as the "who-what-when-where-why-how" or other question lists, asking them to freewrite, or engaging them in other writing and planning activities have become tools of the invention trade. They beguile us into thinking that students will unlock great storehouses of material if given the right tool. But such strategies still ask the writer to confront a piece of blank paper and communicate something of interest on it. The catch here, as Mick Noppen, a peer tutor in a writing lab ("Speaking of Writing") notes, is that students who ask for help when they can't start writing don't seem to profit much from being told to start writing. Some writers can master the use of heuristics, but this still sidesteps the social context of writing, a context that is vividly apparent when someone sitting next to the writer simply (and sincerely) says, "Tell me more."

Useful teacher/student talk about generating more content is the kind of conversation we all engage in when we want to hear more about what someone is telling us:

> *Mr. Emmes:* So what did you do after that?
>
> *Michael:* When we realized how late we were going to be? The coach called ahead when the bus stopped for gas. We were all disappointed because we were sure we'd be disqualified from the semifinals.
>
> *Mr. Emmes:* Yeah?
>
> *Michael:* Well, as it turned out—what happened was the snow delayed several other teams too. What a mess it was when we got there. Really out of joint. The teams who made it were up for it. And it was hard to sit around trying to figure when the games would start. There was a funny kind of atmosphere. On one hand, everyone was tense. We wanted the action to start. But we also felt like celebrating just because we *got* there.

An interested listener helps writers retrieve information more easily, gives them a sense of audience in realizing what the reader would want to know and needs to know, and just as important, validates the subject as having audience interest. Thus I have listened to far too many students who come to writing lab tutorials after spinning endless wheels rejecting topics that are not novel enough ("But the instructor knows all about that, so why would he like my paper?") or topics that seem not to have any worth because they are *too* novel ("Yeah, my dad likes steam engines and we've taken some rides on some old steam trains, but that's not something that interests most people. I need a topic my teacher will be interested in."). The teacher who listens, asks questions, and reacts with interest can help writers knock down these false barriers.

Teacher/student conversation at the generating stage can also provide the writer with useful vocabulary and phrasing practice. When students are beginning to use the language of any discipline, such practice is invaluable. Again, it is an opportunity for socializing, for bringing student writers into the academic community where such language is routinely used. The more practice, the better, particularly at the early stages of handling complex new thoughts. The phrasing does not emerge smoothly or immediately. But as the conversation proceeds, students hear themselves using words and phrases that can be reworked into written form. Conversation with writers as they generate and develop a piece of writing, then, accomplishes several necessary tasks.

Conveying Information and Strategies through Talk

A somewhat different kind of talk has a more overt instructional purpose. Here, we have talk primarily aimed at having writers emerge knowing more about writing in general than they did before, even when the talk may be focused on a particular piece of discourse. When teacher/student talk moves to discussions of general aspects of writing, the temptation for the teacher to lecture, to "tell," is so overwhelming that we constantly have to fight against it. Delivering information, from rules for the comma to strategies for organizing a research paper, can be done economically to large groups, and those writers who understand do not need further help. But for others, those writers who do not completely master what was explained, another round of "tell-it-to-'em-again" in a one-to-one setting is roughly as effective as the "tell-'em-again-but-louder" approach used with those who do not speak English. Instead, the power of interaction in conversation is often the key to helping writers in need:

> *Ms. Niedermann:* You need to use a transition here, a joining word or a phrase, something to help the reader make the connection between this paragraph and the next one. Do you know what "transitions" are?
>
> *LeeAnne:* I guess so. Like using "therefore"?
>
> *Ms. Niedermann:* Sure, that's a good connecting word. But can you see why readers need such words?
>
> *LeeAnne:* I suppose so. I know the book says we should use transitions. And there's that example paragraph in the chapter. But I think it makes my writing sound too formal. Like someone else wrote it, not me. Does that make any sense? Sometimes, I try to use one of those words in that list, but nothing fits. It doesn't sound right. "Therefore" is like something you'd see in an encyclopedia.
>
> *Ms. Niedermann:* Sure, I know what you mean. So what you're saying is that you need a list of words and phrases that are more natural for you. Show me a place where you'd like a connecting word. We'll see what we can come up with together.

The teacher's side of this kind of talk is focused on finding out why the textbook and/or class explanations were not clear. What piece of the puzzle, what prior concept or missing bit of knowledge is needed? How can an abstract concept become a reality for this particular student? What questions does this particular student have? Is some misconception blocking accurate understanding? What first step does this student need in order to think through the problem on her own? Would a demonstration help? In short, what will unlock the door that allows this student to move forward? Writing involves juggling numerous constraints and requires the writer to turn abstract qualities such as "focus," "organization," and "clarity" into specific pieces of text. Because of these complexities, all writers can benefit from talk which specifically addresses their personal concerns and relates abstract concepts about writing to their particular pieces of discourse.

Responding to Writing through Talk

And finally, there is all the talk aimed at providing feedback to writers. Traditionally, teacher response has been in the form of "grading" or writing comments on papers. For such evaluations and responses to be useful, writers need to understand them. But the report from the front is discouraging, as evidence continuing to mount indicates that too many students do not comprehend or profit from written feedback. When C. H. Knoblauch and Lil Brannon (1981) reviewed research on teachers' responses on papers, they concluded that commenting on student essays may be an exercise in futility. Students either do not read the comments or, if they do read them, they do not use the suggestions. Similarly, when Melanie Sperling and Sarah Warshauer Freedman (1987) reviewed the literature on the question of whether students understand teacher comments on papers, their conclusions were similar. They found a disheartening array of studies which show that students either do not understand what is written or think the comments reflect the teachers' confused reading, not the students' confused writing. Sperling and Freedman reflect on what often seems like an uncanny persistence in students to misconstrue, even when the comments are addressed to the most promising students in otherwise successful classrooms.

As an example of how poorly some written responses communicate their messages, consider the findings of a study by Mary F. Hayes and Donald Daiker (1984), when they asked students to react aloud to teacher comments on their papers. The instructor in the Hayes and Daiker study was judged to have offered written response "in keeping with the best pedagogical advice currently offered in our professional literature. That is, she limits her commentary to two or three major points per paper, balances constructive criticism with positive reinforcement, notes students' improvement from paper to paper, and generally avoids abbreviations and correction symbols" (1). Hayes and Daiker clearly did not set up any tenpins to be knocked over. Yet, when one student read the teacher's written comment, "You need to include analysis of the text itself," he commented as follows:

> Analyzing the text. That's kind of hard to figure out because this is more or less an interpretation. It's not so much dealing with—it's not a summary. I guess a summary is the best way to deal with the text, you know, in the paper, and I tend not to summarize. So, uh, I guess I'm confused in that what worked before . . . . (3)

As the conversation with the interviewer continued, it became even clearer that the student thought the teacher was inviting him to summarize rather than analyze as she had said. Another student, when asked what a circle on her paper meant, responded that it had to do with commas: "Yeah. Either it would, depending on the sentence go there or it wouldn't go there, or I need one or I don't. Usually when it's circled, it's not supposed to go there, but sometimes she circles the ones I use well I think"(3). One of Hayes and Daiker's conclusions from all this is that "when a teacher's comment is not immediately clear, students often spend considerable time and effort trying to understand it—and frequently fail"(3).

But in interactive talk, we hear the student's hesitation and the half-articulated questions. Then, we can clarify and amplify our responses. We can also seek feedback from students until we see that they truly understand our comments, a difficult task in the one-way communication of written response. Another goal of oral feedback is to convey to the writer in a more vivid and real manner how the reader actually responds to the writing. Commenting as we read (or just after reading) allows the writer to see and hear the reader's delight in a particular phrase, watch the reader puzzle through a confusing sentence, or become absorbed in a fresh new idea. And the most helpful time for such response is during the writing process, not after the paper is completed. In a study of the response practices of 560 teachers, K–12, judged to be successful teachers, Sarah Warshauer Freedman (1987) found that they considered the individual conference to be more helpful to students than any other type of response (72).

Strategies for Collaboration

If we keep these rationales in mind for using teacher/student talk, our concern then is how to accomplish our goals. How can we talk with students so that the conversation helps them generate content, learn useful strategies for writing, and use our responses productively? In the early stages of a paper, or at any point when writers are searching for ways to develop ideas, the talk is a collaborative search. The teacher is both a partner in the search and also a potential reader asking for information. Being a good listener, as well as offering comments and questions, helps the talk to flow in productive ways. The teacher's collaborative comments are those which help the writer find her direction and the words to get there. A typical exchange might sound like the following brief excerpt in which a teacher and student are working through a problem:

> *Claire:* This doesn't sound right here. Something's missing.
>
> *Mr. Timson:* What if you put that first sentence down here in the next paragraph? It connects with this explanation of why you like special-effects movies in general. But that leaves the other two sentences. What could you do with those?
>
> *Claire:* I guess I don't really need them.
>
> *Mr. Timson:* Wait. Let's not toss them out yet. Since they are about the whole *Star Trek* series, is there something more you could say here? Do you think those *Star Treks* are more examples of good special-effects movies?
>
> *Claire:* No. What I mean is that some movies like *Star Trek* make you use your imagination without special effects. These other movies I talk about here need special effects.
>
> *Mr. Timson:* Oh, I see. You want to point out a contrast.
>
> *Claire:* Sure. Maybe I should explain that more.

This teacher was acting as a collaborator in that he joined in the effort to work through a problem, but he does not do all of the writer's work.

Questions that help the writer get on track are particularly useful. Most often, such questions are the open-ended kind which prompt more than a mere yes/no response. That is, the closed question, "Was that fun?" is likely to produce little more than yes or no. The open-ended form of such a question would be, "What did you enjoy about that?" or "What was the most fun?" Such talk can go on for five to fifteen minutes in some relaxed setting where student and teacher are alone or in a quiet corner together. But it can also go on for just a few minutes as a teacher walks around while students are writing. Amy, a peer tutor in our Writing Lab, realized that even a short bit of talk can work when students are stuck while writing a sentence. She describes her strategy as follows:

> When students keep staring at a sentence, stuck on how to rewrite it, I ask them to try and tell me what they want to write; many

times they are still stuck until I physically remove their papers from view. Then a transformation takes place—suddenly they find themselves able to say what they mean. Once their ideas have crystallized through speech, they are comfortable and can *write* what they just said to me.

When we listen, we will also hear students rejecting what they generate about as fast as they generate it. Encouraging them to turn off their editor is often essential, as students can be unduly harsh critics of the sentences, arguments, or topics they think of. One way to keep the writer from immediately discarding any and every suggestion which does not seem absolutely perfect is to take brief notes as the student talks. Such notes are also useful memory jogs because students can get lost in their talk and not realize how much of what they have talked about can become useful sources for writing. In the early stages of talking with student writers, I was disheartened to see how little of their good talk got translated to paper. And that is exactly the problem. Too many students do not see the relationship between the verbal world they live in and the paper they write on. But we can help students build a bridge by giving them brief written records of their talk—even just a list of phrases from a conversation—which brings together their world of talk and the world of writing. Listen for a moment to this conversation of a teacher talking and taking notes as the student explores an assignment to write about what he learned from some particular experience:

Mrs. Heff: So, you're thinking of writing about being a junior counselor at camp. What part of the experience are you going to concentrate on?

Daniel: I'm not sure yet, maybe how much junior counselors do at camp. Maybe how hard it was. Nah, not that. Maybe . . .

Mrs. Heff: I'll start a list. You said "what junior counselors do." (writes) And "how hard it is." (writes) What things *do* junior counselors do? I suppose the campers never realize how hard the counselor's job is. The kids are there to have a good time.

Daniel: Not always. Some of the kids have to do some growing up. One loudmouth, Brad, he really learned to simmer down and be a part of the group.

Mrs. Heff: Let me add that to the list (Writes "Brad learned to be a part of the group."). I bet teaching Brad to shut up was hard work. Did you learn anything about Brad? Did you learn some interesting strategies for dealing with kids? We're looking for what you learned from being a junior counselor.

Daniel: Well, I wanted the job because I thought it would be fun. My cousin is a counselor there, and she comes back with great stories about what happened. The stories, though, when you are right in the middle of it when it happens, they aren't so funny. Later, though, for Grand Finale night, when everyone says good-bye and the kids put on skits about the camp, then I could see how things get hyped up.

Mrs. Heff: (Laughs and writes "camp stories—hyped up.") Sure, I remember how we did that at camp. Tell me more about it. What do you mean about "hyped up"?

Daniel: Everything gets so dramatized. When there was a big thunderstorm one night, we called it "Noah's Ark Night." Stuff like that. It's fun to make things memorable like that because it's so short. The kids are only there for three weeks. So everything has to be special for them, stuff to go home and remember.

Mrs. Heff: (Writes "make things memorable," "Noah's Ark Night," and "everything has to be special.") Let's look at what you have so far. (They look at the list.)

Daniel: I could write about learning how to make camp special. Well, I didn't really learn how. I mean I did see how things come to be special and how camp stories just grow. I guess I learned *why* everyone hypes up this stuff at camp . . . (pauses and looks over list).

That conference went on for several more minutes as the student and teacher talked about his main point and refined what he wanted to write about. But there are several useful things to note in all that talk. As the conversation flowed, the student explored his topics more thoughtfully as he talked, and the teacher's insistent reminders about what the topic was finally became overt in the student's talk as he, too, asks himself what he learned. Because he was immersed in generating content, even the brief notes will help him recall what he has said and will serve as a stimulus for more when he begins to write.

As drafts develop, there are other helpful things we can do when we are talking with students. A particularly useful strategy is to read the paper aloud for the writer so that she, too, can hear it. When we offer reader comments as we proceed, the writer can see how a reader responds. The teacher/reader can ask questions about context and clarity as they arise and can comment on specific phrases, sentences, ideas, and examples that are particularly effective. Another helpful strategy is to show the writer how the reader is guided by the statement of the topic and by the direction of the sentences and paragraphs. That is, as we read, we can let the writer hear what we anticipate will come next. If that matches with the actual text that we read, the writer hears that she is on target. When some less relevant material intrudes, or when the topic promises one thing and the paper goes a different way, the writer has a vivid lesson in reader confusion caused by the writing. In the following excerpt we can hear the teacher reading and anticipating as he progresses through the student's paper:

> *Mr. Lee:* (reading) "McHenry is not the hero everyone thinks he is because he does not want to get involved." Oh, I see. So you are going to write about McHenry, and the next sentence will show us something about how he doesn't want to get involved. OK, so let's look at what comes next. (reads aloud): "When McHenry hears that Maydene wants to start her own 'rent-a-kid' business, he doesn't want to help." That's a good example of McHenry not getting involved! I see what you mean. (continues to read aloud): "Maydene is always starting new businesses because she always wants to get some money. She is a good organizer." Hmm, I thought I was reading about McHenry, but these sentences are about Maydene. You took a left turn on me here without a signal.
>
> *Cheryl:* Now I want to write about Maydene, too, because she is one of the main characters in the book.
>
> *Mr. Lee:* I see, but you need to explain that to the reader. I got a bit confused there since I was expecting to read more about McHenry. Up here (points to a previous paragraph), I read that the paper would tell us how McHenry changed from the beginning of the story to the end. I didn't expect this paper to be about Maydene too. Why do you want to include Maydene?
>
> *Cheryl:* She's such an interesting character. I liked her and the way she could always come up with new ideas for making money.
>
> *Mr. Lee:* She is pretty imaginative. If you'd like her in the paper, how could you do that? Let's read some more and see if there's a main idea for this paper that will include McHenry and Maydene. (continues reading): "She knows the way to do things." "The way to do things"... Are you saying here that she is talented and does things well? Am I right?
>
> *Cheryl:* No, what I mean is that Maydene knows how to get stuff done. She just knows how things are supposed to happen ... how to get started ....
>
> *Mr. Lee:* Oh, I see what you mean. Can you use what you just said here? It's a lot clearer that way.

Note that in this conversation the teacher offers back to the writer the meaning that he as a reader gets from the text, to allow the student to check it against what she had meant the writing to convey. This bit of teacher/student talk is far from over, but the student has already gotten some information that can be used when revising.

As writers develop their drafts, there are other helping strategies that can be included in the conversation. Asking writers to take stock of where they are and what they need to work on can help them focus their thoughts and can suggest questions that they can begin asking themselves as they write. "What do you like about this paper?" can be a very helpful question as can, "What is giving you problems?" or "Where are you going next?" Becoming a coworker and offering suggestions keeps the conversation truly collaborative. For example, if the writer is relying too heavily on "to be" verbs or on the standard ones that lack vividness, the teacher/collaborator can offer suggestions and examples to help the writer move in the right direction, as in this bit of teacher talk:

> What would help here to let your readers actually see this in their minds would be more specific verbs. For example, I could write, "I'm *sitting* in the chair," but you could see that more clearly in your mind if I write, "I'm *slouching down* in the chair" or "I'm *slumped over* to the side of the chair." Now let's try that part of your sentence about how "Teresa walked out quietly." What about "Teresa *tiptoed out*"? Or "Teresa *snuck out*"?

The writer may opt to select one of the teacher's choices here, an action that may not seem a step forward in making the writer independent. But it does make the conversation collaborative in that the writer sees that the teacher is there as a helper, not a grader. And with an illustration of how to make verbs more vivid, the writer is more likely to be successful in her next attempt on her own.

What I am suggesting here may seem inordinately obvious, the kind of talk we are all familiar with when helping someone. But it is far from obvious to student writers that we as teachers are available as helpers. Teacher/student talk is a powerful means by which we can make students aware of our willingness to assist them in becoming better writers. And by using talk to promote that social awareness that writers need, we are adding a powerful dimension to the writer's awareness of writing for others. Teacher/student talk is, then, that comfortable setting where writer and helper talk about—and work together on—a piece of writing. It is also enjoyable, so much so that I wonder why writing teachers persist in spending so much time lecturing to classes and writing those lengthy marginal comments on papers when, instead, we could be talking individually with writers. Perhaps we, like our students, do not make enough connections between the world of talk and the world of writing. Or we may be deluded by the bias expressed in the old cliche that says "talk is cheap." But for teachers of writing, I would revise that to "talk is better."

Works Cited

Freedman, S. W. 1987. *Response to Student Writing.* Urbana, Ill.: National Council of Teachers of English.

Graves, D. 1983. *Writing: Teachers and Children at Work.* Portsmouth, N.H.: Heinemann.

Harris, M. 1986. *Teaching One-to-One: The Writing Conference.* Urbana, Ill.: National Council of Teachers of English.

Hayes, M. F., and D. A. Daiker. 1984. "Using Protocol Analysis in Evaluating Responses to Student Writing." *Freshman English News* 13, no. 2: 1–4, 10.

Knoblauch, C. H., and L. Brannon. 1981. "Teacher Commentary on Student Writing: The State of the Art." *Freshman English News* 10, no. 2: 1–4.

Noppen, M. 1985. "Speaking of Writing." *Writing Lab Newsletter* 10, no. 1: 9–10.

Sperling, M., and S. W. Freedman. 1987. *A Good Girl Writes Like a Good Girl.* Technical Report No. 3. Berkeley: University of California, Center for the Study of Writing.

11 Talking Life and Literature

Susan Hynds
Syracuse University

Many of us would like to think that discussions about literature help students to understand both the literary text and the world around them. But without realizing it, we sometimes send powerful messages through our classroom talk that stifle creative opinions and silence student voices. By taking a closer look at what we and our students say in discussions about literature, we can begin to uncover and understand the classroom communities that we create. In "talking literature and life," teachers and students can build comfortable environments where students create, explore, and enrich their visions of the literary text and the world beyond.

Eleventh-grade students are discussing Wilde's *The Picture of Dorian Gray*. The teacher has just asked the students to write down one word that epitomizes Dorian and to discuss the reasons for their choices.

Teacher: What about ennui? Who chose ennui?

Craig: I did.

Teacher: Why did you choose ennui?

Craig: Because I think it's about time that we read a real good book instead of a character analysis of a personality type.

Mark: Like *Catcher in the Rye*.

Teacher: Are you attributing this [word] to your feelings or to Dorian?

Craig: No. Dorian was boring. He only killed one person.

Amy: That we know of.

Craig: I'm tired of just reading about these people: "Joe hated himself; Joe hated everybody around him."

Teacher: What would you prefer? Something not about people?

Craig: Something that's got some action in it or something else. Why don't we read like a Stephen King book?

Class: Unintelligible noise.

Teacher: OK. What about the rest of you? Did the mystery of the novel bother you? How did you like being left in mystery?

Class: No response.

Teacher: What about themes now? We're going to have more than one, I'm sure. Who has a theme he or she wants to share?

Some time after her class had engaged in this dialogue, Craig's teacher wrote the following note to herself:

There are 26 students in the class who have opinions. I wish us to hear (16 of 24 students present) participate, so some "on task" conversation must be restricted and some conversations ended to make room for others. The most noticeable attempt at derailment was Craig's shift from the word choice "ennui" not to describe Dorian, but to voice his attitude toward the novel. I know he is undermining the task when he makes the absurd comment, "He only killed one person," from the clamor that resulted. I answer a "mystery" question, the "ennui" interlude in the back of the room ceases, and I use this as a convenient move to "theme."

Two things are interesting in this excerpt of classroom talk. One is Craig's comment that a "good book" is one with a lot of action, rather than a "character analysis of a personality type." How often we encounter students like Craig, who read only books with a compelling plot, and therefore miss the unique power of literature to help them understand their own lives and, in the process, to better understand the people around them. As Louise Rosenblatt once said:

[Literature] offers a special kind of existence. It is a mode of living. The poem, the play, the story is thus an extension, an amplification, of life itself. The reader's primary purpose is to add *this* kind of experience to the other kinds of desirable experience that life may offer. (1983, 278)

And yet, despite the best intentions of English teachers, many students, like Craig, have never learned to "bring life to literature" and, in so doing, to "bring literature to life" (Hynds 1989). Many, like Craig, are "story-driven" readers (Hunt and Vipond 1986), preferring books with a compelling plot and "lots of action" to books about people and their underlying motivations. Others are "information-driven," searching for minute details and facts about the text that might be useful later on for a test or a paper.

What is also interesting about the opening dialogue, however, is that by keeping her discussion "on track," Craig's teacher may be fostering the very disinterest in literature and in character motivation that she seeks to avoid. Subtly and unknowingly, she may be reinforcing and promoting "a-literacy," or the phenomenon where many competent and skilled readers simply *do not* read beyond their years of formal schooling. Although in one sense Craig is undermining the task, on another level he may be entirely honest and straightforward in his personal evaluation of the book. It is clear from the dialogue that an agenda is being derailed. The question is, whose agenda? The student's or the teacher's? What Craig's teacher describes as a "convenient move to theme" may actually be a comfortable move to the teacher-centered classroom, where keeping "on task" becomes more important than exploring a wide range of student opinions and responses.

This chapter operates from two premises: The first is that classroom talk is a powerful vehicle for bridging literature and life. The second is that in order to become competent lifetime readers, students must learn to bring life to literature in the form of literary and social knowledge. Through classroom talk, students and teacher explore interpersonal and social relationships. Literature becomes a window to life, and life becomes a milieu within which readers learn to understand why people and characters do what they do. In so doing, readers develop the "social competence" necessary for reading (Hynds, in press).

Within the classroom, talk is a strong socializing force. Students build personal responses out of the stuff of shared communal response. Through what David Bleich calls "intersubjective negotiation" (1986), students learn what is generally accepted as possible within the text, while maintaining the integrity of their own personal (often idiosyncratic) perceptions. At the same time, talk is the substance through which students and teachers negotiate their classroom community. Teacher talk sends powerful messages to students about what is acceptable literary interpretation, as well as what is acceptable classroom behavior. Student talk sends equally powerful messages about how students perceive "what counts" in English classes and "what is correct" in interpreting texts. Through the constant interpretive process which underlies all classroom talk, students learn "how to succeed in English," how to live in the peculiar social world of the schoolroom, and maybe also how to read and interpret literature.

Reading and Social Competence

As English teachers, we are fond of talking about competence in reading literature. What we mean by "competence," however, often remains vague and undefined in our own minds and in the minds of our students. For some teachers, "competence" means remembering minute details of plot, setting, and theme; for others, "competence" means arriving at inferences about what happened in and beyond the story. Such thinking processes are essential to the reading of literature. However, they fail to take into account "social competence," or the understanding of why people in stories and in real life behave and believe as they do. This "thinking about people" takes place as readers try to interpret the behaviors of story characters, and as they try to understand how their reading relates to people in their everyday lives.

Interestingly, a good many students can memorize literal details about a story, and can even make some pretty sophisticated inferences about the plot, but they fail to understand the complex social explanations behind what characters do, believe, and feel. Let's begin by taking a look at two seventh-grade students' descriptions of the character Chuck in Robin Brancato's "Fourth of July":

> *Becky's description:*
> [Chuck is] shy but not too shy. I mean he isn't as open and straightforward as his friend Bobby. He's really nice and could never hurt someone on purpose. Even though he was really hurt by Sager, he couldn't bring himself to throw the M-80 in his car. He's just a good person, though he is no angel. He is fun and can play pranks. He's really sweet. He knows where he's going—he's going to better himself, but he's not going too fast. He's taking life one step at a time and working hard for the things he wants in life. He also values people's opinions, that's how his girlfriend is getting him to stop smoking, and to be generally a good person.
>
> *Nick's description:*
> Chuck was a man that worked at a gas station. He had a so called friend Sager who stoled money from him. He was a nice person, with a nice girlfriend named Kate. Chuck was a hard working person. He worked hard, so he could buy himself a car. Chuck was a smoker, but he was trying to stop it.

Although both students were doing their best to describe the character, Chuck, in such a way that "a stranger might be able to recognize what kind of person he is from your description," Becky's description demonstrates more social awareness than Nick's does. It is clear that she is using a wide range of internal attributes in her description ("shy," "nice," "hard working"). She also compares Chuck to another story character ("he isn't as open and straightforward as his friend Bobby"), and accepts the contradictions in Chuck's personality without stereotyping or simplifying him (Chuck is "shy, but not too shy"; Chuck is a "good person, though he is no angel"). Finally, she attempts to explain the reasons behind her perceptions with evidence from the story ("He also values people's opinions, that's how his girlfriend is getting him to stop smoking").

In contrast to Becky's description, Nick's description reveals less sophisticated social sensitivity. Although he does mention a few internal qualities ("nice," "hard working"), his impression concentrates mostly on descriptive attributes ("worked at a gas station"), and details of plot ("He had a so-called friend"), rather than details that would enable a stranger to understand what kind of person Chuck was. We might almost bet that Nick's description is a way of demonstrating to the teacher that he has read the story, rather than a clue that he has attempted to understand Chuck's motivations, beliefs, and behaviors.

Richard Beach (1983) has suggested that the reading of literature requires two basic competencies: an understanding of literary conventions (how literary texts "work" on readers) and an understanding of social conventions (how people behave and believe as they do). Readers must not only understand literary technique, they must also develop a knowledge of an empathy for people in a variety of social situations.

From a "skills-based" perspective, teachers and curriculum planners have come to believe that simply equipping readers with necessary comprehension and interpretation skills will somehow guarantee that readers will use these skills outside of the classroom. Over the past few years, however, I have found that students who are able to understand the complex motivations of people in their everyday lives sometimes fail to put these understandings to use in their reading. All too often there is little connection between the ways in which readers view the world of the literary text and the ways in which they view the world of interpersonal communication in which they live (Hynds 1985, 1989).

Not surprisingly, readers who can make the necessary connections between literature and life are those who are more likely to read for their own pleasure outside and beyond the literature classroom (Hynds 1985). For teachers of literature, classroom talk becomes a vehicle for creating a climate that nurtures and promotes those connections between literature and life.

Teacher Talk, Social Competence, and Literary Response

A look at teacher talk can reveal the messages we send students about what it means to read literature and to be a member of a particular literary community (Culler 1975). Consider these three excerpts of teacher talk as an example:

> *Teacher A:* All right. First of all, let's go back and find out—uh, exactly what was happening in *The Pigman*. Remember, I said there are levels of reading? This would be our most basic level of reading. What has just plain happened up until the point of the past scene? Charlie, start us off.

> *Teacher B:* OK. Everybody turn to page 466. When we read "The Tale of Sir Gareth," that is going to be a medieval romance, and you need to know what the characteristics of a romance are. On page 466 we find out that the medieval romance is a form of literature popular throughout Europe during the Middle Ages. Can someone give me the first characteristic of a medieval romance?

> *Teacher C:* OK. Let's spend a minute or two looking at what each other has written, because I did this with fifth period yesterday. They were very diverse in their opinions about Dorian. Some saw him quite differently from other members of the class. That means a good discussion, I think, in how we see Dorian in the novel.

Typically, literature classrooms have been dominated by three overriding perspectives. In discussing these perspectives, however, I want to stress that no one teacher, and few literature lessons, are influenced by only one perspective. I am discussing these positions individually; however, this arbitrary separation is far too "neat" to accurately characterize what really goes on "out there" in classrooms between teachers and students. At the risk, then, of oversimplifying a very complex set of assumptions, I will discuss each perspective, and then try to demonstrate how it might interact with the others.

From a *reading comprehension* perspective, understanding of texts is based upon a "determinate" (Hynds in press) model of "correct meaning." From this viewpoint, students are often overly concerned about arriving at the "right answer" (often the one preferred by the teacher). Thus, Teacher A, in asking for literal details about the text, and Teacher B, in asking for characteristics of a medieval romance, might be sending a message that there is one acceptable response. Of course, teachers do have a responsibility to help students understand plot details and literary genre. However, when they *restrict* literature lessons to only literal recall and knowledge *about* literature, they run the risk of short-circuiting and limiting students' responses.

From a New Critical or "formalist" position, texts are objects to be dissected and studied apart from their surrounding context and the author's possible intention. According to this view, students provide arguments for which meaning is most successfully supported by evi-

Shuttling talk from text, to social reality, to personal experience affirms literature's potential as a window on the world; it is talk that bridges the connections between literature and life. April's comment that her father punished her only because he loved her creates a personal connection to the story, what Richard Beach (in press) calls an "autobiographical association" which opens the way for a much deeper understanding of both the literary text and Beth's social relationship with her father.

It is this constant interplay between personal experience and textual meaning that prompted Louise Rosenblatt to say:

> The ability to understand and sympathize with others reflects the multiple nature of the human being. . . . Although we may see some characters as outside ourselves—that is, we may not identify with them as completely as we do with more congenial temperaments—we are nevertheless able to enter into their behavior and their emotions. Thus it is that the youth may identify with the aged, one sex with the other, a reader of a particular limited social background with a member of a different class or a different period. (1983, 40)

Through talk, literature can become a virtual world within which readers learn vicariously to interpret the events of their lives. Simultaneously, the events of students' lives become a rich milieu within which to understand and formulate their perceptions of literature.

Talking Literature: Promoting Literary Competence

Often, we teach literary techniques and interpretive conventions directly. After all, that's how we learned to define such concepts as "moral," "theme," "onomatopoeia," "iambic pentameter," and so forth. Our classroom talk is punctuated with "minilectures" in which we attempt to help our students "read like writers" (Smith 1984). This teacher, for instance, takes the opportunity to deliver a minilecture, exploring the concepts of theme and symbol, pointing out how each gives literature a certain depth and unforgettable quality:

> *Teacher:* OK, now that's pretty much what happens in the story. I asked you yesterday to think about theme and symbol. And without you realizing it, the story's theme and symbols are part of the story's appeal. If you have just a story that's told, like one of those Harlequin Romances or like a soap opera or something, you are missing a lot of the depth, and when that depth is missing, you may not be so aware of it at the time because you are interested in the plot, but somehow the story does not have the impact. It

doesn't stick with you. And that's one of the differences, perhaps, between a good story that's well-written, and a poorly written story. That you have more than just plot. OK, first of all, refresh our memories, please, Danielle, tell us, if you can, what "theme" means.

In transcript after transcript of classroom talk, one fact stands clear: teachers talk more than students (Rogers, Green, and Nussbaum this volume). To be sure, it is neither possible nor desirable for teachers to avoid the occasional minilecture. We are, after all, more experienced readers than our students. As such, we have many rich insights to enlarge our students' understanding of what happens when they read and how they respond to literary technique and convention.

Unfortunately, however, we are too often the sole navigators of such discussions, ignoring the many opportunities that arise naturally out of students' talk about their own writing and reading. One of the best ways to create such opportunities is to set up writing and reading workshops where students learn about literary conventions and devices through talking about their own "classroom-created literature." Notice, for example, how this teacher weaves a discussion of character development and ambiguous ending into her students' responses to Stacy's short story:

> *Teacher:* OK, let's have some comments about Stacy's story. And remember, if you think that something's good or bad, whatever it is, you can't stop there, you gotta explain what it is, Leslie?
>
> *Leslie:* Well, like it's [the story is] pretty good, except for the fact that it's kind of shocking, like you didn't think—usually people don't come out of their comas and die.
>
> *Stacy:* Yeah, that's what I didn't like. I hated that.
>
> *Leslie:* It's also, uhm, how it's like you don't know what's wrong with her. It's not too bad, but it's just like—it could be that uhm, a little bit more like Sammie talked to her and—I don't know . . .
>
> *Teacher:* So in other words, you're saying that, uhm, that you need more buildup in the beginning?
>
> *Leslie:* Yeah.
>
> *Teacher:* What we call that, we talk about character development. In order for something that tragic to happen to a character, and for us to be involved with these characters as readers before we can ever care if something happens to them, it's like people die every day, but we're not heartbroken, because we don't know them.
>
> *Mark:* You could talk about the good times [between Sammie and her friend], I think.
>
> *Leslie:* Yeah. I sorta wanted to know more about that.

Shortly after his teacher's discussion of the importance of character development, Mark reiterates the same literary response in his comments to Stacy, as revealed in the following excerpt. The ensuing discussion then provides an opportunity for the teacher to discuss another literary technique—the ambiguous ending:

> *Mark:* I mean, it kind of made me like kind of sad, but I didn't really, like if it's a really thick book and you're getting to know the characters, you feel like it's happening to you, and like it feels like your best friend really does die and you just want to cry. But this is like—she dies!
>
> *Gary:* I think she *should* die because so many of the stories, like ... Oh! She lives! And it's like happily ever after. I don't think you should change it.
>
> *Stacy:* Yeah. I definitely want her to die. That sounds horrendous (laughter). That's just what—I mean, it's like every other story I write: "Ha-ha. She lives, and she runs off and marries this guy."
>
> *Teacher:* Well, there is another solution to it other than a happy ending, and that's one of those endings that kind of, you don't know what happens.

There are some noticeable differences between the approaches in the previous excerpts of classroom talk. The teacher in the first excerpt originates the discussion of symbol and theme ("I asked you yesterday to think about theme and symbol."). The discussion arises out of the teacher's desire to define a particular set of literary terms ("Danielle, tell us, if you can, what 'theme' means."). The teacher does attempt to explain how the literary techniques "work" on the reader ("without you realizing it, part of the story's appeal"). However, the task is clearly teacher prescribed, and the goal of the discussion is to define terms with no real student need or context within which to use or understand these definitions.

In the second excerpt, the teacher's minilecture on character development arises, naturally, out of the students' responses to the abrupt death of Stacy's undeveloped character in her short story. Later, Stacy's negative reaction toward stereotypic story endings prompts her teacher to bring up the idea of the ambiguous or open-ended story ending. Thus, this discussion of literary technique and convention grows out of student writers' needs to know how to make language "work" in the minds of readers. The teacher, in this case, acts as a literary consultant, rather than as a resident expert on literary technique.

Thus, when talk emanates not from us, but from the real needs, questions, and insights of our students, teacher talk becomes a welcome vehicle for exploring student concerns, rather than just a tool for teachers to fulfill their classroom objectives.

Creating Classroom Communities through Talk

Our words say many things to our students about the culture of our classrooms. Some classrooms are examination halls, others are comfortable places in which to explore personal insights gained through reading and writing. Consider the interpretive climate reflected in the following discussion. A group of eleventh-grade students and their teacher are talking about the medieval romance. Mary Ann begins by talking about the characters:

> *Mary Ann:* The characters are not ordinary people, they are kings and queens.
>
> *Teacher:* Right, the characters are not ordinary people. They are kings, queens, and knights. Anyone give me another characteristic?
>
> *Grant:* The medieval romance takes place in an imaginary world.
>
> *Teacher:* OK. It does take place in an imaginary world. Can anyone tell me what I mean by an imaginary world?
>
> *Hadyn:* Yes. It takes place in castles, gardens, and forest.
>
> *Teacher:* Yes. Castles, gardens, and forests.

It is interesting that, in response to Grant's comment, this teacher says, "Can anyone tell me what *I* mean by an imaginary world?" How often children must learn to read literature in classrooms where teachers, through the subtle undertones of their talk, ask them to "tell me what I mean." The talk in this classroom is one of recitation (Rogers, Green, and Nussbaum this volume), not of discussion or negotiated meaning. After each student comment, the teacher merely paraphrases or repeats what each student has said and adds an occasional "reinforcer" ("right," "OK," "yes"). There is no building of meaning upon meaning in this classroom, no intersubjective negotiation. Students are reciting facts, not building interpretations.

Teachers need to create classrooms where students are creating unique interpretations, not guessing at predetermined answers—environments where talk about literary form becomes a vehicle for producing responses among readers, and not exclusively a recitation of genre characteristics. Student talk in such classroom communities is directed not only at the teacher, for the purpose of demonstrating

Deer Boy" from the Zuni Indians, she simply recorded the words, as they were dictated, without recording performance features such as tone of voice, or volume:

> One of his uncles caught his mother, and another caught his sister, and another caught his brother. The boy alone came almost to the woods. There his uncle jumped down and ran after him. He ran after him and caught up with him and threw his arms around him. As he clasped him in his arms he struggled. "Oh dear, my boy, stand still, whoever you may be," he said to him. But he did not speak. He just looked into his eyes. Then the people came there. They caught him. (1933, 109)

Compared to a literary story, such a folklore text might appear shorter and stylistically barren, with few details describing characters, and little emotional impact. Unfortunately, the poor quality of many early Native American folklore texts led some critics to disparage the quality of their narratives, claiming that their literary value "is nil" (Tedlock 1972, 114).

Today, however, the new performance approach in folklore studies has stimulated folklorists to make folklore texts that capture more of the total performance (Fine 1984). Compare this 1965 excerpt of the same incident from "The Deer Boy," which was tape-recorded. The folklorist, Dennis Tedlock, has tried to translate the oral dimensions of the performance into print, using line ends to represent half-second pauses, dots to represent two-second pauses, parentheses for soft voice, capitals for loud voice, split lines for chanted lines, and dashes for elongated vowels. To help students appreciate the added power of performance, first have them read the preceding "Deer Boy" tale, and then have them read the following version. Make sure that they try to perform all of the vocal features:

> and ALL THE PEOPLE WHO HAD COME
>   KILLED THE DEER
>   killed the deer
>   killed the deer.
> Wherever they made their kills they gutted them, put
>   them on their backs, and went home.
> Two of the uncles
>
>   •
>
> (then)
> went ahead of the group, and a third uncle
> (*voice breaking*) (dropped his elder sister)
> (his elder brother)

(his mother.)
(He gutted them there)
while the other two uncles went on. As they
    went ON
the boy pretended to be tired. The first uncle
    pleaded: "Tisshomahha!"
"STOP," he said, "Let's stop this contest now."
That's what he was saying as
the little boy kept on running.
As he kept on his bells went telele.
O———n, he went on this way
on until

•

(the little boy stopped and his uncle, dismounting)
(caught him.)

                                        (Tedlock 1978, 21–22)

Clearly this text with vocal performance features recorded is much
more interesting and dynamic than the former one. The performer
creates suspense through the use of pauses and a sense of emotional
intensity with his breaking voice and volume changes. The elongated
vowel "o———n" conveys a sense of motion and duration. When performance features are recorded, folklore can compete well with literature in terms of emotional and stylistic impact.

While examining texts of folk performances reminds us that the
performance is paramount and the text is secondary, how can we
argue that performance is paramount to literary study? After all, most
literary artists do not compose entirely orally in performance, and
their finished products are in print. But, like folk artists, the writer is
striving to capture human experience. Rather than showing us a character's attitude by performing his voice and body movements, the
writer must use certain literary conventions to re-create the tone indi-
cative of that attitude. Through such devices as figures of speech,
punctuation, typography, syntax, and rhythm, writers can imitate human speech, thought, and action. Since writers, in most cases, cannot
appear before their readers to perform the literature themselves, they
must rely on the readers' abilities to reconstruct the intended performances. The marks on the page function to record and store the writer's performance. Thus, literary texts are performance records, or as
Long and Hopkins say, "'arrested performances' of creative writers
that provide readers the signs, clues, cues, and directions for a performance of their own" (1982, 2). As teachers, we must ensure that
students know how to interpret those directions for performance.

Advantages of Student Performance

Teaching literature through performance has enormous advantages. First, performance promotes dialogue between the performer and the classroom audience, and between the performer and the text. A performance is a public statement about a literary work; it is an act of interpretation. When using performance as a pedagogical tool, the teacher should ask the audience members to discuss the performance, comparing it to their own interpretations of the text. Inevitably, students compare their private, silent interpretations to the performed text and begin asking questions or making suggestions. Why did the performer pause in the middle of a line? Should the tone be sincere or ironic? How can the performer show us more of the symbolism? As the performer tries to respond to these questions, he or she must often return to the text, rereading and reperforming. Both the audience and performer gain a new appreciation for the complexity of literary interpretation.

Second, performance is a holistic activity that rescues literature from the fragmenting tendency of criticism. Too often after students have analyzed literature, dissecting its plot, point of view, or other literary features, they are left with a literary experience that is far less than the sum of its critical parts. Performance remedies this situation by forcing students to synthesize all of their research and analysis into a performance that makes sense (Shattuck 1980).

Third, performance is a lively and engaging way to study literature. When students have to perform a text, they feel the pressure of responsibility that performance always entails. Since few students want to appear unprepared before their peers, they work hard preparing their performances. The air is charged with excitement during a performance, as both performer and audience concentrate their energies on the literary experience that is emerging. The performer's facial expressions, gestures, tone of voice, and movements captivate the students, focusing their attention on the literary experience.

In addition to these three primary advantages, performance offers secondary benefits to the performer. Practice reading literature aloud improves both the ear and the voice. The ear becomes more attuned to the sound qualities of literature, and the voice becomes more adept at expressing them. When students perform, they gain greater control over their body language as well. And performing in front of an audience builds confidence in speaking. All of these benefits translate into increased oral communication skills.

Introducing Students to Performance

Although students may not realize it, they have a great deal of experience performing that they can bring to the study of literature. In order to introduce performance in a nonthreatening and positive way, I begin with an exercise called "everyday performances." The first step in introducing this exercise is to point out that, despite their participation in a literate culture, students have a rich oral tradition that is transmitted through performance. To illustrate this point, the instructor can play a simple game of performing the first lines of several types of folklore, and asking the students to complete them. After the class finishes performing each example, the instructor can briefly discuss the genre of verbal art which it represents and its general function in society. Let us see some examples from a hypothetical class:

> *Ms. Jones:* Who can complete these lines, "Thirty days hath September . . ."
>
> *Beth:* "April, June, and November."
>
> *Ms. Jones:* Very good. This is a mnemonic rhyme which most of you were taught in elementary school. The rhyme functions to help you remember important details. Let's try another example of folklore from our oral tradition. Who can complete this? "A stitch in time . . ."
>
> *Tom:* "saves nine."
>
> *Ms. Jones:* Good. What do we call this type of folklore?
>
> *Tom:* Is it a proverb?
>
> *Ms. Jones:* Right. And what do proverbs convey? What is their function in society?
>
> *Tom:* I guess you might say that they teach wisdom.
>
> *Ms. Jones:* You're right. Proverbs convey wisdom, advice, and values. Did anyone ever perform this folklore before? "Cinderella dressed in yellow . . ."
>
> *Lisa:* "Went upstairs to kiss her fellow. How many kisses did she get? One, two, three, four, five, . . . and so on until you miss a jump."
>
> *Ms. Jones:* You've got it. This is an old jump rope rhyme. How many of you know it? And why are jump rope rhymes performed? What is their function?
>
> *Jane:* I think that they are just plain fun. They have a rhythm that kids like to jump to. And sometimes the lines are funny. Remember "Fudge, fudge, call the judge, Mama's got a newborn baby?"
>
> (Several students laugh and the teacher asks the students to perform the whole rhyme.)

his or her characteristics given by the text, they quickly realize that the doctor is defending his decision to commit an act of euthanasia. The ellipsis in the last line indicates some kind of physical demonstration by the doctor, and the class must decide what "slight kind of engine," such as a syringe, might have been used to carry out the mercy killing.

Students usually arrive at two different interpretations of whom the doctor is addressing:

> *Ms. Jones:* Who do you think the doctor is talking to?
>
> *Bill:* He seems to be talking to a jury of his peers, perhaps other doctors who work in the same hospital.
>
> *Ms. Jones:* What gives you this idea?
>
> *Bill:* He keeps referring to "you" on lines 10, 11, 13, and 14. And in line 11, the doctor's request that his audience remember the worst that they know of him suggests that he is talking to people who know him well.
>
> *Tom:* I agree. When he asks the audience to "view yourself as I was, on the spot—" he just has to be talking to someone like other doctors, who could identify with the situation.
>
> *Jane:* I don't think it has to be that way. I picture the doctor talking to himself, in front of a mirror. I think that he is rehearsing the defense that he will use before the jury.
>
> *Ms. Jones:* That's interesting. Now we have two different interpretations to work with. Both seem highly probable. Does the style of the poem work equally well with each interpretation?

To help the students evaluate the conflicting interpretations, the teacher might encourage them to examine the poem's sonnet structure. In each case, the persona is presenting an argument, and the sonnet structure, which is designed to couch philosophical arguments, suits either interpretation well.

From Analysis to Performance

Once students have analyzed Robinson's poem, they are ready to test their interpretations through performance. The Robinson poem works well to introduce three fundamental performance concepts: open and closed speaking situations, subtexts, and prelife and postlife. In an open speaking situation, the persona appears to be communicating directly to anyone who will listen, and thus, makes direct eye contact with the audience. In the Robinson poem, the performer who chooses an open speaking situation would directly address the audience, as if they were his or her jury of peers. In a closed speaking situation, the persona appears to be meditating or talking to some onstage audience. Thus, in a closed situation, no eye contact or direct communication between the performer and audience occurs. To indicate that the doctor is rehearsing the speech in private, the performer would avoid direct eye contact with the classroom audience.

Even though students may intellectually understand the dramatic situation of a poem, they may have problems expressing the persona's attitudes and emotions. Teaching students how to construct probable subtexts for each word of the text helps them recognize, and thus perform, the persona's emotional state. Subtext refers to the under-meanings, the underlying feelings and reasons for uttering the words of a text. For example, the subtext for the first line of the Robinson poem, "They called it Annandale—and I was there" might be: "My friend Annandale was such a physical wreck that the other doctors and nurses spoke of him as an *it*, and used only his last name, and I had to be there." This subtext would cause the performer to emphasize "it" and to perform the line with some sadness and, perhaps, distaste. As an exercise, have students write and discuss a subtext for each line in the text to be performed.

In addition to subtexts, students should discover and perform a "prelife" of the work. That is, they should show the actions and emotions that motivate the first words of the work. The doctor persona in "How Annandale Went Out" might be looking at a picture of Annandale before speaking. Performing a prelife helps the performer get in character and helps the audience understand the dramatic situation. Similarly, at the end of the work, the performer should perform a "postlife." Too often, students tend to cut short the final words of a text and curtail their emotional and philosophical impact. But if they are reminded that the persona must respond to what he or she says, they will learn to show the persona's response to the final words of the text. For example, in the Robinson poem, the performer might have the doctor smile knowingly after he says, "You wouldn't hang me. I thought not."

To encourage students to view performance as a way of studying literature, an exercise round of performances, in which each student performs the same literary selection twice, is most effective. For the first performance, advise the students to memorize their selections so that they will be free to use their voices and bodies to the fullest. They should be instructed to try to re-create the dramatic situation as closely as possible. For example, if the persona is that of an elderly person, they should try to convey that age through appropriate vocal quality and movement. Simple costumes or props often can be used to suggest elements of the dramatic situation. Titles of works give invaluable clues to the dramatic situation, and should be performed. For example, the title, "How Annandale Went Out," clearly indicates that the poem describes how Annandale died, and it also indicates the persona's preference for indirect speech.

After the first performance of the work, students should be asked to discuss the performance and compare it to their own interpretations of the text. Discussion might range over any aspect of the dramatic analysis, and the performer can be asked to try parts of the work in several different ways. After all suggestions have been heard, the performer takes them into consideration and presents the work again in a few days, trying to improve the performance.

Evaluating Student Performances

Evaluation is essential to the learning process. It provides the critical feedback that helps students learn and improve. Performance of literature utilizes many different abilities: analysis, interpretation, and vocal and nonverbal expression. Any of these abilities can be evaluated, depending on the goals of the class. For those English instructors who are also concerned with developing speaking skills or dramatic skills, it makes sense to evaluate such skills as voice projection and articulation. But for those instructors who are primarily concerned with using performance as a means to study literature, it is important to keep evaluations of performances centered on student interpretations of the text. Rather than focusing, for example, on the impact of the performance on the audience, or on the performer's use of voice, facial expressions, gestures, movement, costume, or props as ends in themselves, the instructor should evaluate how well the performance realized the dramatic situation implied by the text. Since there may be several acceptable interpretations of a text, as well as some distorted interpretations, the instructor must establish guidelines for distinguishing plausible from implausible interpretations.

Using the text itself as the blueprint or guide, students must learn to distinguish among four categories of interpretation: certainties, probabilities, possibilities, and distortions (Long 1977). In a poem with a highly defined dramatic situation, such as "How Annandale Went Out," some elements of the dramatic situation are definite, explicitly stated by the words themselves. We know for certain that the persona is a physician, defending a past act. Other aspects of an interpretation are strongly implied by the text; they are weighted likelihoods, or probabilities. For example, given the publication date of the poem (1910), we can infer that the physician is probably male. The text suggests that he is on trial for euthanasia, but does not explicitly state it. Some levels of interpretation rest on slight clues, and may be termed possibilities. Long and Hopkins identify two different possibilities for interpreting the end of the Robinson poem: "The speaker smirks at the jury's decision," or "The speaker is making his claims in good faith; he quietly and humbly accepts the jury's verdict" (1982, 134).

These latter categories—probabilities and possibilities—should remind students that literary texts are rich and complex, offering many levels of interpretation and meaning. Students should be encouraged to explore as many different ways of interpreting a poem as possible. For example, after students have discussed several different probabilities and possibilities for the Robinson poem, the teacher might ask them to prepare performances that would show each different interpretation.

Distortions occur when an interpretation violates a known fact or certainty in a text. The student who performs the persona of the Robinson poem as if the speaker were Annandale, contradicts a certainty that the speaker is a doctor. Ignoring line endings and rhythm patterns, or substituting one's own words for those in the text also distorts the literature. Long and Hopkins identify three types of distortions: "inadequate (when they omit certainties), premature (when they reflect hasty study), or implausible (when they contradict the certainties)" (1982, 134).

To aid in the evaluation and learning process, instructors can require written work. A written dramatic analysis of the text, for example, helps the student analyze the literature and prepare for performance. The teacher might choose to evaluate this written analysis prior to the performance, and suggest other possibilities or point out problems. Alternatively, the teacher can use the student's written analysis as a yardstick by which to measure the performance. He or she might compare the interpretation conveyed by the performance to the student's written interpretation. For example:

> Ms. Jones: In your paper, John, you said that the doctor was talking to other doctors. But in your performance, you seemed to be looking inward, as if talking to yourself. Have you changed your interpretation?
>
> John: No. Was I really gazing inward? I meant to look directly at the class, as if they were the jury.
>
> Ms. Jones: Why don't you try the poem again, and this time focus your eye gaze directly on the students in the room. This would

better convey the open situation of the persona communicating with an audience.

In addition to the written dramatic analysis, instructors may find student journals and performance analyses of use. In the former, students can be asked to keep a log of their analysis and rehearsal process. For example, they might write the subtext of the poem, a paraphrase, or a character analysis. The instructor can use this written log as a means to engage the students in dialogue about the performance as well as to evaluate their preparation. In the performance analysis, the students write about their own performances, describing what they learned through the rehearsal and performance process. This exercise in self-criticism encourages students to view performance as a learning tool, and provides yet another means for the instructor to evaluate student progress.

Conclusion

This brief chapter has presented some basic techniques for using performance to teach literature. We have discussed ways of introducing students to performance by using oral tradition and folklore, and have explored how dramatic analysis, performance exercises, and such basic concepts as open and closed situations, subtexts, and prelife and postlife can be used. The advantages of using performance are considerable. In addition to promoting class discussions, synthesizing criticism, captivating students, and increasing oral communication skills, studying literature through performance undoubtedly improves silent reading as well. Once students have learned dramatic analysis, and have themselves performed, they will be better able to construct performances in the mind's eye, giving life to the printed word and enriching their literary experience.

Additional Resources

The following books, in addition to the references cited, provide useful perspectives and techniques for using performance to teach literature.

Breen, R. S. *Chamber Theatre*. Englewood Cliffs, N.J.: Prentice-Hall.

Fernandex, T. L., ed. 1969. *Oral Interpretation and the Teaching of English: A Collection of Readings*. Champaign, Ill.: National Council of Teachers of English.

Kleinau, M. L. and McHughes, J. L., eds. 1980. *Theatres for Literature*. Sherman Oaks, California: Alfred Publishing.

Long, B. W., Hudson, L. and Rienstra, P. J. 1977. *Group Performance of Literature.* Englewood Cliffs, N.J.: Prentice-Hall, 1977.
Maclay, J. H. and Sloan, T. O. 1972. *Interpretation: An Approach to the Study of Literature.* New York: Random House.

Works Cited

Bauman, R. 1977. *Verbal Art as Performance.* Rowley, Mass.: Newbury House.
Bunzel, R. 1933. "Zuni Texts." *Publications of the American Ethnological Society* 15.
Burke, K. 1945. *A Grammar of Motives.* Englewood Cliffs, N.J.: Prentice-Hall.
Fine, E. 1984. *The Folklore Text: From Performance to Print.* Bloomington: Indiana University Press.
Long, B. W. 1977. "Evaluating Performed Literature." In *Studies in Interpretation,* II, edited by E. M. Doyle and V. H. Floyd, 267–81. The Netherlands: Rodopi.
Long, B. W., and M. F. Hopkins. 1982. *Performing Literature: An Introduction to Oral Interpretation.* Englewoods Cliffs, N.J.: Prentice-Hall.
Robinson, E. A. 1910. "How Annandale Went Out." In *The Town Down the River.* New York: Charles Scribner's Sons.
Tedlock, D. 1972. "On the Translation of Style in Oral Narrative." In *Toward New Perspectives in Folklore,* edited by A. Paredes and R. Bauman, 114–33. Austin and London: University of Texas Press.
Shattuck, R. 1980. "How to Rescue Literature." *The New York Review of Books* 27: 29–35.
Valéry, P. 1954. "The Course in Poetics: First Lesson." In *The Creative Process: A Symposium,* edited by B. Ghiselin. Berkeley: University of California Press.

13 Dramatic Improvisation in the Classroom

Betty Jane Wagner
National College of Education

Educators in a wide variety of disciplines recognize that dramatic improvisation, role-playing, can provide powerful learning experiences. After all, when students engage in role-playing, they truly do experience the subject they are studying. But how can we ensure that dramatic improvisation will result in meaningful learning, and not just in time off-task. Teacher-imposed structure and intervention are not antithetical to successful improvisation; in fact, they are critical ingredients. The trick is in knowing what kind, how much, and when to impose structure.

This chapter shows how improvisational drama can be used to learn: not only to extend the range, vocabulary, and tone of oral language, but also to deepen understanding of human experience. Here is an example:

An adult stood in front of a group of children, looking helpless. She had assumed the role of an injured soldier in the time of George Washington. By standing there, looking pained, she evoked a response from the children in role as adult care-givers trying to aid the injured in time of war.

"How did you hurt your arm?"

"Did you fall off your horse?"

The adult in role replied weakly, "I didn't fall; my horse reared and threw me off."

The children gently led the injured soldier to a long table they had set up as a bed. "Let's give him water."

"I can put a pillow under his arm."

"We can make like a tourniquet."

"Let's cover him up."

The children's response to the adult whom their teacher has set up as a soldier reflects not only appropriate adult language but solicitous care-giving as well. By trying on adult roles, children have a chance to

195

discover modes of talk they might not otherwise need to employ. As they use language in a new way, they extend the range of registers and vocabulary they can control and use with confidence.

Improvisational drama, perhaps more obviously than other oral language activities, ties directly into both literacy and nonverbal knowing. Dramatizing a story one has just read, or pantomiming a poem or story as it is presented orally, helps children internalize the meaning of language, extend their range of understanding, or make unfamiliar words their own. Often a classroom drama deliberately leads into writing or reading, as well as talk.

Improvisational drama often feels familiar to children because it is close to the spontaneous pretend play of early childhood. As children assume roles, they enter into appropriate postures and use apt physical gestures. Because drama stimulates the imagination, it engages children's attention and generates energy. They make decisions and, in so doing, have the opportunity to actively discover why people behave as they do. Role players are under pressure to bring to a drama relevant understandings of real-world social interaction and apply them to a different challenge. The result can be the surprise of a new awareness.

Improvisational drama is process-centered, not audience-centered as theater is. Whereas the word *theater* is derived from the Greek term meaning "to see or to view," *drama* comes from the Greek word meaning "to do, struggle, or live through." In improvisational drama, role players do not have scripts; instead, they live *as if* they were someone else, talking and acting in an unrehearsed fictive situation. Typically, they have no other audience than the other participants in the classroom, which may range from one—or as small as a single partner—to as large as the rest of the class. Unlike the goal of a theatrical performance, which is to create an experience for an audience, the goal of improvisation is to create an experience and understanding *for the role players themselves.* As they begin to believe in the moment they are creating together, improvisational drama students have an opportunity to penetrate and understand other human beings who have found themselves in similar circumstances. The goal is not to put on a play, but to learn through fictive experience.

The key here is learning, not through manipulation of the real world in front of their eyes, but through bringing the imagination into play to make the present setting disappear and through willing another reality to take its place. When students are working together to create a drama, they must at least tacitly agree to stay in the imagined reality and to believe the setting and roles they have decided upon. This means they must concentrate on a fictive moment in time, and must believe that moment. This takes enormous commitment and alertness—qualities even preschoolers engaging in spontaneous drama have been shown to exhibit. Whenever anyone in the drama says something, the rest of the group is challenged to concentrate on the implication of those words and to respond aptly within the fictive reality all have agreed to create. To break that reality is to destroy the drama for the whole group. Improvisational drama is successful if the talk is purposeful and disciplined to a highly social end. What one says in role constrains everyone else in the group. To keep the drama going, each participant has to take account of whatever the others have contributed. Thus, a fictive conversation is even more demanding than a real-world one, for a participant who is not listening finds it difficult to reenter the dialogue when it is words alone that are creating the drama the group is believing. Drama in the classroom entails unremitting pressure to develop listening and conversational skill.

We shall illustrate here two different kinds of dramatic improvisation. One is *story drama*: acting out or pantomiming a story or poem, the plot or substance of which is known in advance, or acting out a scene that is not actually in the story but could be; the other is *theme-oriented drama*: identifying with a particular person in a moment in time and living that person's responsibility and feelings in order to discover, to know what this particular situation would be like. In story drama, there is often a beginning, middle, and end. In theme-oriented drama, the students are not given a story or poem as a starting stimulus, but instead, they find themselves in a situation and are pressed to respond as persons might in a similar real-world situation. The student is often given a task or a challenge. Often theme-oriented drama begins by having students perform a task in pantomime; as they do so, their role in a larger social setting begins to take shape, and responses to others in the drama start to ring true. The goal for all improvisational drama is for participants to reach a level of feeling that comes from total engagement, a level that forges authentic and spontaneous oral language.

Learning through Story Drama

The simplest way to improvise a story is to have the whole class simultaneously pantomime the action as the teacher or a student reads the text aloud. They can stay near their seats for this activity if they choose. A second approach is for the entire class to plan the dramatization ahead of time, to decide on the setting for the action, and to plan in advance the sequence of the action. Volunteers then take the role of each of the characters and act out the story, with the rest of the class watching. After members of one group have finished, the class discusses their performance, and then another group of volunteers replays the scene. The two versions can then be compared. We shall not consider in this chapter performances where parts are learned from a script; that is a type of performance of a text which was the subject of the previous chapter, by Elizabeth Fine.

A third way to set up improvisational story drama is for a small group of students who have just finished reading a myth, fable, legend, folk tale, poem, or piece of contemporary literature to discuss how it made the children feel and how it might be dramatized. Such discussion helps prime the pump for later dialogue. Children select a central and interesting scene and act it out, for themselves first, and then perhaps for the rest of the class. A whole class might act out a single scene or different scenes simultaneously. The disadvantage of such simultaneous dramas is that the teacher is not available to help each group get to a serious and deeper level; the advantage, however, is that students are allowed to solve problems on their own.

A fourth way is to have the students dramatize a scene that is not actually a part of the plot of the story or novel they have read. It is something that might have happened in the context of the story, but it was not presented in the text as a developed scene. The goal of such a drama is to help students imagine in more vivid detail the scenes they are going to read later.

In a class of seventh graders, for example, who had been having some difficulty reading *Johnny Tremain* by Esther Forbes, I had students assume the roles of inhabitants of Boston in 1773.[1] They had read only the first chapter of the novel when I initiated this drama. In that chapter, Forbes introduced the characters associated with the main family in the novel. John Hancock had come into the silver shop where Johnny was an apprentice and had asked to have a creamer wrought. Johnny had determined to duplicate the fine workmanship his master, Mr. Lapham, had been able to do forty years before. Thus the scene was set by the novelist, but the students had little idea why Mr. Lapham and John Hancock would have different views about political matters. Although the seventh graders had read about the historical

---

[1]For this illustrative drama, I am grateful to an able teacher, Charlotte Willour, who invited me to coteach one of her classes at Thomas Junior High School in Arlington Heights, Illinois.

events in Boston during the prerevolutionary years, what they needed was a vehicle to put themselves emotionally back into that time. They needed a way to make the events that had taken place just before the onset of the Revolutionary War come alive.

I began by asking them to decide who they would be for this drama. Naturally, some of the class members chose the roles of Johnny and members of the Lapham family. Others decided to be heroes of that time—Samuel Adams, John Hancock, Paul Revere, et al. Some were tailors, sail makers, ship owners, fishers, blacksmiths, etc. One chose to be a French trapper who had been forced to stop in the city of Boston because of the blizzard up north. He wanted to have no part of this quarrel between these colonists and their mother country.

After their roles were chosen, I showed a picture of one of the original Tea Party ships, Brig Beaver II, and I told them that three ships were now moored in the Boston Harbor. "British crews are waiting there to unload their cargo and, by law, to charge us the tax Parliament has levied on tea." I had the class choose where the townspeople of Boston might meet to talk about what to do about these ships: they chose to gather at the Boston Common in the middle of the morning with the December weather raw and bitter cold. Then I pushed the desks back and had them gather in a large circle. I guided them in a low voice:

> You are now waking up on a December morning in 1773 in your house in Boston. It may be a large house up on Beacon Hill; it may be a small room or two above your shop on the wharf. You may be rich; you may be poor.

I asked the students to pantomime getting dressed for this day. I kept them in role by reminding them:

> Everything you put on is made by someone you know. Shake out each garment and look at it. Think about the person who made it. Was it someone you loved? Had you purchased it from one of the village tailors or cobblers? Put on your outer garment and something to cover your head. Now before you leave your home, look at yourself in the mirror. What age is that face staring back at you? What attitude do you see there? Are you proud, tired, timid, determined, lighthearted, lonely, content, afraid, in pain, eager?

Then the students took hold of the basket or bundle of goods or lead rope of the cow they were taking to pasture in the Common, and they began to walk slowly in a circle. A few giggled, and I stopped them, acknowledging that it was very hard to stay in role, but if they did not, they would destroy the drama work of the others, so they settled into a quiet pantomime that I sustained as long as I could. When I stopped them, we went around the circle and introduced ourselves. I began with:

> "I am Prudence Eaton. I am the mother of four sons, ages 17–27. My brother lives in England, and I feel certain there is a letter from him in the cargo of one of those three ships in the harbor. I think we should allow them to unload. The tea tax is not excessive."

I chose the role of a Tory because I sensed that the students would most likely choose to be patriots, and I wanted them to get the feel of a time when it was not easy to decide which was the "right" side and when the outcome of their decisions and actions was not yet known. The students introduced themselves:

> "I am Sam Adams and I want us to fight for our freedom."

> "I am an escaped slave, Fridgi, sister of Crispus Attucks. Those mean old British shot my brother dead, and I'm mad at them."

Then we walked a bit further in pantomime, and then arrived at the Common. We greeted one another in role and talked about the problem posed by those three ships laden with tea. Whenever the students addressed me, I reminded them:

> "We are English. If we resist this tiny tax on tea, we may start a war against our fathers and brothers who live across the sea. King George will send my brother's sons to kill my sons. Our children's children will look back and curse this day."

I told the boy who had chosen to be the vicar that his homily last Sunday disturbed me:

> "It sounds as if you believe God is on the side of those who would rise up against our king."

> "I do," he said. "Even Jesus had to stand by what he thought was right!"

In the middle of the greeting of each other and the arguing over the fate of the ships in the harbor, a boy who had chosen the role of Sam Adams got up on a table and read this announcement I had previously given him:

> Friends! Countrymen! The detested tea has now arrived in the harbor. Every friend to his country, to himself, and to posterity, is now called upon to meet at Faneuil Hall, at one o'clock tomorrow. The bells will ring to make united and successful resistance to this last, worst, and most destructive Tyranny.

As the tension of the challenge we faced became increasingly reflected in our voices, more and more of the students joined in. Three girls, however, were not yet in the drama. One of them, who had chosen to be an old, deaf woman, was hobbling about with her imagined cane and squawking in a high voice, her hand cupped behind her ear: "Eh, I can't hear you. What'd ya' say?" Her two companions, in role as her daughters, found this very funny. In role, I stepped in and shouted:

> "Old woman, can you hear me?"
>
> "Eh?"
>
> "Can you hear me?"
>
> "A little."
>
> "I'll give you this dollar if you'll vote as I tell you tomorrow."
>
> "OK. Can I have the dollar now?" she asked, grabbing for the bill.
>
> "Of course."
>
> "Hey, you can't do that!" one of the daughters complained. "It's not fair!"
>
> "We are free to vote as we choose in this country," asserted the other daughter.
>
> "Yeah, this is America!"
>
> "A vote isn't something you can buy. It belongs to a citizen. It is one of our freedoms! We'll go to war for our freedom!"

That is all it took to get those three girls into the drama.

The next scene was that night, back in their homes. I had the students sit in their chairs around the sides of the room, and I turned off the classroom lights and pulled the shades. I lit a candle that I had brought in, one in an old-fashioned brass holder with a handle on the side, and placed it on a table in the middle of the circle. As they sat quietly, I asked them to see themselves sitting beside that table with only that candle to warm the darkness:

> The rest of the family have all gone to bed. The clatter of horses' hooves no longer echoes from the cobblestones. The peddlers crying their wares have all gone to rest. The screaming gulls in the harbor are quiet. The clock in the church steeple chimes the hour. As you look into the flickering flame, go back in your mind over the events of the day. What will you do if those three ships of tea do not unfurl their sails and return to England? How do you feel about Sam Adams's plea? What will your prayer be this night? How will you vote on the morrow? What are the words you write in your diary?

The power of the earlier drama showed vividly in the accounts they wrote. One boy, who had played the role of a young fishmonger's son eager for the excitement of war, wrote that it was not until he talked with one of the Tories that it hit him. His life could be blown out as quickly as this little candle flame. Another wrote:

> I am here in my house on Beacon Hill. I see the Rebellion coming ever closer. Many men will die so another may live in prosperity and dignity. Many people criticize me, but I believe in my cause. Our representation in Parliament is all important. Though I can now say that possibility is growing evermore harder to reach.

Then came a poignantly mature simile:

> As the light wanes this night so does England's hold on us. We have tried ever so hard, but to no avail.

But the next paragraph was pure eleven-year-old:

> My family believes in this cause as strongly as me. And I think even my pets do. I am sure they too would die for our cause. . . .

After the students had read the second chapter of *Johnny Tremain*, we had another drama—this time of a meeting of Johnny and Dove after the accident they read about that crippled Johnny's hand. To prepare for the drama, the teacher had the students draw a cluster; they began with the word "Johnny," with a circle around it, in the middle of a page; all the things they could think of about Johnny were arrayed in circles around the central one and connected to it with spokes. Then they did the same for Dove. An example of one student's cluster appears on page 203.

After they arranged their clusters, they compared them with a partner, adding to their own clusters if they chose. Then the whole class met in pairs and simultaneously played a meeting between Johnny and Dove, an event that does not actually happen in the book. They decided where they would meet and improvised a dialogue that might have taken place between them. Here is a typical exchange:

> "Hi, Johnny."
> "You pig of a louse! I hate you!"
> "Hey, I didn't mean to hurt you."
> "Oh yeah? You knew that crucible was cracked."
> "Honest, I didn't dream you'd fall into it."
> "I'll never forgive you—not ever!"
> "Please, Johnny! I didn't mean to do it."

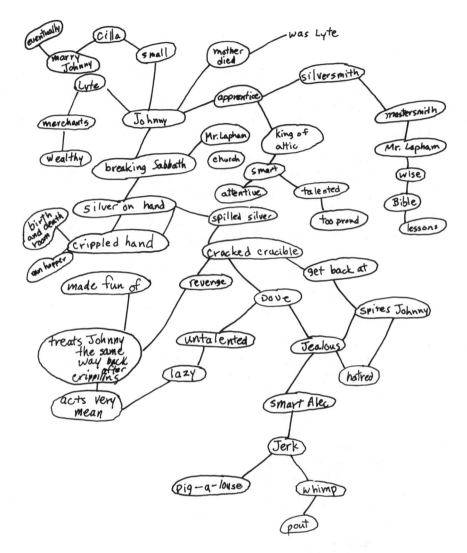

Preparing for a story drama: An example of one student's cluster.

"You've ruined my hand *and* my dream. Just you wait! I'll get
even with you someday."

The next part of the drama took place in their beds that night. While
the students were sitting at their desks, their teacher asked them to
choose the role of Johnny or of Dove and to reflect on their feelings
about what had happened. Then they wrote another diary entry. A
boy who chose the part of Dove wrote:

> It's night and the crickets are chirping outside. In the distance a
> seagull cries. I'm feeling kind of guilty about giving him that
> cracked crucible then having it brake apart then having the silver
> pour all over the top of the furnace. That's not really what I'm
> feeling guilty about, but having his hand in it that's why. It wasn't
> all my fault. True, I did give him the cracked crucible, but if he
> would have cleaned up the beeswax which melted onto the floor
> he most likely wouldn't have slipped and stuck his hand in it. All
> I wanted to do is make a fool out of Johnny. But he deserved it.
> Always bossing Dusty and me around. Also, we had to do all of the
> chores when he didn't have to do anything. One thing I really hate
> is him saying I am fat. I don't think I am. I am hungry, I wish I had
> something to eat.

When the students went back to the *Johnny Tremain* book, they took
with them a sense of the tension of the times and of the hatred and
remorse of the characters, Johnny and Dove.

Learning through Theme-Oriented Drama

Now we look at an example of theme-oriented drama. A teacher who
wanted to help a group of six-to-eight-year-olds understand the differences between a modern hospital and medical care in George Washington's time, started by having the class role-play hospital personnel
in a present-day setting, one that was more familiar to them. Then,
after two days in a modern hospital, the next day's drama was set 200
years earlier.

The teacher, Dorothy Heathcote, started the first day in the modern
hospital by having the children role-play janitors sent to clean up a
brand-new hospital which had been left a mess after the builders left.
The whole first day of the drama was devoted to hauling away rubbish
and scrubbing floors and walls because the teacher wanted the children to start feeling responsible and caring enough about the hospital's future patients to work very hard on their behalf. The second day
she gave them a set of drawings of hospital equipment, each done with
a deliberate tension and possibility of a problem. For example, one

drawing was of a wheelchair, with the brake colored in red and a warning under it: "Be sure the brakes are set on all wheelchairs." Another large card had on it a set of three pictures of a hand holding a key. Beside each hand was a little cabinet with a very prominent lock on it. On one cabinet were the words "Medical Drugs," on another, "Chemicals for Deep Cleaning," and, on the third, "Germ Killers." Under the pictures was the warning, "Keep your keys safe at all times." There were several pieces of tagboard, with telephones drawn on them. Under each was a sign: "Remember, keep calls in this hospital very short."

She also had a set of hand-lettered signs for the children to use in the drama: Occupational Therapy, Emergency Room, Accidents!, Out-Patient Unit, Maternity, Recovery Room, Operating Room, Patient Check-In, Blood Bank, Intensive Care, X-Ray, Prenatal Unit, Cafeteria, etc. Thus, she had created an environment loaded with information. Her goal was to lure the class into using more sophisticated language, but never once did she lapse into a presentational teaching mode. Instead, she invited the class to pick up any information they were ready to use to make their own statements sound authentic.

In addition, everything was set up to keep the children's attention on the notion of caring. She arrayed the pictures of the hospital equipment and the signs depicting different areas of the hospital on a table where the children could puzzle them out. Her goal was to evoke a drama created largely by the children. She knew that to give them too many facts would distract them from the one thing they had to experience if the drama was to do its work: the feeling that they were persons of great expertise, persons on whom patients could depend. She addressed them as experts, and even when they were trying to sound out the word "Maternity" on one of the signs, she did not tell them what it meant. She simply sounded it out with them, musing, "I wonder what that means." If one of the terms on a sign was already in the child's passive vocabulary, he or she might gradually gain control over it in the process of using it in role.

Both the pictures of equipment and the signs helped the children create a belief in their own power. If they chose to take a piece of machinery back to one of the tables set up in the room, they knew they were expected to know how it operated. For example, a shy little girl, who chose a huge X-ray machine, found herself with the responsibility implied in the warning, "Be sure not to use with women who are expecting babies. Attendant must wear lead apron at all times."

Heathcote began the drama by addressing the assembled hospital personnel in the role of the hospital administrator. First, she welcomed them as the new staff. They were made to feel important by having to sign their names on a large sheet of chart paper titled "Duty Roster," July 14. It had a column to check "On Duty" and "Off Duty." After each child had signed his or her name, the teacher read all the names in a very dignified fashion and asked, "Tom, shall I mark you in or out today? Giri, are you on duty today?" She put a big check mark in the "On Duty" column as each answered yes. Then she congratulated her staff. "This is marvelous. Not many hospitals have such dedicated staffs. Imagine, no absences—every single staff member reporting for work this morning. I certainly appreciate that." Thus, she acknowledged and confirmed their commitment to the drama and started to instill in the children a sense of pride in their hospital and their dedication to their work. Children will be more likely to produce oral language they presume to be characteristic of adults if their sense of importance is enhanced and their contributions acknowledged. It is generative to upgrade both the children's sense of importance as they are in role and to provide a model of more sophisticated language.

The next thing the group did was to read a message left for them the day before: "We are sorry we didn't get everything perfect. Signed, The Cleaners." Of course, the day before, this group of children had *been* the cleaners, but today they were primarily doctors and nurses. They spent the one-hour class session unpacking their equipment, trying it out, complaining that the electricity was going out, etc. The teacher would not let them move on to the next stage, namely working with patients, until she was satisfied that they were really believing in the reality of that modern hospital with all its sophisticated equipment; her goal was not the same as the children's—to "play doctor." She wanted to help them learn something about the dedication and caring that must go into an enterprise that is going to serve a community's health needs.

As they worked, the children began to use words such as X-ray, operation, pediatric doctor, stethoscope, and special diet. Their assumption of the role of expert pulled them to an uncharacteristic seriousness and responsible behavior. The doctors started calling for their nurses, only to find that the telephones did not work. They took their problem to the teacher in role as hospital administrator, who told them to make a list of all the problems they faced, the equipment that needed fixing, or the new supplies they needed. She told one girl who said she did not know how to spell "dustpan" to draw a picture instead "so we will know what we need." By withholding information in a drama, the teacher pushed the children to assume responsibility and do what they could. This pressure to cope despite limitations of knowledge is one of the most effective strategies for enabling students to demonstrate their competence, to discover what they did not know they knew.

The next day the children involved in the hospital drama had a new surprise. This time there was a group of patients (a few teachers in role) waiting outside the hospital. Each one had a hint of the dress of the eighteenth century, an obvious injury or illness of some kind, and a large placard with name and malady pinned to him or her: "Timothy Morgan, who burned his hand while forging a horseshoe," "Martha Mather, who swallowed a pin while sewing," etc. The teacher introduced them to the assembled doctors and nurses: "These patients here are from the time of Gen. George Washington." So their medical care needed to be that of the time of Washington. This meant they had none of the sophisticated machinery of the day before. They had to make do with bandages, herbs, soap and water, and ointments.

The teacher got them to believe in this old-fashioned hospital by having them roll imaginary bandages long enough and repetitively enough that they began to sense the feel of the cloth and the tightness of the roll in their hands. Even this simple task is made up of a number of separate actions and sensory experiences which, when remembered, become a source of insight. Verbal fluency for a child often flows more freely in the presence of actual or imagined objects or actions. Fully realized, but imagined, concrete experiences provide the basis for the development of more abstract thought at a later stage. In addition, most concrete experiences are fused with emotion which gives them power, and which in turn energizes speech. The children chanted softly with the teacher, "The nurses work; the doctors work; roll, roll, roll, roll bandages." She would not let them roll too fast; she kept the pace slow in order to give time for imaginations to grow. They kept a tally of the number of bandages they had rolled, writing on the white butcher paper that covered each of the tables where they worked.

Then they took branches of herbs from the imaginary baskets the teacher handed them, and they rolled the leaves in their hands until they had a fine powder that they scooped up to put into jars. The teacher showed them how to shake the powder down in the jar so it could hold more ground herbs. Then they looked in their imaginary drawers for ointments and salves. They drew onto the chart paper pictures of the jars they found. The students were working very hard, feeling themselves to be doctors and nurses on whom others depended.

The adults in role as patients had been coached to push the children into the role of experts by assuming they as patients did not know much about how to deal with their illness or injury. The teacher, as hospital administrator, introduced each of the patients to a child: "This is Dr. Jerry; he'll help you if he can." The patients would ask questions about how to treat their problem. After the child explained what to do, the patient would somewhat hesitantly repeat what the doctor said, and then say something like, "I have a short memory. Will you show me again what to do? Would you mind writing the directions down for me?" If a child introduced an anachronism, such as telling the patient to keep an ice pack in the freezer, the adult patient would not correct him or her, but instead she might ask, "Ah, this freezing, do you mean to put it on the ice block in my root cellar? You mean I fill this pack with the part of the river that is cold and solid?" Such questions supply information at the same time they ask for it. They feed in clues which a direct question like "What is a freezer?" does not. When a child suggested using paper towels to catch the blood, the patient asked if she meant old but clean rags that were as thin as paper. Such responses acknowledged the contribution the doctor or nurse had just made and, at the same time, guided the child into a new level of awareness.

The power of improvisational drama is the pressure it exerts on problem solving for an unpredicted situation. For example, when faced with the patient who had swallowed a pin, the teacher asked the child, in role as nurse, "Would it be best to let the pin go on through, or should we try to make her spit it up?" The six-year-old nurse who was treating the patient said, "What we need to do is get a small magnet and then we can put it on the end of a string so she can swallow it." The child's logic was impeccable; she was putting together what she knew about pins and magnets in her search for a way to deal with this medical emergency.

When a child brought in some "sleeping medicine" for one of the patients, the teacher asked, "How much should we give him?"

"One bottle full," was the reply. The teacher let misinformation go uncorrected in the attempt to get to what the drama was set up to accomplish—children assuming the initiative of oral language in a role they were only beginning to explore. Through using oral language in an imagined hospital, the children were coming to understand the real world better. By not letting them "operate," as modern children playing doctor might choose to do, and by insisting that this hospital be set long ago, the teacher led them into other, less dramatic, but no less important, ways of caring for the ill or injured: providing solace, comfort, and empathy.

Improvised drama can be a window into a student's thinking. The social pressure of the medium takes role players into realms they did not know they could experience. In some theme-oriented dramas, like the hospital one described here, both oral and written language are evoked. The teacher made it clear to the children that, in a hospital, it is important that accurate records be kept. The teacher told each one to put a pencil behind his or her ear and to be ready to keep track of each patient's progress. Then she said, "When a doctor is off duty, the hospital still needs to know what has been done for a patient so they can continue to care for the patient properly, isn't that so? So we will need to keep all the information, our records, in our archives, our big folders, right?" She was not teaching the children how to keep records; she was just reminding these emergently literate persons that in the "real world" written records are important and must be created with care.

The Role of Improvisation in Language Arts Instruction

Teachers who employ improvisational drama sometimes look as if they are not really teaching because they are seldom in the familiar "imparter of information" role. Their goal is to set up a situation that allows for maximum student initiative. Perhaps the most difficult part of learning to use drama is learning to trust that students will make good use of this initiative and will not merely waste time. Teachers who first try small-group discussions have this same concern. To develop oral language, students simply *must* talk. Listening to teacher-talk alone will not do the job. But, of course, at first, students do not know how to talk appropriately or aptly. Teachers need to find ways to reflect back the flaws in their oral language without obviously "correcting" them. In a drama, they can do this in a nonobvious way, either by sensitive side-coaching or by a response in role in the drama that reflects accurately the time period being depicted and an appropriate tone and dialect.

Once, when I was teaching in a lower socio-economic, all-black eighth grade in Chicago, I had the students role-play a job interview. Without my mentioning a need for standard English, all but three of the students were able to handle the role of the interviewer (in this case an owner of a gas station) without lapsing into the vernacular black English, which was the only dialect I had previously heard them use. Where had they learned this? Perhaps the models on TV had taken root. Perhaps this was the first time in my classroom that they had seen any point in speaking the "phony" way their white teachers talked. In any case, the drama provided just the right pressure: it was OK to use "teacher dialect" if they were in role, but they risked losing status if they talked that way to each other. Needless to say, our dramas in that class continued, with community leader roles such as lawyer, landlord, mayor, or school superintendent. They explored the sound of standard dialect as they relished the feel of the authority of their new roles.

Value of Improvised Drama

Because most students *enjoy* engaging in drama, its educational import is sometimes underestimated. What onlookers may fail to perceive is that when a person tries to enter the physical, emotional, and intellectual center of another person, he or she must get beyond superficial imitation and empathize with that person's inner world in order to respond appropriately. This means the role player must operate on at least a tacit understanding of another person's worldview. Through improvised drama, students can build social skills and become more sensitive listeners and more apt and mature conversationalists. They also grow in their capacity to send and receive increasingly complex and mature verbal messages effectively, independently, creatively, and symbolically.

As the illustrations above demonstrate, improvisational drama is a powerful medium for learning. The recognition that such drama is an effective way to develop oral language goes back more than a century. In the 1880s, Francis W. Parker, as head of the Department of Didactics at Martha's Vineyard Summer Institute, urged the use of simple improvised activities as an excellent technique for the development of oral expression.

James Moffett wrote more than two decades ago that drama and speech are central to a language arts curriculum. He implored teachers to see them as base and essence, not desirable additions to a good solid academic program. He reminded us that we experience the world first with our muscles and bodily sensations, then with our senses, later with our memory, and only after all of that, with our reason. Improvisational drama educates the whole person—muscles, senses, memory, and reason.

Improvising or inventing is at the heart of all oral language develop-ment. Toddlers never mature as speakers simply by imitation; they must make up sentences they have never heard before. They play with options, try out new words, experiment with more complex struc-tures, and project a wider range of registers. Dramatic improvisation—invented conversation that mirrors the interactions of real life—pro-vides a powerful stimulus for a continuation of this valuable enterprise.

Recommended Readings

Cottrell, J. 1987. *Creative Drama in the Classroom.* Lincolnwood, Ill.: National Textbook Company.

Heinig, R. 1987. *Creative Drama Resource Book, K–3.* Englewood Cliffs, N.J.: Prentice-Hall.

_____. 1987. *Creative Drama Resource Book, 4–6.* Englewood Cliffs, N.J.: Prentice-Hall.

McCaslin, N. 1987. *Creative Drama in the Primary Grades.* White Plains, N.Y.: Longman.

_____. 1987. *Creative Drama in the Intermediate Grades.* White Plains, N.Y.: Long-man.

Morgan, N., and J. Saxton. 1987. *Teaching Drama.* Portsmouth, N.H.: Heinemann Educational Books, Ltd.

O'Neill, C. 1985. *Drama Guidelines.* Portsmouth, N.H.: Heinemann Educational Books, Ltd.

O'Neill, C., and A. Lambert. 1985. *Drama Structures.* London: Hutchinson.

Salisbury, B. T. 1986. *Theater Arts in the Elementary Classroom, Kindergarten through Grade Three.* New Orleans, La.: Anchorage Press.

_____. 1986. *Theater Arts in the Elementary Classroom, Grades Four through Six.* New Orleans, La.: Anchorage Press.

Spolin, V. 1986. *Theater Games for the Classroom, Teacher's Handbook, Grades 1–3.* Evanston, Ill.: Northwestern University Press.

_____. 1986. *Theater Games for the Classroom, Teacher's Handbook, Grades 4–6.* Evan-ston, Ill.: Northwestern University Press.

Wagner, B. J. 1976. *Dorothy Heathcote: Drama as a Learning Medium.* Washington, D.C.: National Education Association.

14 Learning to Listen and Learning to Read

Sara W. Lundsteen
University of North Texas

In many classrooms, the instruction to "Listen up!" is understood as an order to students to "Shut up!" But listening is not the same thing as being quiet, not the same as being a passive sponge for someone else's verbal output. In fact, effective listening is just the opposite; it is an active process. If we fail to exert energy in listening, we are likely to be distracted, or to draw faulty inferences, or the like. Helping students to become effective listeners is a worthy instructional goal, indeed. Helping teachers to become effective listeners from time to time is not a bad idea either.

Listening is not only the heart of human interaction, but also the heart of teaching and learning. Yet listening is rarely—too rarely—a matter for conscious awareness. In many classrooms, the call to "Listen up!" translates into the teacher directives, "I talk; you don't." In an effort to help us all appreciate the richness of a proper study of listening, this chapter presents an overview of the topic. I will explore ways of defining chief characteristics of listening: (1) a process with at least eight components; (2) a goal-driven activity adapting itself according to its varying purposes; (3) a developmental ability; and (4) a communication art related to reading. I suggest the central importance of listening as a tool for learning language arts and content-area knowledge. Finally, I developed the notion of "metacognitive listening," awareness of listening patterns and specific listening strategies, as central to effective listening and as a productive objective for English/language arts instruction.

Multifaceted Listening in One Primary Grade Classroom

A classroom scene introduces several important concepts for learning/ teaching about listening and reading. In the larger context of a listening unit, a teacher and a small group of children had been exploring the sound made by shaking the contents of a paper bag which selected students had brought for group work:

> *Teacher:* Now listen again, but in a *new* way. Of what does the sound remind you? Berta, you've done this before in small groups, so I leave you in charge. (Teacher moves to another small listening group.)
>
> *Berta:* Think about the sound you hear . . . when I shake whatever's in Otto's paper bag—listen . . . in a fresh, new way.
>
> *Max:* Piggy banks.
>
> *Berta:* Old sleigh bells.
>
> *Ernst:* A rattlesnake.
>
> *Ester:* A box of curtain clips.
>
> *Teresia:* Poker chips.
>
> *Berta:* Thanks for those ideas.
>
> *Otto:* I'll open my bag. This time it was . . . (dramatically pouring them out)—pennies! Max, you were close.
>
> *Berta:* Ernst, it's your turn to choose one of the ideas for drama, an improvised scene.
>
> *Ernst:* The rattlesnake.
>
> *Berta:* Where might it be? Brainstorm a place.
>
> *Teresia:* In the school yard. (Group suggests other ideas before settling on Teresia's.)
>
> *Berta:* Who discovers it?
>
> *Ester:* A lady with a small child—the child discovers the snake.
>
> *Berta:* A unicorn finds it.
>
> *Max:* A principal finds it.
>
> *Berta:* . . . Choose, Ernst.
>
> *Ernst:* A mother with a small child.
>
> *Berta:* Who will play the part of the snake? . . . Thanks, Otto. . . . Of the mother. . . . Thanks, Teresia. . . . Of the small child. . . . Well, I will. The rest of you are listeners. OK? (Signaling) Now, go to it. (Side coaching) Great hissing, Otto! (In role) Mommie, look at . . . short rubber hose, (Coaching Teresia). What does the mother say?
>
> *Teresia:* I'm scared. I mustn't panic. Freeze where you are, child. And listen to your mother, for once! (Scene continues for a few minutes.)
>
> *Teacher:* (Interrupting groups) I can tell you're really getting warmed up to this. I'd like to give some options—one, to take out your pencils and blank play-script booklets if you'd like to work independently, fleshing out the rest of your improvised scenes.

Later, we'll have time to read what you wrote with your listening partners.

Another option is to add to your listening journals. Think over the listening you've done today so far and write about that. For example, during improvised drama time, what and who did you listen to; what did you learn; what helped; what didn't? I'll write some other ideas on the board. (Writes: 1. How I think about listening. 2. How I feel about it. 3. What I've decided to do about it.)

Berta: (To teacher) Are you going to write in your journal about those three things?

Teacher: Yes, I've started a listening section. I'm also going to describe how much time I think I've talked today, and log how much time I observe the class has gotten to interact. I'm audio taping myself today, so I can play it back and see for sure. I think I've already talked too much. (After the students settle into chosen writing and reading of their writings, teacher begins writing in log.)

The teacher in the preceding scene used many naturally occurring events in the classroom to teach listening/speaking/reading/writing, not just games and drama. Some natural events occurred during peer sharing, during committee work on the listening and communication unit. Alert, the teacher capitalized on all manner of incidents. The activities illustrated in this scene can span a wide range of ages. Readiness at any age is individual and depends in large part on previous experience. The aim is starting with natural student listening interests and needs occurring in the classroom. Then the teacher builds classroom listening experiences from such natural events. Such is the most meaningful and motivating of instructional strategies for listening. But just what is the nature of listening in the classroom? The next section amplifies.

Characterizing and Defining Classroom Listening

Is good listening in school always a matter of listening dutifully to adults? Teachers can accomplish a much sought goal of getting children to listen to them; but not by admonishing. The teacher in the previous scene never admonished the children to "listen." Let's consider some significant aspects.

Components of a Listening Process

Most people and children have an oversimplified idea of what listening is. ("It's just 'hearing,' isn't it?") A definition of listening has so many important concepts that only a few can be dealt with here. First of all, listening is a *process*. It is an *active* comprehension process, including: (1) receiving, (2) focusing, (3) attending, (4) discriminating, (5) assigning meaning, (6) monitoring, (7) remembering, and (8) responding to auditory messages. The children and teacher in the previous scene did all of these things as they listened *and* responded.

For example, they *received* through their physical auditory systems ideas about the scenario as they exchanged messages. They *attended* to these messages rather than to the multitude of other auditory stimuli that might have distracted them in a typical school context. They were *discriminating* the relevant from the irrelevant stimuli. They *assigned meaning* to the options and choices presented for enacting the drama. They *monitored* their own attentive, evaluative responses to these choices, *remembering* them for a sufficient length of time so that they could finally choose and concur or disagree about options. Thus they *responded* to messages and fashioned a scenario.

Observers of this classroom would notice that listeners use many visual cues to guide their listening comprehension and responses. Individuals "listen with eyes" as well as with ears. The students in the scene were picking up visual cues from the teacher, group leaders, and one another—cues that said: "It's OK; brainstorm; get out many ideas; there are not going to be any 'bad' ideas." (Body movements and stance inform listeners much of the time as they use this auditory comprehension process.)

Purposes for Listening

Another part of a definition of effective listening deals with a wide variety of purposes. Individuals read for many aims, too. Consider five of these:

1. Sometimes purpose is merely following a *ritual* (e.g., answering when the roll is called in school).

2. Sometimes the purpose is to be *informed*. For example, in the opening scene the group leader sought previous personal, oral information as to what could have caused the sound in the paper bag, and of what the sound might remind one.

3. The latter is known as *imaging*. Being informed can also help us solve problems and predict.

4. Sometimes the purpose is to listen with *feeling* and aesthetic appreciation. For example, "That made my ears happy!" said a kindergartner in response to an autoharp. Without restorative

joy, teachers and students accomplish far less in school. School programs need to include memorable listening material of high quality, just as students need such material for reading. Having chances to listen to fine literature each day stretches a student's listening language store, though the idea here is not just to read quality materials to a class every day. Aesthetic listening experiences could additionally include recorded resources that students use in centers or for individual projects. The idea is also to avoid materials for listening that are trivial, unrelated to needs and feelings, and below dignity at any age. The idea is to put joy from listening into the lives of students who starve for beauty just as they starve for food.

5. Sometimes the purpose is to listen *critically* when the listener is *being controlled* or persuaded. For example, one member of the group in the previous scene might try to influence another by saying, "Everyone else is choosing the rattlesnake." The listener then may wonder if the message sent is really in their and the group's best interests. They might ask, "Who is 'everyone' and what's the cost?" (Lundsteen 1989, Ch. 10).

Relations between Listening and Reading

Listening is the aural counterpart of *reading*, with auditory symbols compared to print symbols. Reading is visual, space oriented. Reading may be "cooler." The reader is likely to be more objective, less emotionally influenced by print. A reader can scan in any direction. But listening is usually one way or sequential. Listening has peculiar time pressures that reading does not. A reader can go back and read it again, and again, a sustained visual opportunity, usually lacking in listening. However, in the listening mode one can sometimes replay a tape or stop the speaker and ask for clarification. The responsibility for successful communication is in this latter case more evenly shared by speaker and listener than by reader and writer (Lundsteen 1979).

Too often in real-life listening, however, the individual gets only one chance at the message and its brief auditory images. In listening, in a formal audience or mechanical context, one normally has minimum control; with reading, you typically have maximum control. Teachers who repeat and repeat may reinforce bad listening habits and fail to reflect the real world. A remedy is to let another successful student listener volunteer for any necessary repeating. Teachers can cue children for attention and purpose; then say it *once* (Lundsteen 1989, Ch. 3).

When students have learned something about the process of listening comprehension, they can immediately apply the learnings to the context of reading comprehension. A teacher might say, "Could you use what you learned about spotting purpose and organization while listening when you're reading? Tell how." Or, "We practiced forming pictures in our minds when listening; how could we use that when you're reading a new book?"

A caution: To try to integrate by turning a reading test into a listening test is not an accurate reflection of typical listening material and context. Although there is overlap in vocabularies, listening material is not necessarily the same as reading material (the written word). The spoken language is much more likely to be redundant, as people stutter, stammer, and try to find words to express their meanings. Spoken language tends to be incomplete, as the referents are in the heads of individuals, and they are often too egocentric to remember that others cannot know exactly what they know. The language listened to is often disorganized, as senders strive to shape spoken thoughts and sometimes do not know what they know until they have voiced it.

But as the teacher places listening material and reading materials dealing with the same topic side by side in different versions in a listening center, children can grasp the interrelatedness of a composing and comprehending process. Children can see that orally presented materials can be well organized and memorable. Such an integration of listening and reading could be fruitful. Let's listen in on a bit of dialogue at such a center:

> *Harriet:* (Taking off the earphones, having listened to Danny Kaye's partly musical rendition of Hans Christian Andersen's "The Ugly Duckling.") I could listen and listen and listen all day to that. (Whistles softly and sings a snatch of the tune.) 'I'm not such an ugly duckling, not me.'
>
> *Rufus:* Yeah, but you oughta see this book version here. This one's illustrated by Monika Laimgruber. Like stained glass. With lots of little dots. And different borders around the pictures.
>
> *Terry:* And listen to this from the book: "An old house stood bathed in the sunlight. It was surrounded by a deep moat, and between the house and the moat grew giant coltsfoot leaves." I wonder what a *coltsfoot leaf* looks like.
>
> *Rufus:* I bet this is one here in the picture hiding the mother duck and her hatching ducklings.
>
> *Glenda:* (Picking up another book) I like this version illustrated by Robert Van Nutt. The pictures are so beautiful, especially when the ugly duckling finally realizes it has turned into a swan. Besides, it's a bit easier to read.

Harriet: I still don't think you can beat listening to Danny Kaye. But, well, maybe, it's good to know both ways. You know, I'm going to write a story about an ugly—child. A beautiful story, illustrated, with borders.

The Importance of Listening as a Tool for Learning

Listening is important to all school learning as well as to the other language arts. Optimally teacher and children work through the question of the importance of listening together as they reflect across the curriculum. They examine their real-life needs and experiences. Mentionable is the value of listening in other tool and academic school subjects. Other values are found in social and language development, in problem solving, and in the impact of listening on reading.

If a student cannot comprehend a message through listening, it is unlikely that she will comprehend that message through reading. Further, if a student cannot compose a text from a message presented to the ears, it is unlikely that she will be able to compose a text for herself using print symbols for that message. Because listening is a prerequisite for so many abilities, one may make the statement that nearly all remedial listeners will be remedial readers. There are, of course, many other causes of need for remedial reading; so not all remedial readers will be remedial listeners.

Why does listening have a ceiling effect on the other language arts? For one thing, remember that listening vocabulary is typically the largest of the four vocabularies (listening, speaking, reading, and writing). Figure 1 illustrates this with reference to typical elementary school children.

Skills common to both reading and listening are likely to be best learned first in the listening mode. What student does not read a selection more effectively after listening to it dramatically and memorably rendered? ("Students who read were read to," goes the slogan.) Moreover, punctuation is rooted in oral language. A student can notice that a drop in pitch and a definite pause in oral language have a correspondence to a period in written language. A broad, general background of comprehending through listening face to face helps reading comprehension.

To move across the curriculum, consider the following example from a preschool math lesson where learning through listening took place. The children, working on different tasks and consulting with each other, were seated in small groups at tables using abaci, Cuise-

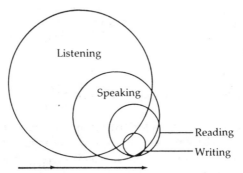

(Arrows suggest movement through time.)
Are all vocabularies basically dependent on listening?

Fig. 1. Four overlapping vocabularies used in school. (Figure from *Language Arts: A Problem Solving Approach* by Sara W. Lundsteen. Copyright © 1989 by Sara W. Lundsteen. Reprinted by permission of Harper & Row, Publishers, Inc.)

naire rods, counting frames, and hundreds boards. One group of five had a large box of pencils. One of the children speaks:

> *Antonio:* (recording the counting for the group) We have thirty-five pencils in that box.
>
> *Teacher:* There are five of you. How many groups of five can you make? With those thirty-five pencils? How many for each? Talk with each other about it. (Much consultation among the children follows.)
>
> *Sofia:* Why don't we put the sticks in piles of five? Lupe: We can see how many piles we get. (Starts.)
>
> *Laura:* No, no, she said "five," Lupe, not "six." There are five of us. Listen, will you.

Back to reading, teachers can help some children in beginning reading by giving guided experiences in discriminating groups of sounds. Of course, mere sounds are not the significant part of language; significant meanings in complex extended discourse are. Some students are more ready for listening instruction than for reading instruction. To ignore listening is to hurt reading (and writing, and speaking). In sum, effective listening helps communication and other skills and content learnings. When you ask some children about the importance of listening, a common response is that it "helps you do good in school."

But simply being aware of the importance of listening is not sufficient. A helpful aspect coming from more recent study is referred to as metacognitive listening.

Metacognitive Listening

Self-monitoring has been researched extensively in the areas of reading and writing, and now research is beginning in the field of listening. The technical term is "metacognitive listening," or thinking about your thinking while you are listening. During this process, one has something of a split-mental focus that can correct and enhance meaning. Long ago, however, related productive (and less productive) listener patterns were pointed out (Nichols and Stevens 1957). The instructional point is to help children become aware of patterns, and to guard against those unproductive ones when the occasion warrants. Essential skills in monitoring communication are (1) realizing that problems can occur, (2) recognizing when they do, and (3) knowing how to remedy them (Revelle, Wellman, and Karabenick 1985).

Four listener patterns (Fig. 2) are typical during use of leftover thinking space. These patterns show alternate ways of interacting with material. The first pattern, small departure, is effective for literal listening, and the other three are not (Lundsteen 1989).

Sometimes the metacognitive strategy of telling ourselves that the "very next words may completely change our lives" helps even those students whose thoughts are most prone to wander. Up to a certain

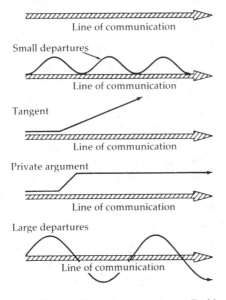

Fig. 2. Listener patterns. (Figure from *Language Arts: A Problem Solving Approach* by Sara W. Lundsteen. Copyright © 1989 by Sara W. Lundsteen. Reprinted by permission of Harper & Row, Publishers, Inc.)

point, we can help children learn to quiet themselves and discipline their attention. They can visualize on target so as to enhance the message with an appropriate amount of relevant, image-enriching experience during leftover thinking space. Figure 2 represents all four listener patterns. Younger children might dramatize the first three patterns with puppets, after modeled examples. Older students might role-play all four contrasting patterns (Tway and Lundsteen 1989, Ch. 3).

Strategies for Metacognitive Listening

The following self-monitoring techniques can reveal some strategies children choose from when they realize and recognize that a listening problem has occurred:

1. *Attention directing*, which may receive a boost with note taking in the case of students who can write. This strategy is used mainly to keep attention focused on the line of communication and to provide a record for later reading. Picking a focus also helps ("I'm listening for anything that shows the character was really brave."). In essence children tell themselves, "Get ready; get set; tune out all else; select a purpose; LISTEN."

2. *Memory enhancing* is a strategy or action that children can take when the problem seems to be memory overload. Basics that help are imposing organization on the seemingly unorganized message, categorizing, labeling, and rehearsing. Applying the organization of the different speaker patterns mentioned earlier may help. *Word signals* may help. Younger children can watch for word cues such as "first," "second," "third"; older students can watch for "in contrast," and "as another example." The use of an *advance organizer* (outline, web, study guide) helps a child with labels and categories—fewer concepts for the young child, more detail for the older ones. Most individuals *chunk* phone numbers, saying, "dial 361 thirty-four, twenty-four" (instead of 3,4,2,4). Many students unconsciously use the strategy of *rehearsal*, repeating under their breath over and over.

3. *Enhancing the communication* is a strategy pertaining to requests for clarity, active feedback, paraphrasing, and parasupports. Examples of parasupports are head nodding, phrases such as "Did you really!"; "Well!"; "Uh-huh." Enabling words of active feedback might be, "Would this be an example of what you mean?" Words related to paraphrasing might be, "What I've learned so

far is . . ."; "Is this what you're saying, that . . . " Active feedback and summarizing can help memory, attention, and meaning during listening.

4. *Enhancing the meaning* is a strategy in which listeners elaborate messages with appropriate mental images, pictures in the mind, referral to previous experience, and self-questioning. Here is an example from a four-year-old: "I 'membered where you said to put it; I walked backward in my mind" (Bosma 1986). Even some young children aged three and four can realize ambiguities and puzzlements in communication, and will rather directly seek to clear them up after monitoring a situation highly *meaningful* to them (Revelle, Wellman, and Karabenick 1985). Most at any age, however, could use some improvement.

The main point for teachers is to know the learners and help them with the following tasks: (1) selection of appropriate *strategies*; (2) *monitoring* of the effectiveness of a selected listening strategy; and (3) *revision* of an ineffective listening strategy (or ineffective reading strategy, too, for that matter). Teachers can help children attend and give self-alerts when the listening activity is not proceeding properly (Flavell 1981; Flavell et al. 1981; Robinson and Robinson 1982).

Teachers need to find appropriate places for instruction regarding strategies and to not use isolated practice of this split-mental focus. That is, they avoid seeking to clarify or summarize when nothing needs it. Instruction is not a matter of fifteen minutes here and there with a metacognitive listening cap on; it is not a matter of a "quick fix." Instruction involves a sense of communication responsibility that teachers as models can seek to transfer to children's own use when it comes up naturally in the course of each day. The foregoing ideas on metacognition apply to reading as well as to listening.

Summary

In sum, what is listening? In brief, it is an active (often interactive), predominantly auditory comprehension process. Listening includes (but is not limited to) the following: hearing, receiving, focusing, attending, discriminating, assigning meaning and interpreting, monitoring, organizing, synthesizing, evaluating, remembering, and responding to messages. It is a "sister" process to reading, but with peculiar demands as to person, acoustics, noise, and linear and sometimes mechanical context. A number of strategies useful across the curriculum exist for enhancing listening. Most children and adults could profit from becoming students of their metacognitive listening process and applying appropriate strategies. Unfortunately, few if any strategies are typically at a sufficient level of awareness and conscious use by children. Detail on relevant self-monitoring techniques alert the listener to success and to failures in communication with this tool for learning.

Consider once again the classroom interaction episode displayed at the beginning of this chapter where children pretended to discover a reptile. As in that case, listening as well as reading can become an interactive comprehending process that is meaningfully, powerfully, and joyfully interconnected. Then effective listening can help get some of those miscommunication "snakes" out of our schoolrooms and serve children as a valuable tool for learning.

Works Cited

Andersen, H. C. 1986. *The Ugly Duckling*. Illustrated by R. Van Nutt. Adapted by J. Tuber and C. Stites. New York: Alfred A. Knopf. Available narrated in audio and video cassette.

_____. 1982. *The Ugly Duckling*. Illustrated by M. Laimgruber. English text by A. Stewart. New York: Greenwillow Books.

Bosma, B. 1986. "The Nature of Critical Listening: Its Base and Boundaries." Paper presented at the open meeting of the NCTE Committee on Critical Thinking and the Language Arts, Annual Convention of the National Council of Teachers of English, San Antonio, Texas, November 21.

Flavell, J. H. 1981. "Cognitive Monitoring." In *Children's Oral Communication Skills*, edited by W. P. Dickson, 35–58. New York: Academic Press.

Flavell, J. H., J. R. Speer, F. L. Green, and D. L. August. 1981. "The Development of Comprehension Monitoring and Knowledge about Communication." *Monographs of the Society for Research in Child Development* 46, no. 5: serial 192.

Lundsteen, S. W. 1989. *Language Arts: A Problem-Solving Approach*. New York: Harper & Row.

_____. 1979. *Listening: Its Impact at All Levels on Reading and the Other Language Arts*. Urbana, Ill.: National Council of Teachers of English.

Nichols, R., and L. A. Stevens. 1957. *Are You Listening?* New York: McGraw-Hill. The first full-length book on listening.

Rankin, P. T. 1952. "The Measurement of the Ability to Understand Spoken Language." Doctoral dissertation. University of Michigan, 1926. *Dissertation Abstracts International* 12: 847.

Revelle, G. L., H. M. Wellman, and J. D. Karabenick. 1985. "Comprehension Monitoring in Preschool Children." *Child Development* 56, no. 3: 654–63.

Robinson, E. J., and W. P. Robinson. 1982. "Knowing When You Don't Know Enough: Children's Judgments about Ambiguous Information." *Cognition* 12: 267–80.

Tway, E., and S. W. Lundsteen. 1989. *Choose Your Own Activity Book*. New York: Harper & Row.

15 Oral Activities in the English Classroom

Phil Backlund
Central Washington University

Many people's stereotypes about "speech" in the classroom are associated with a speech-a-week public speaking curriculum: heavy on evaluation and anxiety, low on authentic communication. But speaking activities can instead present students with genuine opportunities to exert influence in their classroom communities and to explore their own understandings of the world about them. Later, in a developmental sequence, teachers can help students monitor the form of their oral messages.

Teacher (fifth-grade class): OK, class, next we are going to work on our social studies. Please get out your social studies book.

David: Mr. Rubin, Mr. Rubin?

Teacher: Yes, David?

David: Could we do our social studies later this afternoon?

Teacher: Why would you want to do that, David?

David: Let's do that oral stuff, that's cool.

Teacher: It's called oral communication. Anyway, we have to do our social studies.

David: Gee, Mr. Rubin, I can think of at least three reasons why it'd be good to work on our oral communication right now.

Teacher: Oh, what are they?

David: Well, we need more work on them. You saw how we did yesterday; we just didn't do so hot. Second, we can do oral communication and social studies at the same time. See, we work in groups and give oral reports on the social studies stuff. And last, we have such a good time with oral communication. What do you think, Mr. Rubin? Can we, please?

Teacher: Well, OK, David. Those are three pretty good reasons. We can work on both oral communication and social studies at the same time. And you're right, you didn't do so hot. OK, let's get going.

David and class: Thanks, Mr. Rubin.

227

Pretty fanciful dialogue? It represents a specific point—the student was able to persuade the teacher to change his mind. Mr. Rubin listened to David's arguments and changed his class plans based on them. Is this a good idea, or is Mr. Rubin losing control of his classroom?

The above example points to the heart of this chapter. As language arts teachers, one of the most important things we can do for our students is to give them the belief that they can use language to influence the world around them, including us. If students develop that belief, they will attempt to use language to attain goals more readily, they will be less reluctant to participate in classroom activities, and they will improve their behavior in other aspects of their education and in aspects of their social life. If their language behavior is reinforced by having persuasive efforts work, then students will come to realize the power of language.

We, as teachers, need to do everything we can to promote the oral language development of our students as a means of empowering them to function more effectively in the world. As stated above, they need to believe they have the power to use language with effect. How might you promote this belief in your classroom? This article will describe activities in public speaking, reporting, and debate that will enhance students' language skills and help them develop confidence to effectively use both oral and written language.

Many people, when they hear the words "oral communication" or "speech," think to themselves, "Oh, this is about public speaking." This chapter is about public speaking, but it is also about many other kinds of activities that promote the ability of students to use oral communication with confidence. We are not just interested in students' confidence in front of a group, but also in their confidence in social and interpersonal situations. We are interested in their efficacy and power in communication in all situations. To this end, the chapter develops three points in a rationale for including oral activities in the English classroom and provides examples of activities that can meet the challenge of oral language skill development. These will be divided into the areas of social knowledge, self-knowledge, and content knowledge. The last section of the chapter covers some information on the classroom evaluation of oral communication activities.

Am I suggesting that children currently do not believe they can influence the world around them through language? You and I have seen too many examples to the contrary to believe that fully. Yet, many students do not have that belief and many others use it inappropriately. Clearly, some students have the belief to the point of arrogance. It is my contention that, through appropriate instruction, a teacher can empower students to use oral and written communication effectively and appropriately. Let us look at each of the three areas of knowledge mentioned above.

Social Knowledge

One clear function of education is to help children develop an effective sense of society and social roles. The primary vehicle for this "sense" is language and communication. In fact, many scholars believe that society exists in language. For example, Hugh Duncan (1962, 76) said, "The self and society originates in communication." From the time of ancient Greece, oral communication activities (public speaking, persuasion, rhetoric) have been used for both the public and private good. Oral communication activities in the classroom can give the student a sense of how to use communication to relate effectively to others, as an understanding of the social system, and as a confidence builder in attempting to influence that social system.

There is at least one other good reason for attempting to help students develop their power to use oral expression. The effective use of oral power can become a substitute for physical power. Research in this area comes from Basil Bernstein (1958), who describes two types of language codes—elaborated and restricted. Essentially, children who used restricted-code language were those children who had a low facility in language, whose language use rarely reflected a sensitivity to the viewpoint of the other person, and whose language skill was insufficient to fully express their thoughts and feelings. On the other hand, children with a more elaborated code used language with qualities that enabled them to take into account the viewpoint of the other person, express thoughts and feelings effectively, and use language to influence the world around them. Not surprisingly, Bernstein found that restricted-code children were more apt to resort to violence to resolve interpersonal conflicts and more likely to "act out" their frustrations than children with elaborated codes. Bernstein's research creates a powerful argument for oral language skill development as a means to help children integrate themselves more effectively into society (whether the classroom society or society at large) and to deal with that society effectively.

Developing the Elaborated Language Code

Cecilia Vogt uses a technique called "unfinished stories." She bases her class discussions on a small pamphlet published by the National

Education Association titled *Unfinished Stories for Facilitating Decision Making in the Elementary Classroom* (Weiner 1980). The book contains fifty-two short stories divided into the areas of "Responsibility and Commitment to Others," "Personal Shortcomings," and "Shortcomings of Others." Each story presents a short scene that describes a moral dilemma and ends with "what should———do?" In one example from the book, Gwen is a sixth-grade student who finds it very difficult to voice her opinions in class. One day, the teacher tells her to do something she does not wish to do, but the words stick in her throat, she cannot get them out. Gwen obeys the teacher but feels bad that she cannot stick up for her own feelings. Vogt asks her students what they would do in those circumstances; the various student responses are discussed, debated, written about, and generally hammered out. She also uses this exercise as the basis for a wide range of written assignments. Through such an exercise, she meets many different educational goals, including the development of decision-making skills, oral communication skills, values, and a sensitivity to the social process. Vogt's technique works well for her. She capitalizes on a situation that Davison (forthcoming) refers to as an "ill-structured" problem. Davison makes the point that ill-structured problems are highly useful in developing reflective thinking and reasoning skills—skills that support and are supported by high language arts skills.

Teaching Persuasion

The goal of activities which hone these skills is to help the student understand what it takes to persuade someone to do something. For example, Mark Redmond, a fifth-grade teacher, picks out a number of potential real-life activities: joining the Boy or Girl Scouts, volunteering for a social service group such as the Red Cross, helping clean up the school grounds, etc. He tries to select activities that the students would actually take part in, if persuaded. For example, if the students were to join the Boy Scouts (if that was the persuasive goal), the persuasive goal would not just be to develop a speech or a written argument, but to persuade students to actually do something different in their lives.

A persuasive dialogue in Redmond's class went something like this:

Johnny: Sarah, you know, you should join Camp Fire. It's lots of fun.

Sarah: Yeah, right. What's so cool about it?

Johnny: Well, I like it, Camp Fire accepts boys now, and I have a lot of fun.

Sarah: Neat, what do you do?

Johnny: We help with a preschool. I like playing with those little kids, and we work on projects, and just have fun.

Sarah: Well, it sounds OK, but I don't have too much time.

Johnny: We only meet once a week for an hour. That's not bad, plus you will meet lots of kids that you will like. So, you will join, won't you? Please?

The main goal of the aforementioned exercise is that the students direct their persuasive efforts directly at each other on a topic that relates directly to that student's life. This kind of a dialogue can serve as a prewriting or prespeech activity to help the students focus their efforts. It also opens up lots of possibilities, including the fact that persuasion might not take place. But ideas for and against can be easily and fully explored. Students learn a lot about what is effective and what is not. Redmond believes that this exercise helps develop the students' persuasive powers. Persuasion clearly has a central place in helping students develop a sense of their own power in communication.

Using Historical Examples

A related activity that helps point out the power of persuasion in the classroom consists of exercises that examine and reenact public speech events of the past. Jim Brantley, a middle school history teacher, uses the writing and signing of the Declaration of Independence as the basis of a series of oral communication activities. His students examine the speeches, analyze how they might have formed opinions at the time, and judge how times have changed. As an example, Brantley asks a student to find, learn, and recite Patrick Henry's "Give me liberty or give me death" speech. He asks his students: "Would the words be as effective today?" "Could you imagine people putting their lives on the line for an ideal now?" Brantley has students role-play other characters and use their own words to convey the ideas of the times. He also uses the assignment as a basis for written work. An English teacher at the same school uses the same approach in teaching one of her literature classes. Role playing helps the students both understand more completely the feeling of various times in history and develop their communication skills by using role models from the past.

Classroom activities that focus on social roles, on social persuasion, and on reenactment of scenes that help illustrate some important points in history all accomplish two things. First, they help give students a greater knowledge of social roles, mores, and rituals. Second, and more important, they help give students the ability to use that knowledge to develop effective persuasive messages that work. Thus students develop confidence in their ability to make language work.

Self-Knowledge

A primary goal of education is to develop a healthy sense of self on the part of the child. The more the children understand their needs, values, reactions, etc., and how those factors mesh with the other people in their world, the more effectively they will be able to function. Their greater self-awareness also helps promote a greater level of self-confidence. There is a wide variety of language activities that can help promote this self-awareness.

One interesting idea on the relationship of self-awareness to language comes to us from the sociologist George Herbert Mead (1934). Mead once said, "The self rises in resistance." It is an interesting thought, but what does it mean? Mead believed that people begin to learn more about themselves as they meet resistance to their efforts. For example, Mary Fisher, a third-grade teacher, uses gentle resistance to help students examine and clarify their own beliefs. If a child expresses the opinion that "I think Seattle is a bad place to live," Fisher probably will not let that pass. If she did, not much learning would take place. Instead, she is likely to challenge the student with some simple questions such as "Oh, how did you arrive at that conclusion?" or "As compared to what?" Then the student needs to defend the statement, sometimes in writing, sometimes orally. Increased probing brings increased explanation. Students learn the extent to which they can support their opinions, where the holes are in their arguments, what they do not know, and which arguments may work more effectively than others. As someone once said, "How do I know what I think until I say it?" Encouraging students to explore, examine, and evaluate their own points of view through gentle and effective challenges can do much to promote effective thinking and develop more effective verbal skills.

Testing Other Alternatives

One activity with a long history in oral communication is debate. There are many ways to practice debate in a class, and some do not promote effective thinking or effective listening. But handled well, debate is highly effective. Here are a few examples of how it might work:

One of my personal favorites is known as "parliamentary debate," which involves the entire class. I pick a topic that relates specifically to the students in the class, such as a school dress code, a planned activity, or perhaps a wider social issue. One example I used recently was the issue of fast-food packaging: McDonald's uses Styrofoam, while Burger King uses cardboard. The debate was over which type of packaging is more environmentally sound. I asked two students to volunteer for each side of the issue and had them prepare their points of view. When both sides had prepared their arguments, the fun began. I divided the classroom physically into two halves, to represent both sides of the issue. I asked the students in the class to sit on the side that represented their point of view (paper or Styrofoam). Then, as the debate progressed, I encouraged students to move to the other side of the class if they were persuaded by what the debaters said. The students in the audience were allowed to heckle, to ask questions, and to challenge the speakers. This resulted (as usual) in a highly energetic, interactive, and lively session. I use this exercise to help teach the power of arguments—which arguments work, how to deal with challenges, and how to back a point of view. Plus, the students usually have a lot of fun. Again, this assignment could be easily adapted to include a wide variety of written assignments. The students could turn in written arguments, written critiques of the speeches, and written revisions of speeches that did not work.

One further activity that helps support self-awareness and oral communication skill development can be done just about anytime during the school day. The activity revolves around something that is known as "meta-talk," which means literally, "talk about talk." In an English classroom, it could be "talk about writing." Students can be asked about how and why certain selections were made in their communication decisions. For example, a dialogue might go something like this:

Mrs. Fisher: Mary, when you tried to convince David to recycle his newspapers, what alternatives did you consider before you chose to say what you did say?

Mary: Well, I was going to tell him how much money he could make, but then decided not to say that because you really can't make very much on newspapers. So I told him about all the trees that are being cut down.

Mrs. Fisher: I noticed that you really leaned toward David as you were talking to him. Did you intend to do that? Did you use any other body actions?

Mary: Yes, I did kinda lean close. I tried to get him to think I was really interested. I also looked right at his eyes, and used a lot of facial expressions.

Dialogues like this that probe students' awareness of their own behavior can do much to improve their communication skills. Students develop a sharper knowledge of the choices they make in their own communication behavior as they are encouraged to talk about what they are doing. The more students practice this, the more precise they can become in their descriptions. As they develop the ability to describe what they do, they achieve a control over what they do. Thus they can more carefully and easily communicate in the manner intended.

Although students may become "deceptive" if they become "too" aware of what they are doing, this potential problem can be avoided if the teacher and the student discuss beforehand the ethical and appropriate uses of the power the student is developing over the spoken and written word.

Content Knowledge

The third area of knowledge that can be developed by effective use of oral communication activities is content knowledge. "Content" generally refers to the subject being taught at a particular time—social studies, arithmetic, language arts, health, or any of the other subjects taught in the public schools. The goal of education is not only to teach the students about the content, but to give them power over the content, to master it and make it their own. Not surprisingly, there are a number of oral communication concepts and activities that can do much to promote mastery over content.

The primary objective of using oral communication activities in the teaching of content is to provide opportunities for the student to *talk* about the content. For example, hundreds of studies have shown that the lecture method is not very effective in helping students learn, primarily because students are not actively involved in the learning process—they are just sitting there. At the other end of the spectrum, there is the old dictum, "If you want to learn something, teach it." There is some truth to that, truth that points to helping students talk and write about what they have learned. "If you can't communicate it, you probably don't know it." Chris Thaiss, in his book *Language across the Curriculum in the Elementary Grades* (1986), makes three strong points on this subject:

1. Children will understand, and thus remember, only what they have the opportunity to talk about (and, perhaps, to write about, sing about, draw, make plays about, etc.) (6).
2. Children can learn to read and listen beyond mere word recognition only if they regularly practice expressing their own meanings in speech and writing to themselves and others (8).
3. Children learn only if knowledge is defined in action as a dialogue, or conversation, between teacher and student, student and student, student and the text, and student and the world (11).

Thus, encouraging students to talk about what they are doing, to think out loud, and to verbalize their thought processes is a powerful part of the learning process.

Something different seems to come into play when students verbalize their thought processes. Research by Vygotsky (1962) showed that children who spoke out loud about what they were doing, while they were doing it, were able to accomplish tasks more quickly and more efficiently than students who did not. Vygotsky's findings suggest that external vocalization of a task might focus thinking and make it more complete. The children are not only thinking through it, but also listening to themselves describe what they are doing. This extra step gives the children another chance to evaluate what they are doing. Normal activities can be modified to accommodate this technique simply by asking the child to describe out loud what he or she is doing. Sample dialogue might run like this:

> *Teacher:* Sharon, what were you thinking about when you worked on that essay, OK?
>
> *Sharon:* Well, first, I thought about my main idea, then I thought about the things I wanted to say about it and what order I wanted to put them in.
>
> *Teacher:* How did you decide which order to use?
>
> *Sharon:* Well, since I'm writing about how to do something, I decided to use a time sequence.
>
> *Teacher:* Good job, Sharon.

Such dialogue exemplifies a number of things. First, it gives the teacher an opportunity to check the thinking process of the students for accuracy and procedure. Next, it helps students clarify their own thinking processes. Finally, it gives them one more opportunity to develop verbal skills.

A related idea here is the somewhat complicated but highly useful notion of "decentering." Decentering is a concept that describes our ability to step "outside" of ourselves and examine and talk about ourselves as another person might. Our ability to talk is the vehicle that allows us to decenter, to attain a perspective about ourselves. Decentering is valuable to students in a number of ways. First, helping students develop this ability can do much to increase their self-awareness—they begin to see themselves as others see them. Second, as this ability develops, they can more clearly analyze their own behavior and comment effectively on it. They can give themselves feedback and adjust their own behavior and not depend on someone else to do that for them. Third, decentering can help them develop the ability to step outside of a situation and analyze it for themselves. They can more clearly understand the form and effect of the situation around them. One of my favorite writers on language, Neil Postman, describes decentering this way:

> The fundamental strategy of [decentering] is to put ourselves, psychologically, outside the context of any semantic environment so that we may see it in its entirety, or at least from multiple perspectives. From this position—or variety of positions—it is possible to assess meaning and quality of talk in relation to the totality of the environment in which it occurs, and with a relatively high degree of detachment. We become less interested in participating in semantic environments, and more interested in observing them. (1976, 34)

The ability to decenter may best be developed by asking questions of the students during various activities. Just about any activity will do. For example, the following questions may be useful: What are you trying to accomplish here? What things might keep you from achieving your goal? How do you have to adapt your efforts to meet the rules of the situation? What about other people in the situation; what do you think they are trying to accomplish? What is their role here; what is yours? Does your goal complement or conflict with the other people involved? How do you think the other person will respond to you? What does the situation suggest as to how you should behave? These are just samples of the potential questions you might ask. As you can see, all the questions are designed to get students to analyze the situation, their role in it, and how they might be affecting others. Questions such as these will not only develop the students' ability to use language more effectively, but will also develop a much higher degree of awareness of how students fit into the situation and gain control over it—thus becoming empowered.

Giving the student power over content means giving the student the ability to "handle" the content, which in turn implies that the student needs tools to do the handling. Thus emerges one of the most useful distinctions in education, the distinction between "form" and "content." Generally, form refers to the way content is structured, or put together. For example, the content of a speech is the topic the student describes. The form is the way the student chooses to put the content together. The distinction is similar in written work. For students to have power over content, they also need power over the forms that convey that content. Power over form in a subject can give students power over any content. This notion is summed up by the old saying, "Give a man a fish and he will eat today. Teach him to fish and he will eat the rest of his life."

Distinguishing between Form and Content in the Classroom

First, it would help to simply make your students aware of the two concepts. Let them know the power of knowing the "form" of knowledge. Even children in the primary grades can understand the distinction. In each assignment (this may be stretching it), point out the form you are teaching and the form you would like them to follow on the assignment. Analyze and talk about assignments and concepts for both content and form.

As an example, Steve Hall uses a study of advertisements in his middle school English classroom. He finds an ad in a magazine and he leads the students through a discussion of the content of the ad, what product is being sold, what the ad is saying about the product, and what the ad would like the reader to believe. *Then* Hall leads the students through a discussion of the form of the ad, how it is structured and laid out, how the various parts of the ad relate to each other, and options that might be tried to put the ad together differently. Hall uses the advertisement to study both form and content. He maintains that by leading the students through a discussion of both topics, their writing improves much more quickly.

The same format can be used in analyzing student work. Lead the class or the student through a discussion of the content, but then also discuss the form. What other way could the student have put the content together? Point out that in many areas, people make as many important judgments about the form of something as they do about the content. In the university teaching that I do, the quality of the product the student turns out is based on solid content, but it is equally based on effective form.

I have found it very helpful to give the students a set of options for the forms of an assignment. For example, a wide variety of organizational patterns exists for a public speech, which means that a student must select the best one for this particular speech. Usually, the selection is based on an analysis of the topic, the audience, the occasion, and the speaker's purpose. If students have a series of options to choose from, they have a much higher chance of success if the most effective form is selected. I encourage students in class to discuss the options with classmates:

> *Sheila:* Let's see, this is a persuasive speech, so maybe the problem-solving organizational pattern will work the best.
>
> *Tom:* Well, I don't know. Since there are only two solutions to the problem, I think a compare-and-contrast pattern would be more effective.
>
> *Sheila:* Yeah, I think you're right. I'll use that one.

Helping students talk through and understand the forms available in learning, learning how to select the best form to fit the situation, and how to apply the various forms to different contents are some of the most powerful abilities a teacher can develop in students. Activities based in oral communication can do much to give the student this power.

Evaluation of Activities

Barbara Wood (1984) makes the point that many students see a negative relationship between talk and grades. The more you talk in class, the worse your grade. It is the quiet student, working diligently, who seems to get the positive evaluation from the teacher. Unfortunately, many teachers' evaluations of students do little to allay students' fears of talking in the classroom. Wood describes four beliefs that seem to guide many teachers' approaches to student talk in the classroom:

1. I must retain the floor as much as possible.
2. I must insist on complete quiet from my students in order to retain control.
3. Students cannot gain access to the floor without first getting my invitation. (I call on them.)

4. Students should not ask questions or make comments about the topic until the proper time. (Such time is rarely provided.)

Such teachers' beliefs seem to invite passive behaviors from children:

1. I must remain quiet as much as possible. I know I am being very good when I remain quiet.
2. Unless I am really lost with an assignment, it is better not to raise my hand and ask a question because the teacher will think I am stupid or get mad at me.
3. Wait until the teacher asks if we have questions before I ask—otherwise I will get punished.

Giving students the power of language is the most important function of education. If a teacher believes this, then the classroom becomes a place where talk is valued, supported, and encouraged. It becomes a place where students can try new ideas and skills, and get careful, nurturing feedback on those efforts. Yet it cannot be a place of unbridled talk, of meaningless and pointless language. Evaluation of some type is in order.

Some writers believe that we should not evaluate language attempts at all. Some believe that it is important that teachers not criticize their students' use of language. Burnes (1968) notes that "as soon as we begin to hamper the child's desire to express him or herself by criticism of that expression, we begin to destroy his or her ability to communicate at all" (40). There is enough truth in this idea to warrant a careful approach to evaluating students' talk in the classroom. Badly done, it can do much to decrease self-confidence, increase apprehension, and heighten the chances that the student will avoid saying something next time. Yet handled well, evaluation can do much to increase skill, develop confidence, and promote effectiveness.

Suggestions for Evaluating Student Talk

Promote Interaction

Early in the class, at the beginning of the year, do much to promote interaction between you and the students and among the students. I use activities that require, in a nonthreatening way, every student to say at least two things the first day of class. I want them to get in the habit early of contributing, orally, to the class. Have you ever been in a meeting where you wanted to say something, but the longer you waited for an opportunity, the harder it became to break in? That holds true for a lot of students. So try to get them to say something right away. It breaks the ice and begins to get them used to saying things in class.

Develop Outside Boundaries

Early student efforts at talking in class should be answered with minimal feedback or evaluation. The best approach is to develop outside boundaries, such as specific time frames, for their comments and interactions, with other time periods devoted to specific instruction. "Time" is a convenient beginning boundary, followed by the boundaries of topic, channel (who can talk to whom), and other boundaries that might be appropriate.

Use Descriptive Feedback

After the students have realized that talking in class is not necessarily wrong, and after they have gotten used to the idea of boundaries (two things that aren't hard for them to grasp), you will be ready to move to descriptive feedback on their communication efforts. Descriptive feedback focuses on message effects, and then compares the effect to the original goal, thus following an *intent/act/effect* model. Such an evaluation technique asks the student to describe, with perhaps some probing from the teacher, what his or her original intent was for the conversation, what communicative acts the student used, and what the subsequent effect was. When these three things are described (either orally or in writing), it becomes easy for the teacher to probe and suggest alternatives in each area. Perhaps the original intent was incomplete or inappropriate for the situation, perhaps different communication acts would have been more effective, and perhaps these changes would have led to different effects in the conversation. The intent/act/effect model is a powerful tool in getting the student to see options in communicative behavior. A sample dialogue might run something like this. (In this example, the student is trying to persuade another student to join Camp Fire as in the example described earlier):

> *Teacher:* Well, Johnny, did you talk Sarah into joining Camp Fire?
>
> *Johnny:* Nah, she said she'd think about it, but I don't think she will join.
>
> *Teacher:* Let's talk about it for a while, OK? What did you say to try to convince her? (No opinion from the teacher, just doing some information gathering)
>
> *Johnny:* I told her about the fun we have, the projects we do, and how much time it takes.

Teacher: Hmm, those seem like good points. Why do you think they didn't work? (Asks for his opinion on effectiveness)

Johnny: Well, it seems like she is already having fun in other things she is doing. She doesn't have time for another activity.

Teacher: Oh, I see. That sort of thing happens to a lot of people, even adults. We get so busy we can't do something new even if we wanted to. Do you think you could have done anything to convince her?

Johnny: The only thing I can think of is showing her how Camp Fire is better than one of her other activities, and convince her to drop something to add Camp Fire.

Teacher: That's a really good idea. It might not have worked, you can't change people's minds all the time, but it would have been worth trying. Maybe if you are in a situation like that some other time, you can use that point to convince someone else.

Johnny: I'll give it a try, thanks.

In the example above, the teacher is not giving direct advice, though sometimes advice helps a lot. She is probing Johnny's thoughts on why he was not successful and helping him see alternatives that he might use next time. This kind of descriptive evaluation focuses on Johnny's original goal, whether or not it was accomplished, the alternatives he used, alternatives not used, and the potential effects of the alternatives. The evaluation helps Johnny see the connection between his communication efforts and the potential effect they might have on others. Johnny winds up judging and evaluating his behavior, while the teacher merely helps him think through it by focusing on descriptions of what happened.

Set Up a Specific Objective

In addition to such after-the-fact evaluation, before-the-act evaluation is a good focal point for teachers. The latter follows a more traditional teaching model in that the teacher sets up a specific objective to work on in communication behavior. It could be virtually any objective in interpersonal, group, or public speaking. The teacher sets it up, shows the students how it works, helps them practice, and then helps them to try it out in as real a situation as possible. Evaluation is done afterwards in the sense of "Did it work? Why or why not?"

Employ Traditional Testing

The last point in evaluation is traditional testing. Examples and ideas of how to do assessment of oral communication skills is beyond the scope of this chapter, but material can be found in Backlund (1982),

Bock and Bock (1981), Larson et al. (1978), Rubin and Mead (1984), and Stibbs (1979).

Evaluation is difficult, but necessary. It clearly takes some time, and it takes working with students on an individual basis fairly frequently, but in the long run, it is a far more educationally powerful method. If evaluation follows the basic intent/act/effect model described above, and focuses on description of behaviors, then evaluation can be a powerful learning tool that helps students see the connection between their communicative efforts and results in the real world. That belief, and that sense of power, is what we are after.

Conclusion

Just about the time our first son was born, in 1971, I read an article by Robert White (1965) titled "The Experience of Efficacy in Schizophrenia." In his article, White pondered the roots of mental illness, specifically forms of schizophrenia. Among other ideas, White came to the conclusion that some aspects of schizophrenia could be traced to early childhood and to early language development. He noted that one symptom of schizophrenia is the belief on the part of the patients that their efforts do not matter. It does not make any difference what they do; it won't affect anyone anyway. Schizophrenics tend to see no relationship between their actions and any effect on the outside world. White was interested in how this belief might have originated. The conclusion he came to was interesting and had a large impact on my role as a father and teacher. He concluded that infants need to develop the connection early in life between their own actions and an effect on their outside world. White maintained that if an infant cried, something should happen—the infant should be picked up, held, changed, fed, or whatever it took to meet the needs of the infant at that time. According to White, the first six months were critical for the infant; this was the time that the infant began to believe that he or she could affect the world, could mold it to meet needs, and could begin to feel a sense of power. White opined that a child could not be "spoiled" before six months of age; after that, some tempering was in order to avoid developing an overindulged child.

For me, language development means this: My kids should be able to use language to influence the world around them. They should see that their efforts to influence through spoken language would have some effect. Who was the most influential part of their world? My wife and I. So, from the time our children could put together a basic sentence, we would let them change our minds occasionally. If one of our sons gave a sufficiently good reason, we would change our minds and go along with his request. As two-year-olds, their arguments were very simple. As a sixteen-year-old, our oldest son's reasoning got pretty elaborate. In most situations, we would listen to the request, the reason, and if there was sufficient rationale, we would change our minds. I believe that this strategy has worked. We have three boys who are highly verbal, effective socially, and have a solid degree of self-confidence. Now I am not saying that this one strategy was the sole reason for the way they are turning out, but I think it helped. Each son knows he will not always get what he wants, but each knows that it is worth the effort to ask. They know it is worth the effort to ask the teacher, the principal, the boss, the friend. The effort may not succeed, but each boy knows that if he puts together a well-thought-out argument, sometimes things will go his way.

This tack will also serve us well as teachers. If we are truly interested in helping our students build confidence in language skills, we need to provide a classroom environment that supports and encourages their efforts. In such an environment, students will develop more confidence in their relationship with society, with themselves, and with the subject matter being taught in their classes.

Works Cited

Bernstein, B. 1958. "Some Sociological Determinants of Perception: An Inquiry into Subcultural Differences." *British Journal of Sociology* 9: 159–74.

Bock, D., and E. Bock. 1981. *Evaluating Classroom Speaking.* Annandale, Va.: Speech Communication Association/ERIC.

Burnes, D. J. 1968. "Using Audiovisual Materials for Teaching Children to Communicate." *Audiovisual Instruction* 13: 40–43.

Cooper, P., and L. Stewart. 1987. *Language Skills in the Classroom.* Washington, D.C.: National Education Association.

Duncan, H. D. 1962. *Communication and Social Order.* New York: Bedminister Press.

Larson, C., P. Backlund, M. Redmond, and A. Barbour. 1978. *Assessing Functional Communication.* Annandale, Va.: Speech Communication Association.

Mead, G. H. 1934. *Mind, Self, and Society.* Chicago: University of Chicago Press.

Postman, N. 1976. *Crazy Talk, Stupid Talk.* New York: Delacorte Press.

Rubin, D., and M. Mead. 1984. *Large-Scale Assessment of Oral Communication Skills: Kindergarten through Grade 12.* Annandale, Va.: Speech Communication Association.

Stibbs, A. 1979. *Assessing Children's Language: Guidelines for Teachers.* London: Ward Lock Educational/National Association for the Teaching of English.

Thaiss, C. 1986. *Language across the Curriculum in the Elementary Grades*. Urbana, Ill.: ERIC Clearinghouse on Reading and Communication Skills and the National Council of Teachers of English.

Vygotsky, L. S. 1962. *Thought and Language*. New York: John Wiley & Sons.

Weiner, E. 1980. *Unfinished Stories for Facilitating Decision Making in the Elementary Classroom*. Washington, D.C.: National Education Association.

White, R. 1965. "The Experience of Efficacy in Schizophrenia." *Psychiatry* 28: 199–211.

Wood, B. 1984. "Oral Communication in the Elementary Schools." In *Speaking and Writing, K–12: Classroom Strategy and Research*, edited by C. Thaiss and C. Suhor. National Council of Teachers of English.

III Talking across Cultural Boundaries

16 Language Diversity and Learning

Lisa D. Delpit
Morgan State University

A nonstandard language variety is a stubborn thing. Teachers seeking to help students acquire standard English as a second dialect sometimes think that all they are asking of their students is some technical linguistic achievement. They forget that students' community speech patterns are loaded with emotional investment for those students. They forget, also, that speech style is not just composed of discrete linguistic elements, but is also composed of broader styles of interaction and expression. Finally, teachers sometimes forget that speech which may deviate from some standard does not necessarily reflect thought patterns that deviate from any logic. Ability to learn is not hindered by the boundaries between language varieties.

A brand-new black teacher is delivering her first reading lesson to a group of first-grade students in inner-city Philadelphia. She has almost memorized the entire basal-provided lesson dialogue while practicing in front of a mirror the night before.

> "Good morning, boys and girls. Today we're going to read a story about where we live—in the city."
>
> A small brown hand rises.
>
> "Yes, Marti."
>
> Marti and this teacher are special friends, for she was a kindergartner in the informal classroom where her new teacher-student taught.
>
> "Teacher, how come you talkin' like a white person? You talkin' just like my momma talk when she get on the phone!"

I was that first-year teacher many years ago, and Marti was among the first to teach me the role of language diversity in the classroom. Marti let me know that children—even young children—are often aware of the different codes we all use in our everyday lives. They may not yet have learned how to produce those codes or what social purposes they serve, but children often have a remarkable ability to discern and

247

identify different codes in different settings. It is this sensitivity to language and its appropriate use upon which we must build to ensure the success of children from diverse backgrounds.

One aspect of language diversity in the classroom—*form* (the code of a language, its phonology, grammar, inflections, sentence structure, and written symbols)—has usually received the most attention from educators, as manifested in their concern about the "nonstandardness" of the code their students speak. While form is important, particularly in the context of social success, it is considerably less important when concern is lodged instead in the area of cognitive development. This area is related to that aspect of language diversity reflected in Marti's statement—language *use*—the socially and cognitively based linguistic determinations speakers make about style, register, vocabulary, and so forth, when they attempt to interact with or achieve particular goals within their environments. It is the purpose of this paper to address a broad conception of language diversity as it affects the learning environments of linguistically diverse students; it focuses on the development of the range of linguistic alternatives that students have at their disposal for use in varying settings.

Acquiring One Language Variety and Learning Another

The acquisition and development of one's native language is a wondrous process, drawing upon all of the cognitive and affective capacities that make us human. By contrast, the successful acquisition of a second form of a language is essentially a note-learning process brought to automaticity. It is, however, a process in which success is heavily influenced by highly charged affective factors. Because of the frequency with which schools focus unsuccessfully on changing language form, a careful discussion of the topic and its attendant affective aspects is in order.

The Affective Filter in Language Learning

Learning to orally produce an alternate form is not principally a function of cognitive analysis, thereby not ideally learned from protracted rule-based instruction and correction. Rather, it comes with exposure, comfort level, motivation, familiarity, and practice in real communicative contexts. Those who have enjoyed a pleasant interlude in an area where another dialect of English is spoken may have noticed a change in their own speech. Almost unconsciously, their speech has approached that of those native to the area. The evidence suggests that had these learners been corrected or drilled in the rules of the new dialect, they probably would not have acquired it as readily.

Stephen Krashen (1982), in his work on second language acquisition, distinguishes the processes of conscious *learning* (rule-based instruction leading to the monitoring of verbal output) from unconscious *acquisition* ("picking up" a language through internalizing the linguistic input-derived immersion in a new context—what happens, say, when the North American enjoys a visit to the Caribbean). Krashen found unconscious acquisition to be much more effective. In further studies, however, he found that in some cases people did not easily "acquire" the new language. This finding led him to postulate the existence of what he called the "affective filter." The filter operates "when affective conditions are not optimal, when the student is not motivated, does not identify with the speakers of the second language, or is overanxious about his performance, . . . [causing] a mental block . . . [which] will prevent the input from reaching those parts of the brain responsible for language acquisition" (1984, 22). Although the process of learning a new dialect cannot be completely equated with learning a new language, some processes seem to be similar. In this case, it seems that the less stress attached to the process, the more easily it is accomplished.

Effects of Correction

The so-called affective filter is likely to be raised when the learner is exposed to constant correction. Such correction increases cognitive monitoring of speech, thereby making talking difficult. To illustrate with an experiment anyone can try, I have frequently taught a relatively simple new "dialect" in my work with preservice teachers. In this dialect, the phonetic element "iz" is added after the first consonant or consonant cluster in each syllable of a word. (*Teacher* becomes tiz-ea-chiz-er and *apple*, iz-ap-piz-le.) After a bit of drill and practice, the students are asked to tell a partner why they decided to become teachers. Most only haltingly attempt a few words before lapsing into either silence or into "standard English," usually to complain about my circling the room to insist that all words they utter be in the new dialect. During a follow-up discussion, all students invariably speak of the impossibility of attempting to apply rules while trying to formulate and express a thought. Forcing speakers to monitor their language for rules while speaking, typically produces silence.

Correction may also affect students' attitudes toward their teachers. In a recent research project, middle-school, inner-city students were interviewed about their attitudes toward their teachers and school. One young woman complained bitterly, "Mrs.——always be interrupting to make you 'talk correct' and stuff. She be butting into your conversations when you not even talking to her! She need to mind her own business."

In another example from a Mississippi preschool, a teacher had been drilling her three- and four-year-old charges on responding to the greeting, "Good morning, how are you?" with "I'm fine, thank you." Posting herself near the door one morning, she greeted a four-year-old black boy in an interchange that went something like this:

> *Teacher:* Good morning, Tony, how are you?
>
> *Tony:* I be's fine.
>
> *Teacher:* Tony, I said, How *are* you?
>
> *Tony:* (with raised voice) I be's *fine.*
>
> *Teacher:* No, Tony, I said *how are you?*
>
> *Tony:* (angrily) I done told you I *be's fine* and I ain't telling you no more!

Tony must have questioned his teacher's intelligence, if not sanity. In any event, neither of the students discussed above would be predisposed, as Krashen says, to identify with their teachers and thereby increase the possibility of unconsciously acquiring the latter's language form.

Ethnic Identity and Language Performance

Issues of group identity may also affect students' oral production of a different dialect. Nelson-Barber (1982), in a study of phonologic aspects of Pima Indian language found that, in grades 1–3, the children's English most approximated the standard dialect of their teachers. But surprisingly, by fourth grade, when one might assume growing competence in standard forms, their language moved significantly toward the local dialect. These fourth graders had the *competence* to express themselves in a more standard form, but chose, consciously or unconsciously, to use the language of those in their local environments. The researcher believes that, by age 8–9, these children became aware of their group membership and its importance to their well-being, and this realization was reflected in their language. They may also have become increasingly aware of the school's negative attitude toward their community and found it necessary—through choice of linguistic form—to decide with which camp to identify.

A similar example of linguistic *performance* (what one does with language) belying linguistic *competence* (what one is capable of doing) comes from researcher Gerald Mohatt (personal communication), who was at the time teaching on a Sioux reservation. It was considered axiomatic amongst the reservation staff that the reason these students failed to become competent readers was that they spoke a nonstandard dialect. One day Mohatt happened to look, unnoticed, into a classroom where a group of boys had congregated. Much to his surprise and amusement, the youngsters were staging a perfect rendition of his own teaching, complete with stance, walk, gestures, *and* standard English (including Midwestern accent). Clearly, the school's failure to teach these children to read was based on factors other than their inability to speak and understand standard English. They could do both; they did not often choose to do so in a classroom setting, however, possibly because they chose to identify with their community rather than with the school.

Appreciating Linguistic Diversity in the Classroom

What should teachers do about helping students acquire an additional oral form? First, they should recognize that the linguistic form a student brings to school is intimately connected with loved ones, community, and personal identity. To suggest that this form is "wrong" or, even worse, ignorant, is to suggest that something is wrong with the student and his or her family. On the other hand, it is equally important to understand that students who do not have access to the politically popular dialect form in this country, i.e., standard English, are less likely to succeed economically than their peers who do. How can both realities be embraced?

Martha Demientieff, a native Alaskan teacher of Athabaskan Indian middle school students, finds that her students, who live in a small, isolated village, are not fully aware that there are different codes of English. She analyzes their writing for features of the dialect that has been referred to by Alaskan linguists as "Village English." Half of a bulletin board is then covered with words or phrases from students' writing, which she labels "Our Heritage Language" (e.g., "We go store."). On the other half of the bulletin board she puts the equivalent statements in standard English, which she labels "Formal English," and sometimes refers to as "political English." ("We went to the store.")

She and the students savor the phrases and discuss the nuances of their "heritage English," as she says to them, "That's the way we say things. Doesn't it feel good? Isn't it the absolute best way of getting that idea across?" The class then turns its attention to the other side of the board. Martha tells the students that there are people, not like those in their village, who judge others by the way they talk or write:

> We listen to the way people talk, not to judge them, but to tell what part of the river they come from. These other people are not like that. They think everybody needs to talk like them. Unlike us, they have a hard time hearing what people say if they don't talk exactly like them. Their way of talking and writing is called "Formal English." We have to feel a little sorry for them because they have only one way to talk. We're going to learn two ways to say things. Isn't that better? One way will be our Heritage way. The other will be Formal English. Then, when we go to get jobs, we'll be able to talk like those people who only know and can only really listen to one way. Maybe after we get the jobs we can help them to learn how it feels to have another language, like ours, that feels so good. We'll talk like them when we have to, but we'll always know our way is best.

Martha continues to contrast the notions of Formal and Heritage (or informal English), telling the students that everyone in the village speaks informally most of the time unless there's a special occasion:

> You don't think about it, you don't worry about following any rules—it's sort of like how you eat food at a picnic—nobody pays attention to whether you use your fingers or a fork, and it feels so good. Now, Formal English is more like a formal dinner. There are rules to follow about where the knife and fork belong, about where people sit, about how you eat. That can be really nice, too, because it's nice to dress up sometimes.

The students then prepare a formal dinner in the class for which they dress up and set a big table with fancy tablecloths, china, and silverware. They speak only formal English at this meal. Then they prepare a picnic where only informal English is allowed.

What Martha has done is to support the language her students bring to school, provide them input from an additional code, and give them the opportunity to use the new code in a nonthreatening, real communicative context. Other teachers have accomplished the same goal by having groups of students create bidialectal dictionaries of their own language form and standard English. Some have had students become involved with standard forms through various kinds of role-play. For example, memorizing parts for drama productions will allow students to "get the feel" of speaking standard English while not under the threat of correction. Young students can create puppet shows or role-play cartoon characters. (Many "superheroes" speak almost hypercorrect standard English!) Playing a role eliminates the possibility of implying that the *child's* language is inadequate, and suggests, instead, that different language forms are appropriate in different contexts. Some other teachers in New York City have had their students produce a news show every day for the rest of the school. The students take on the persona of some famous newscaster, keeping in character as they develop and read their news reports. Discussions ensue about whether Walter Cronkite would have said it that way, again taking the focus off the child's speech.

Activities for Promoting Linguistic Pluralism

It is possible and desirable to make the actual study of language diversity a part of the curriculum for all students. For younger children, discussions about the differences in the ways television characters from different cultural groups speak can provide a starting point. A collection of the many children's books written in the dialects of various cultural groups can also provide a wonderful basis for learning about linguistic diversity, as can audiotaped stories narrated by individuals from different cultures.[1] Mrs. Pat, a teacher chronicled by Shirley Brice Heath (1982), had her students become language "detectives," interviewing a variety of individuals and listening to the radio and television to discover the differences and similarities in the ways people talked. Children can learn that there are many ways of saying the same thing, and that certain contexts suggest particular kinds of linguistic performances.

Inevitably, each speaker will make his or her own decision about the appropriate form to use in any context. Neither teachers nor anyone else will be able to force a choice upon an individual. All we can do is provide students with the exposure to an alternate form, and allow them the opportunity to practice that form *in contexts which are non-threatening, have a real purpose, and are intrinsically enjoyable.* If they have access to alternative forms, it will be their decision later in life to choose which to use. We can only provide them with the knowledge base and hope they will make appropriate choices.

Ethnic Identity and Styles of Discourse

Thus far, we have primarily discussed differences in grammar and syntax. There are other differences in oral language with which teachers should be aware in a multicultural context, particularly in discourse style and language use. Michaels and other researchers identified differences in children's narratives at "sharing time" (Michaels and Cazden 1986). They found that there was a tendency among young white children to tell "topic-centered" narratives—stories focused on one event—and a tendency among black youngsters, especially girls, to tell "episodic" narratives—stories which include shifting scenes and are typically longer. While these differences are interesting in themselves, what is of greater significance is adults' responses to the differences. Cazden (1988) reports on a subsequent project in which a white adult was taped reading the oral narratives of black and white first graders, with all syntax dialectal markers removed. Adults were asked to listen to the stories and comment about the children's likelihood of success in school. The researchers were surprised by the differential responses given by black and white adults.

In responding to the retelling of a black child's story, the white adults were uniformly negative, making such comments as "terrible story, incoherent" and "[n]ot a story at all in the sense of describing something that happened." Asked to judge this child's academic competence, all of the white adults rated her below the children who told "topic-centered" stories. Most of these adults also predicted difficulties for this child's future school career, such as, "This child might have trouble reading," that she exhibited "language problems that affect school achievement," and that "family problems" or "emotional problems" might hamper her academic progress (18).

The black adults had very different reactions. They found this child's story "well formed, easy to understand, and interesting, with lots of detail and description." Even though all five of these adults mentioned the "shifts" and "associations" or "nonlinear" quality of the story, they did not find these features distracting. Three of the black adults selected this story as the best of the five they had heard, and all but one judged the child as exceptionally bright, highly verbal, and successful in school (18).

When differences in narrative style produce differences in interpretation of competence, the pedagogical implications are evident. If children who produce stories based in differing discourse styles are expected to have trouble reading, and viewed as having language, family, or emotional problems, as was the case with the informants quoted by Cazden, they are unlikely to be viewed as ready for the same challenging instruction awarded students whose language patterns more closely parallel the teacher's. It is important to emphasize that those teachers in the Cazden study who were of the same cultural group as the students recognized the differences in style, but did not assign a negative valence to those differences. Thus, if teachers hope to avoid negatively stereotyping the language patterns of their students, it is important that they be encouraged to interact with—and willingly learn from—knowledgeable members of their students' cultural groups. This can perhaps best become a reality if teacher education programs include diverse parents, community members, and faculty among those who prepare future teachers, and take seriously the need to develop in those teachers the humility required for learning from the surrounding context when entering a culturally different setting.

Questioning Styles

Heath (1982) has identified another aspect of diversity in language use which affects classroom instruction and learning. She found that questions were used differently in a southeastern town by young black students and their teachers. The students were unaccustomed to responding to the "known-answer" test questions of the classroom. (The classic example of such questions is the contrast between the real-life questioning routine: "What time is it?" "Two o'clock." "Thanks." And the school questioning routine: "What time is it?" "Two o'clock." *"Right!"* [Mehan 1979].) These students would lapse into silence or contribute very little information when teachers asked direct factual questions which called for feedback of what had just been taught. She found that when the types of questions asked of the children were more in line with the kinds of questions posed to them in their home settings—questions probing the students' own analyses and evaluations—these children responded very differently. They "talked, actively and aggressively became involved in the lesson, and offered useful information about their past experiences (124)." The author concludes not only that these kinds of questions are appropriate for all children rather than just for the "high groups" with which they have typically been used, but that awareness and use of the kinds of language used in children's communities can foster the kind of language and performance and growth sought by the school and teachers.

Oral Styles in Community Life

I would be remiss to end this section without remarking upon the need to draw upon the considerable language strengths of linguistically diverse populations. Smitherman (1978) and many others have made note of the value placed upon oral expression in most African-American communities. The "man (person) of words," be he or she preacher, poet, philosopher, huckster, or rap song creator, receives the highest form of respect in the black community. The verbal adroitness, the cogent and quick wit, the brilliant use of metaphorical language, the facility in rhythm and rhyme, evident in the language of preacher Martin Luther King, Jr., boxer Muhammad Ali, comedian Whoopi Goldberg, rapper L. L. Cool J., singer and songwriter Billie Holiday, and many inner-city black students, may all be drawn upon to facilitate school learning.

Other children, as well, come to school with a wealth of specialized linguistic knowledge. Native American children, for example, come from communities with very sophisticated knowledge about storytelling, and a special way of saying a great deal with a few words. Classroom learning should be structured so that not only are these children able to acquire the verbal patterns they lack, but that they are also able to strengthen their proficiencies, and to share these with classmates and teachers. We will then all be enriched.

The Demands of School Language—Orality and Literacy

There is little evidence that speaking another dialectal form per se negatively affects one's ability to learn to read (Sims 1982). For commonsensical proof, one need only reflect on nonstandard-dialect-speaking slaves who not only taught themselves to read, but did so under threat of severe punishment or death. But children who speak nonmainstream varieties of English do have a more difficult time becoming proficient readers. Why?

One explanation is that, where teachers' assessments of competence are influenced by the dialect children speak, teachers may develop low expectations for certain students and subsequently teach them less (Sims 1982). A second explanation, which lends itself more readily to observation, rests in teachers' confusing the teaching of reading with the teaching of a new dialect form.

Cunningham (1976-77) found that teachers across the United States were more likely to correct reading miscues that were dialect related ("Here go a table" for "Here is a table") than those that were nondialect related ("Here is the dog" for "There is the dog"). Seventy-eight percent of the dialect miscues were corrected, compared with only 27 percent of the nondialect miscues. He concludes that the teachers were acting out of ignorance, not realizing that "here go" and "here is" represent the same meaning in some black children's language.

In my observations of many classrooms, however, I have come to conclude that even when teachers recognize the similarity of meaning, they are likely to correct dialect-related miscues. Consider a typical example:

Text: Yesterday I washed my brother's clothes.

Student's rendition: Yesterday I wash my bruvver close.

The subsequent exchange between student and teacher sounds something like this:

T: Wait, let's go back. What's that word again? [Points at *washed.*]

S: Wash.

T: No. Look at it again. What letters do you see at the end? You see "e-d." Do you remember what we say when we see those letters on the end of a word?

S: "ed"

T: OK, but in this case we say wash*ed.* Can you say that?

S: Wash*ed.*

T: Good. Now read it again.

S: Yesterday I wash*ed* my bruvver . . .

T: Wait a minute, what's that word again? [Points to *brother.*]

S: Bruvver.

T: No. Look at these letters in the middle. [Points to *th.*] Remember to read what you see. Do you remember how we say that sound? Put your tongue between your teeth and say /th/ . . .

The lesson continues in such a fashion, the teacher proceeding to correct the student's dialect-influenced pronunciations and grammar while ignoring the fact that the student had to have comprehended the sentence in order to translate it into her own dialect. Such instruction occurs daily and blocks reading development in a number of ways. First, because children become better readers by having the opportunity to read, the overcorrection exhibited in this lesson means that this child will be less likely to become a fluent reader than other children who are not interrupted so consistently. Second, a complete focus on code and pronunciation blocks children's understanding that reading is essentially a meaning-making process. This child, who understands the text, is led to believe that she is doing something wrong. She is encouraged to think of reading not as something you do to get a message, but something you pronounce. Third, constant corrections by the teacher are likely to cause this student and others like her to resist reading and to resent the teacher.

Robert Berdan (1980) reports that, after observing the kind of teaching routine described above in a number of settings, he incorporated the teacher behaviors into a reading instruction exercise which he used with students in a college class. He put together sundry rules from a number of American social and regional dialects to create what he called the "language of Atlantis." Students were then called upon to read aloud in this dialect they did not know. When they made errors he interrupted them, using some of the same statements/comments he had heard elementary school teachers routinely make to their students. He concludes:

> The results were rather shocking. By the time these Ph.D. candidates in English or linguistics had read 10–20 words, I could make them sound totally illiterate. By using the routines that teachers use of dialectally different students, I could produce all of the behaviors we observe in children who do not learn to read successfully. The first thing that goes is sentence intonation: they sound like they are reading a list from the telephone book. Comment on their pronunciation a bit more, and they begin to subvocalize, rehearsing pronunciations for themselves before they dare to say them out loud. They begin to guess at pronunciations. . . . They switch letters around for no reason. They stumble; they repeat. In short, when I attack them for their failure to conform to my demands for Atlantis English pronunciations, they sound very much like the worst of the second graders in any of the classrooms I have observed.
>
> They also begin to fidget. They wad up their papers, bite their fingernails, whisper, and some finally refuse to continue. They do all the things that children do while they are busily failing to learn to read. Emotional trauma can result as well. For instance, once while conducting this little experiment, in a matter of seconds I actually had one of my graduate students in tears. (78)

The moral of this story is not to confuse dialect intervention with reading instruction. To do so will only confuse the child, leading her away from those intuitive understandings about language that will promote reading development, and toward a school career of resistance and a lifetime of avoiding reading. For those who believe that the child has to "say it right in order to spell it right," let me add that English is not a phonetically regular language. There is no particular difference between telling a child, "You may *say* /bruvver/, but it's spelled b-r-o-*t-h*-e-r," and "You say /com/, but it's spelled c-o-m-*b*."

For this and other reasons, writing may be an arena in which to address standard forms. Unlike unplanned oral language or public reading, writing lends itself to editing. While conversational talk is spontaneous and must be responsive to an immediate context, writing is a mediated process which may be written and rewritten any number of times before being introduced to public scrutiny. Consequently, writing is amenable to rule application—one may first write freely to get one's thoughts down, and then edit to hone the message and apply specific spelling, syntactical, or punctuation rules. My college students who had such difficulty talking in the "iz" dialect, found writing it, with the rules displayed before them, a relatively easy task.

We must be careful in attending to standard forms in writing, however, that we not substitute "correctness" for communicative competence. By illustration, a black second grader wrote a story which she volunteered to share with the class. She began: "Once upon a time there was an old lady, and this old lady ain't had no sense. . . ." At this point the teacher interrupted her. "Doris, that sounds like it's going to be a wonderful story, but can you put the beginning in standard English?" Doris looked at her paper for a moment, and then proffered, "There was an old lady who didn't have any sense." She paused, put her hand on her hip, and said emphatically, "But *this* old lady ain't had *no* sense!" Doris had developed a very sophisticated sense of language, understanding the power of "nonstandard" forms to better portray some meanings, just as many brilliant authors have done before her. (Consider Alice Walker's Pulitzer Prize-winning *The Color Purple*.)

Styles of Literacy

There are other culturally based differences in language use in writing as well. In a seminal article arguing for the existence of "contrastive rhetoric," Robert Kaplan (1966) proposes that different languages have different rhetorical norms, representing different ways of organizing ideas.

Such style differences have also been identified in public school classrooms. Gail Martin, teacher-researcher in Wyoming, wrote about her work with Arapaho students:

> One of our major concerns was that many of the stories children wrote didn't seem to "go anywhere." The stories just ambled along with no definite start or finish, no climaxes or conclusions. I decided to ask Pius Moss [the school elder] about these stories, since he is a master Arapaho storyteller himself. I learned about a distinctive difference between Arapaho stories and stories I was accustomed to hearing, reading, and telling. Pius Moss explained that Arapaho stories are not written down, they're told in what we might call serial form, continued night after night. A "good" story is one that lasts seven nights. . . .
>
> When I asked Pius Moss why Arapaho stories never seem to have an "ending," he answered that there is no ending to life, and stories are about Arapaho life, so there is no need for a conclusion.

My colleagues and I talked about what Pius had said, and we
decided that we would encourage our students to choose which-
ever type of story they wished to write: we would try to listen and
read in appropriate ways. (Cazden 1988, 12)

Similarly, Martha Demientieff, the Native Alaskan teacher mentioned above, has discovered that her students find "book language"
baffling. To help them gain access to this unfamiliar use of language,
she contrasts the "wordy," academic way of saying things with the
metaphoric style of Athabaskan. The students discuss how book language always uses more words, but how in Heritage language, brevity
is always best. Students then work in pairs, groups, or individually to
write papers in the academic way, discussing with Martha and with
each other whether they believe they have said enough to "sound like
a book." Next they take those papers and try to reduce the meaning to
a few sentences. Finally, students further reduce the message to a
"saying" brief enough to go on the front of a tee shirt, and the sayings
are put on little paper tee shirts that the students cut out and hang
throughout the room. Sometimes the students reduce other authors'
wordy texts to their essential meanings as well. Thus, through wind-
ing back and forth through orality and literacy, the students begin to
understand the stylistic differences between their own language and
that of standard text.

Functions of Print

Print may serve different functions in some communities than it does
in others, and some children may be unaccustomed to using print or
seeing it used in the ways that schools demand. Shirley Brice Heath,
for example, found that the black children in the community she called
Trackton engaged with print as a group activity for specific real-life
purposes, such as reading food labels when shopping, reading fix-it
books to repair or modify toys, reading the names of cars to identify a
wished-for model, or reading to participate in church. There was seldom a time anyone in the community would read as a solitary recrea-
tional activity; indeed, anyone who did so was thought to be a little
strange (Heath 1982).

     The children in Trackton, in short, read to learn things, for real
purposes. When these children arrived in school they faced another
reality. They were required, instead, to "learn to read," that is, they
were told to focus on the *process* of reading with little apparent real
purposes in mind other than to get through a basal page or complete
a worksheet—and much of this they were to accomplish in isolation.

Needless to say, they were not successful at the decontextualized, individualized school reading tasks.

Researchers have identified other differences in the use of language in print as well. For example, Ron Scollon and Suzanne Scollon report that, in the Athabaskan Indian approach to communicative interaction, each individual is expected to make his or her own sense of a situation and that no one can unilaterally enforce one interpretation. Consequently, they were not surprised when, in a story-retelling exercise intended to test reading comprehension, Athabaskan children tended to modify the text of the story in their retellings (Scollon and Scollon 1979). The school, however, would be likely to interpret these individually constructed retellings as evidence that the students had not comprehended the story.

Talk across the Curriculum

A debate over the role of language diversity in mathematics and science education was fueled recently by the publication of a book by Eleanor Wilson Orr titled *Twice as Less: Black English and the Performance of Black Students in Mathematics and Science* (1987). Orr is a teacher of math and science who, as director of the elite Hawthorne School, worked out a cooperative program with the District of Columbia to allow several Washington, D.C., public high school students to attend the prestigious school. Orr and her colleagues were dismayed to find that despite their faithfully following time-tested teaching strategies, and despite the black D.C. students' high motivation and hard work, the newcomers were failing an alarming percentage of their math and science courses.

Noting the differences in the language the black students used, Orr decided to investigate the possibility that speaking black English was preventing these students from excelling in math and science. In a detailed argument she contends that the students' nonstandard language is both the cause and the expression of the real problem—their "nonstandard *perceptions*" (30). She cites student statements such as, "So the car traveling *twice as faster* will take *twice as less* hours," to support her thesis, and suggests that it is the difference between black English and standard English forms in the use of prepositions, conjunctions, and relative pronouns that is the basis for the students' failures.

It is important to critique this position in order that the failures of those responsible for teaching mathematics and science to poor and black students not be attributed to the students themselves, that is, so that the victims not be blamed. There are many problems with the Orr argument. One is her assumption that black students, by virtue of speaking black English, do not have access to certain concepts needed in mathematical problem solving. For example, she makes much of the lack of the "as——as" comparison, but I have recorded black-English-speaking 6–11-year-olds frequently making such statements as, "She big as you" and "I can too run fast as you."

A second problem is that Orr compares the language and performance of low-income, ill-prepared students with upper-income students who have had superior scholastic preparation. I contend that it was not their language which confused the D.C. students, but mathematics itself! Any students with a similar level of preparation and experience, no matter what their color or language variety, would probably have had the same difficulties.

The most basic problem with the Orr argument, however, is Orr's apparent belief that somehow mathematics is linked to the syntactical constructions of standard English: "[T]he *grammar* of standard English provides consistently for what is *true mathematically*" (emphasis added, 149). What about the grammar of Chinese or Arabic or German? Orr's linguistically naive determinist position can only lead to the bizarre conclusion that speakers of other languages would be equally handicapped in mathematics because they, too, lacked standard English constructions!

Even though Orr asserts that the cause of the problem is the speaking of black English, she seems unaware that her proposed solution is not linked to this conceptualization. She does not recommend teaching standard English, but rather, teaching *math* through the use in instruction of irregular number systems which force students to carefully work out concepts and prevent their dependence on inappropriate rote memorized patterns. One can surmise that as students and teachers work through these irregular systems, they create a shared language, developing for the students what they truly lack, a knowledge of the *content* of the language of mathematics, not the form.

Interviews with black teachers who have enjoyed long-term success teaching math to black-dialect-speaking students suggest that part of the solution also lies in the kind and quality of talk in the mathematics classroom. One teacher explained that her black students were much more likely to learn a new operation successfully when they understood to what use the operation might be put in daily life. Rather than teach decontextualized operations, she would typically first pose a "real-life" problem and challenge the students to find a solution. For example, she once brought in a part of a broken wheel, saying that it came from a toy which she wished to fix for her grandson. To do so, she had to reconstruct the wheel from this tiny part. After the students tried unsuccessfully to solve the problem, she introduced a theorem related to constructing a circle given any two points on an arc, which the students quickly assimilated.

Another black math teacher spoke of putting a problem into terms relevant to the student's life. He found that the same problem that baffled students when posed in terms of distances between two unfamiliar places or in terms of numbers of milk cans needed by a farmer, were much more readily solved when familiar locales and the amount of money needed to buy a leather jacket were substituted. I discovered a similar phenomenon when my first-grade inner-city students did much better on "word problems" on standardized tests when I merely substituted the names of people in our school for the names in the problems.

All of these modifications to the language of instruction speak to Heath's (1982) findings in Trackton—some youngsters may become more engaged in school tasks when the language of those tasks is posed in real-life contexts than when they are viewed as merely decontextualized problem completion. Since our long-term goal is producing young people who are able to think critically and creatively in real problem-solving contexts, the instructional—and linguistic—implications should be evident.

Conclusion

One of the most difficult tasks we face as human beings is communicating meaning across our individual differences, a task confounded immeasurably when we attempt to communicate across social lines, racial lines, cultural lines, or lines of unequal power. Yet, all U.S. demographic data points to a society becoming increasingly diverse, and that diversity is nowhere more evident than in our schools. Currently, "minority" students represent a majority in all but two of our twenty-five largest cities, and by some estimates, the turn of the century—a mere eleven years away—will find up to 40 percent nonwhite children in American classrooms. At the same time, the teaching force is becoming more homogeneously white. African-American, Asian, Hispanic, and Native American teachers now comprise only ten percent of the teaching force, and that percentage is shrinking rapidly.

What are we educators to do? We must first decide upon a perspective from which to view the situation. We can continue to view diversity as a problem, attempting to force all differences into standardized boxes. Or we can recognize that diversity of thought, language, and worldview in our classrooms cannot only provide an exciting educational setting, but can also prepare our children for the richness of living in an increasingly diverse national community. (Would any of us really want to trade the wonderful variety of American ethnic restaurants for a standard fare of steak houses and fast-food hamburgers?)

I am suggesting that we begin with a perspective that demands finding means to celebrate, not merely tolerate, diversity in our classrooms. Not only should teachers and students who share group membership delight in their own cultural and linguistic history, but all teachers must revel in the diversity of their students and that of the world outside the classroom community. How can we accomplish these lofty goals? Certainly, given the reality of the composition of the teaching force, very few educators can join Martha Demientieff in taking advantage of her shared background with her culturally unique students and contrasting "*our* Heritage language" or "the way *we* say things" with "Formal English." But teachers who do not share the language and culture of their students, or teachers whose students represent a variety of cultural backgrounds, can also celebrate diversity by making language diversity a part of the curriculum. Students can be asked to "teach" the teacher and other students aspects of their language variety. They can "translate" songs, poems, and stories into their own dialect or into "book language" and compare the differences across the cultural groups represented in the classroom.

Amanda Branscombe, a gifted white teacher who has often taught black students whom other teachers have given up on, sometimes has her middle school students listen to rap songs in order to develop a rule base for their creation. The students would teach her their newly constructed "rules for writing rap," and she would in turn use this knowledge as a base to begin a discussion of the rules Shakespeare used to construct his plays, or the rules poets used to develop their sonnets (personal communication 1988).

Within our celebration of diversity, we must keep in mind that education, at its best, hones and develops the knowledge and skills each student already possesses, while at the same time adding new knowledge and skills to that base. All students deserve the right both to develop the linguistic skills they bring to the classroom and to add others to their repertoires. While linguists have long proclaimed that no language variety is intrinsically "better" than another, in a stratified society such as ours, language choices are not neutral. The language associated with the power structure—"standard English"—is the language of economic success, and all students have the right to schooling that gives them access to that language.

While it is also true, as this chapter highlights, that no one can force another to acquire an additional language variety, there are ways to point out to students both the arbitrariness of designating one variety over another as "standard," as well as the political and economic repercussions for not gaining access to that socially designated "standard." Without appearing to preach about a future which most students find hard to envision, one teacher, for example, has high school students interview various personnel officers in actual workplaces about their attitudes toward divergent styles in oral and written language and report their findings to the entire class. Another has students read or listen to a variety of oral and written language styles and discuss the impact of those styles on the message and the likely effect on different audiences. Students then recreate the texts or talks, using different language styles appropriate for different audiences (e.g., a church group, academicians, rap singers, a feminist group, politicians, etc.).

Each of us belongs to many communities. Joseph Suina, a Pueblo Indian scholar, has proposed a schematic representation of at least three levels of community membership. He sets up three concentric circles. The inner circle is labeled "home/local community," the middle circle is "national community," and the outer circle represents the "global community" (personal communication 1989). In today's world it is vital that we all learn to become active citizens in all three communities, and one requisite skill for doing so is an ability to acquire additional linguistic codes. We can ignore or try to obliterate language diversity in the classroom, or we can encourage in our teachers and students a "mental set for diversity." If we choose the latter, the classroom can become a laboratory for developing linguistic diversity. Those who have acquired additional codes because their local language differs significantly from the language of the national culture may actually be in a better position to gain access to the global culture than "mainstream" Americans who, as Martha says, "only know one way to talk." Rather than think of these diverse students as problems, we can view them instead as resources who can help all of us learn what it feels like to move between cultures and language varieties, and thus perhaps better learn how to become citizens of the global community.

Note

1. Some of these books include *All Us Come Cross the Water* by Lucille Clifton (New York: Holt, Rinehart and Winston 1973); *I Am Eskimo—Aknik My Name* by Paul Green, aided by Abbe Abbott (Juneau, AK: Alaska Northwest Publishing, 1959); *Once Upon a Bayou* by Howard Jacobs and Jim Rice (New Orleans, LA: Phideaux Publications, 1983); *Yaqua Days* by Cruz Martel (New York: Dial, 1976); *Santa's Cajun Christmas Adventure* by Tim Edler (Baton Rouge, LA: Little Cajun Books, 1981); and a series of biographies produced by Yukon-Koyukkuk School District of Alaska and published by Hancock House Publishers in North Vancouver, British Columbia, Canada.

Works Cited

Berdan, R. 1980. "Knowledge into Practice: Delivering Research to Teachers." In *Reactions to Ann Arbor: Vernacular Black English and Education*, edited by M. F. Whiteman. Arlington, Va.: Center for Applied Linguistics.

Cazden, C. B. 1988. *Classroom Discourse*. Portsmouth, N.H.: Heinemann.

Cunningham, P. M. 1976-77. "Teachers' Correction Responses to Black-Dialect Miscues Which are Nonmeaning-Changing. *Reading Research Quarterly* 12.

Heath, S. B. 1982. *Ways with Words*. New York: Cambridge University Press.

Kaplan, R. 1966. Cultural Thought Patterns in Intercultural Education. *Language Learning* 16: 1-2.

Krashen, S. D. 1982. *Principles and Practice in Second Language Acquisition*. New York: Pergamon.

Mehan, H. 1979. "Asking Known Information." *Theory Into Practice* 28: 285-94.

Michaels, S., and C. Cazden. 1986. "Teacher-Child Collaboration as Oral Preparation for Literacy." In *Acquisition of Literacy: Ethnographic Perspectives*, edited by B. Schieffer. Norwood, N.J.: Ablex.

Nelson-Barber, S. 1982. "Phonologic Variations of Pima English." In *Language Renewal among American Indian Tribes: Issues, Problems, and Prospects*, edited by R. St. Clair and W. Leap. Rosslyn, Va.: National Clearinghouse for Bilingual Education.

Orr, E. W. 1987. *Twice as Less: Black English and the Performance of Black Students in Mathematics and Science*. New York: W. W. Norton.

Scollon, R., and B. K. Scollon. 1979. "Cooking It Up and Boiling It Down: Abstracts in Athabaskan Children's Story Retellings." In *Spoken and Written Language*, edited by D. Tannen. Norwood, N.J.: Ablex.

Sims, R. 1982. "Dialect and Reading: Toward Redefining the Issues." In *Reader Meets Author/Bridging the Gap*, edited by J. Langer and M. T. Smith-Burke. Newark, Del.: International Reading Association.

Smitherman, G. 1978. *Talkin and Testifyin*. Boston: Houghton Mifflin.

17 Bilingual/ESL Learners Talking in the English Classroom

Sarah Hudelson
Arizona State University

The demographics of American education are changing at a dizzy-
ing pace. In 1982 fewer than 2 million school-age children were
dominant in a language other than English. Projections show that
two decades later, in the year 2000, over 3 million students will be
non-English dominant, and two decades after that, American
schools will house 5 million such students. Multilingualism is not
an issue that can be shut out of mainstream classrooms and shunt-
ed off to a limited number of second language specialists. The most
effective classroom strategy available to teachers is simply to
listen to the students whose proficiency in English is limited.
When we do listen, students learn how to communicate in English.
Equally important, when we do listen, teachers and students learn
about a world broader than their own immediate cultural horiz-
ons.

Introduction

Imagine this classroom setting: a fifth grade of twenty-eight children
in Atlanta, Georgia. What would the children be like? If you envision
a group of Black and Anglo children you are only partially correct
because nine of the learners come from outside the United States, and
all of them, speakers of seven different native languages, are learners of
English as a Second Language (ESL). To give you an idea of their
linguistic and cultural variety, here are brief sketches of three of the
children:

Xiancuong came from the People's Republic of China. Xiancuong
was quiet, almost withdrawn, for the first several months of school, so
he often went unnoticed. He was good at math but less interested in
language work. His passion was origami, and he often entertained one
or two classmates by creating all kinds of animal creatures. Early in the
year, Xiancuong's father was injured in an automobile accident, an
event which cast a shadow over him for several months.

267

Miguel was a recent arrival from Mexico. The only boy in a single-parent family, he was fun loving and not really interested in school work. He enjoyed sports, games, and travel. If left to his own devices he would have spent his days socializing. Miguel and Xiancuong became friends early in the school year, and they could often be found creating origami figures.

Hanh had come to Georgia via a refugee camp two years earlier. She and her family had escaped from Vietnam and then had been in Thailand before arriving in the United States. Hanh assumed adult responsibilities in her home, doing much of the cooking and cleaning. This adult role carried over in the classroom, where she took a motherly stance with many of her classmates. Generally a quiet child, she was a willing worker and stood out more in small groups.

For the classroom teacher without special training faced with this array, such questions as the following are only natural: What are they like? How do I teach them? What do I do to help them? How do I work with them without taking away from the others I am teaching? One way to respond to this challenge is to use information about bilingual/second language learners and language learning in planning classroom instruction. This chapter will look at bilingual/second language learners from the following perspectives: the learners' efforts to acquire English and to use it as a tool for communication; the learners' natural use of both of their languages; the learners' needs to adapt to American classrooms; the learners as individuals. Implications for instruction will follow. These will include suggestions both for teacher actions and for peer work.

Bilingual/Second Language Students
Learn English as a Tool for Communication

In order to achieve school success in the United States, learners must be able to use English, in both oral and written forms, to carry out their own and school tasks. Students need to communicate effectively in English and use this language to learn school content. For non-English speakers, then, a major school task is learning and using English. The following sample, featuring eight-year-old, Spanish-speaking Ariel, illustrates the ESL learner's active involvement in using his still-developing English to communicate with his teacher:

Ariel: Mrs. Pelaez! Mrs. Pelaez!
Teacher: What is it, Ariel?

Ariel: Roberto throw things in the, to the childrens. He, he, and then he throw *tiro* to———. Roberto he throw to something in he eyes. And then he got, the teacher looks him and *dice* go the corner now and then he go and then he jump, he play.

Teacher: What did he throw?

Ariel: Crayah

Teacher: Crayons? (Ariel nods). Did he hit you?

Ariel: No.

Teacher: Who did he hit?

Ariel: The childrens.

Teacher: Which ones?

Ariel: The Cheri that sits there (points to one of the tables in the classroom where one of two girls usually sits)

Teacher: Chica?

Ariel: No. The Cherins.

Teacher: Oh, Cherin.

Ariel: Yeah.

Teacher: Roberto hit Cherin in the eye?

Ariel: Yeah.

Teacher: Thank you, Ariel. Tell Mrs. P. I'll be right there.[1]

In spite of Ariel's errors, it is not impossible to understand what he is struggling to say. Ariel rushes in to tell his teacher that Roberto, a classmate, has thrown something at some other children's eyes and that another teacher has told Roberto to stand in the corner. Roberto has obeyed the teacher momentarily, but he is now playing and jumping instead of standing in the corner. As the conversation progresses, it becomes clear that Roberto hit Cherin—another student in the class—in the eye with the crayons he was throwing. Apparently, Ariel wants to move his teacher to action, and he is successful in doing so.

Ariel's conduct illustrates several important points made by educators concerned with second language development: (1) the overriding goal of the second language learner is to be able to use the new language with other speakers. Because the learner already knows one language, the learner is aware of what language does, of how language may be used. So the learner is focused on being able to use the new language for a variety of functions and purposes. (Ariel's purpose is to explain to this teacher that something has happened and to persuade his teacher to take action.) (2) Second language learners work hard to make their meanings and intentions as clear as possible to others. To

---

[1] I am grateful to Gloria Pelaez for this example.

do this, they use whatever linguistic resources are available to them at a given time. (As Ariel talks, he uses the English action words he knows, but he relates an incident in the past using verb forms in the present tense.) (3) Second language learners are actively involved in figuring out the rules for the language they are learning. The process of second language acquisition is essentially a process of creative construction of the new language, construction of the rules resulting from continued hypothesis generation, testing, and revision. Through ongoing experimentation second language learners finally generate the rules for the second language. (4) Given the process of creative construction, learners necessarily and naturally will make mistakes as they work to figure out how the new language works. Many of the errors learners make will resemble errors made by children acquiring English as their native language (for example, Ariel's overgeneralization of the rule for forming the plural in the addition of the "s" to children). Other errors may be traced to using the rules of the native language to create the second language. There are also times when learners will actually slip back into the native language or use words from the native language. All of these errors are proof of learners working to figure out the second language systems (Ellis 1985, Lindfors 1987).

And what of the teacher in this excerpt? In her role as conversational participant, she exhibits many characteristics that facilitate students' second language development. She attends closely to the learner's utterances, making concerted efforts to understand what is being said. (The questions she asks Ariel make it clear that she is trying to make sense of his talk.) She repeats some of the learner's words (crayons and Cherin) in adult English as a way of checking their comprehensibility. She extends some of the learner's incomplete utterances, thus providing samples of well-formed English sentences (for example, she formulates the sentence about Roberto hitting Cherin in the eye). She does not correct all of the learner's mistakes, but rather focuses on understanding and responding to the learner's messages. (The teacher does not ask Ariel to repeat himself in correct English.) In these ways, the teacher provides input that focuses on the situation at hand, input that she strives to make easily understood by the learner. (Ellis 1985, Krashen 1982, Long and Porter 1985).

Fundamentally, the learner and teacher in the previous example illustrate a point that second language educators have been making with ever-increasing confidence in the past few years: the processes of first and second language acquisition are more alike than they are different. Second languages develop much as first languages do, as learners in language-rich and supportive environments experiment with their new language (in both oral and written forms) and gradually become ever more capable of using that language to fulfill their own and others' purposes (Allen 1986, Krahnke and Christison 1983, Lindfors 1987, Rigg and Enright 1986).

What this means for classrooms is that the kinds of integrated, whole language experiences this and many other publications advocate for native speakers will also be beneficial for second language learners. As with native speakers, the focus for second language learners should be on using English to do something (a focus on content rather than on the language itself), rather than drilling language forms (Allen 1986, Krahnke and Christison 1983, Rigg and Enright 1986). Even as second language learners are learning to speak English, they need to speak about meaningful content. As among native speakers, interactive group work where learners work together will benefit both content and language learning. In group work ESL learners may work effectively both with other second language learners and with native speakers (Long and Porter 1985). As with native speakers, there will be significant individual differences in rates of learning and willingness to use the language (Lindfors 1987). As in native language settings, the teacher's role is to facilitate both content and language exploration and experimentation, to focus on learners' understandings and misunderstandings, to respond to what the learners are trying to do (Rigg and Enright 1986).

Bilingual/Second Language Students Switch between English and Their Native Language

It would be a mistake to assume that all second language learners in English classrooms are struggling with English. Many are fluent bilinguals, meaning that they already communicate easily both in English and another language. While these learners do not have problems communicating in English, and using English to learn, it is quite probable that they will behave linguistically in a way that may seem strange to listeners not used to it. They will use both their languages in the same interaction, alternating between the two at the word, phrase, clause, or sentence level. This phenomenon is called code-switching, and researchers interested in bilingualism have documented that virtually all bilinguals code-switch at one time or another, although some code-switch with greater frequency than others (Valdes-Fallis 1977). Even in school settings where the language of the school is English, bilingual students will code-switch with each other, particularly if they are working in small-group settings.

Many who listen to code-switching assume that bilinguals are mixing the two languages indiscriminately, that they switch because of a language deficiency, that they do not know either language well and that, therefore, they use both languages. In fact, only fluent bilinguals are able to code-switch. Code-switching does not occur simply because the speakers do not know how to say something in one language. Rather, bilinguals naturally use both languages in communicating with other bilinguals, because making use of the resources of both languages serves their communicative needs. The following two examples, taken from transcripts of Spanish-English bilingual Cuban-American children in small-group settings in English language classrooms, demonstrate how bilingual learners may make use of both of their languages to accomplish school tasks. To facilitate reading, the Spanish utterances have been italicized and then translated into English. In the first excerpt, second grader Diana has been asked to help another student, Alex, with his math word problems. The tutoring proceeds in this way:

> *Diana:* OK. Let's begin with No. 1. Mary has three balls. Carlos has four balls. How many altogether? *Entendiste?* (Did you understand?)
>
> *Alex: Si. Cómo lo pongo?* (Yes. How do I put it?)
>
> *Diana:* Mary has what?
>
> *Alex:* Three balls.
>
> *Diana:* OK. Write a three. *Ahora* (Now), is it plus or minus?
>
> *Alex: Qué?* (What?)
>
> *Diana:* Are you going to add them together or take away, *quitar* (take away)?
>
> *Alex:* Add three and *lo que tiene* Carlos.
>
> *Diana:* OK. *Vamos. Son tres mas cuatro.* (Let's go. It's three plus four.) How much does it equal? *Alex, pon tres dedos. Ahora cuatro dedos. Cuéntalos.* (Alex, put three fingers. Now four fingers. Count them.)
>
> *Alex:* Ah, seben (seven).
>
> *Diana:* Right. OK. Look at No. 2. Susan had five balloons. Ted took two away. Alex. *Atiende.* (Pay attention.) (Alex drops his pencil under the table and looks down.) *Cójelo. Está debajo de la mesa. Atiende.* (Pick it up. It's under the table. Pay attention.)
>
> *Alex: Ya lo cojí. OK. Dónde?* (I picked it up. OK. Now where?)
>
> *Diana:* How are you going to do it?

Alex: Put, eh, five plus two equals seben (seven).

Diana: No. Ted took away from Susan. If you have five balloons and I take away two how many do you have?

Alex: Three.

Diana: Right. OK. *Cómo lo pones? Qué número va primero?* (OK. How are you going to put it? What number goes first?)

Alex: *El cinco.* (The five.)

Diana: OK. Then——

Alex: Two.

Diana: OK. Is it plus or minus?

Alex: Minus.

Diana: What's the answer?

Alex: Three. *Oye, esa mesa tiene los libros. Vamos. Mira el libro de Peter Pan.* (Listen, that table has books on it. Let's go over there. Look at the Peter Pan book.)

Diana: *Mira la maestra.* (Look at the teacher.) We have to finish. You better pay attention. Alex, stop playing, OK? *Se lo digo a la maestra.* (I'll tell the teacher.)

Alex: OK. *Yo no estoy jugando.* (I'm not playing.)

Diana: Alex, you better listen one more time. Look at No. 3. I'll read it and you open your ears.

Alex: OK, man.[2]

And the tutoring continues until Alex has finished all the problems.

The classroom language is English, and the teacher has used English to request that Diana help Alex. Diana begins in English, reading the first word problem. But Diana is aware that Alex also speaks Spanish. In fact, Alex addresses her in Spanish, perhaps signaling to her that he needs some native language assistance. So Diana uses Spanish selectively, to check Alex's comprehension, to provide additional explanation of the processes, to get Alex's attention, to keep Alex on task, and to control Alex's behavior, which includes threatening to tell the teacher about his misbehavior. In order to assure that Alex completes his work, Diana makes use of both of her languages.

The second example comes from a sixth-grade class, where the children are carrying out a science project. The teacher has divided the class into small groups. One group, made up of three Spanish-English bilingual students—Ricardo, Pedro, and Mario—is going to dissect a frog. Ricardo quickly assumes the leadership role of the group, and uses both Spanish and English as he takes over the task.

---

[2] I am grateful to Maria Morffi for this example.

Ricardo: (sits at round table) Miss——, today's the day we're going to dissect the frog.

Teacher: Yes, you're right. I'll be back in a few minutes to tell your group what to do.

Pedro: (sitting next to Ricardo) Hey, what does that big word mean? Where'd you get that big word?

Ricardo: At home. My Uncle Frank is a doctor, and last night I was explaining to him that we were studying about animals. I told him about our assignment today, that we have to open a frog, to cut up and study the skeleton and to answer why the frog is a vertebrate. He was listening and then he told me that all the work with a dead animal is a dissection and the verb is dissect.

Mario: (sitting with the other two) Who's talking about verbs? I don't like verbs. *Hoy no quiero hablar sino de ciencias. Recuerdan que hoy vamos a abrir una rana.* (I only want to talk today about science. Remember that we're going to open a frog today.)

Ricardo: Eso es lo que estábamos diciendo que hoy tenemos que abrir una rana para estudiar su cuerpo, sus organos, sus músculos, pero tenemos que hacer la desección con cuidado para no cortar lo que no debemos cortar. (That's what I was saying, that today we have to open a frog to study his body, his organs, his muscles, but we have to do the dissection carefully so that we don't cut what we shouldn't cut.)

Pedro: Bueno, en eso yo soy un tremendo. Yo he operado muchas lagartijas. Yo ya se como hacerlo. (Good, I'm great at that. I've operated on a lot of lizards. I know how to do it.)

Mario: Oh, yeah. He is *el bravo de la película* (the movie hero). You know something. This is something you need to follow directions for.

Ricardo: Of course. This is a science project. It's work that has to be done with a sequence, step by step. *Primero un paso seguido de otro más complicado hasta terminar de sacar todos los músculos de la rana y dejarla en el esqueleto.* (First one step followed by another more complicated one until you finish taking away all the frog's muscles and leave only the skeleton.)[3]

As is obvious from the excerpt, Ricardo is not a learner who has trouble expressing himself in English. Rather, Ricardo demonstrates that he is able to use both of his languages to consider the content of the lesson and to control the situation. Ricardo sets himself up as the one with information and expertise on the subject of dissection and, in both English and Spanish, provides the others information about frogs. This demonstration of expertise results in the others' choosing him to cut open the frog. As the dissection continues, Ricardo retains control of the activity, telling the others what to do and getting them to do as he

---

[3]I am grateful to Olga Cardet for this example.

wishes. To help him accomplish this, he uses both English and Spanish.

As is also obvious from the context, the language of the classroom is English, and the children are expected to turn in their observations in English. This they are able to do, jotting down notes in English even as they use both English and Spanish orally. So the natural use of Spanish by these bilingual learners does not mean that they do not know English, that they must use their other language as a crutch. Rather, the native language is an additional tool or resource that they may call on when they are interacting with other bilinguals.

What implications might this natural behavior of bilinguals have for English educators concerned with promoting talk and learning? In the first place, it seems important to see code-switching as normal rather than abnormal, as a communication strategy rather than a linguistic deficiency, and to understand that code-switching does not necessarily mean that learners do not know English, or are too lazy to use the language (Valdes-Fallis 1977). Such a recognition suggests that teachers would not automatically seek to prevent bilingual students from code switching as they work together.

Second, it is important to recognize that bilinguals sense the language abilities of the people they are interacting with and may switch to make others more comfortable and to facilitate their understanding. So bilingual learners working cooperatively with less fluent English speakers may switch into their native language because they can see that their peers need some native language assistance, translation, paraphrasing, summarization, examples, etc. This sensitivity to the comprehension of peers is something that teachers may want to encourage rather than discourage, as peers assist each other. As English language fluency increases, the amount of native language assistance given by the fluent bilinguals will naturally decrease.

Bilingual/Second Language Students Must Often Adjust to New Norms for Classroom Talk

While human beings grow as individuals, they also develop within a particular cultural framework. Part of this framework involves such physical or concrete aspects of culture as food, clothing, celebrations, the arts, forms of recreation, and so on. In addition, each culture has its own rules or norms for behavior, including rules or norms for talking with others and for participating in conversations and activities of the particular group. Children growing up within a particular culture early on learn the rules for how to interact and participate successfully within their own family and community settings. By the time they enter school they have become competent communicators in their particular culture; they have learned their group's participant structures (Philips 1983).

Schools are also cultural settings, and classrooms operate according to particular rules or norms for participation. When the home and community language-use rules that learners bring to school are significantly different from those of the school, learners may not respond to instruction and direction as teachers expect them to. Miscommunication, conflict, lowered expectations, and lack of learning may result. Philips (1983) has demonstrated this reality by contrasting the rules for participation that children from a Native American community in Oregon acquired at home to those expected in school.

Philips found that the Native American students, from a very early age, frequently had trouble acting appropriately in traditional classrooms where the teacher was the authority and the children were expected to follow the teacher's lead. Children often forgot to raise their hands or did not wait to be called on before speaking. Children often moved around or spoke to other children while the teacher was talking and did not respond to questions the teacher posed directly to individuals. Students often did the exact opposite of what the teacher directed.

By examining home participation structures Philips discovered that the children became accustomed, at an early age, to determining a lot of their own actions, to being somewhat independent from their elders. Children were raised in extended families, where many adults—not just a single authority figure—took part in child rearing. Older children assumed responsibilities in caring for younger siblings. Children were expected to demonstrate their competence at tasks by performing silently rather than by talking. At the community level, too, Philips discovered that activities were carried out without the direct verbal leadership of a single person; activities were open to all, and individuals could choose to be involved or not.

These rules for participation were very different from those that the traditional classrooms expected. As a result, the children frequently did not participate appropriately, and the teachers often assumed that they either would not or did not want to learn. Philips also examined some classrooms where children from the same Native American group were successful. She found that the teachers in these classes had adjusted the rules for participation in their classrooms in ways that were more congruent with what the children were used to in the community. Group work and voluntary participation in groups and in some activities was allowed. Teachers did not single out individuals to answer questions but let many students contribute to an answer. When students worked at their desks, teachers were available as resources, but they did not initiate interactions with the students, so that less attention was called to individual students. These adjustments made the students more comfortable in class, and they more readily participated, demonstrating their abilities.

Work with native Hawaiian children (speakers of Hawaiian creole) also has demonstrated that adjusting classroom interaction patterns may have a positive effect on student performance (Au and Jordan 1981). One of the features of traditional Hawaiian culture is that story-telling is a group, rather than an individual, activity. One individual may begin to tell a tale, but others soon join in and jointly construct the story. Children growing up in this culture soon adopt this technique. Concerned with the low achievement of native Hawaiians in reading, educators decided to experiment with this idea of joint narration in terms of reading comprehension instruction. Teachers adapted their reading instruction by moving away from the traditional format of teacher question and single individual response to allowing and encouraging children to build on each other's ideas as they responded jointly to questions and ideas in the stories they were reading. As an example, in the following sequence, the teacher asks a question, looking at Child 1, and then the children take over, together creating the response which the first child repeats at the end of the sequence:

> *Teacher:* If you're gonna use it for bait, what do you have to do with that frog? You just throw it in the water?
>
> *Child 1:* Uh-uh.
>
> *Child 2:* Put it on a hook.
>
> *Teacher:* Oh, no! He's gonna have to stick it on a hook.
>
> *Child 3:* And den go like dat, an den dat (gestures casting).
>
> *Teacher:* And throw it in the water and
>
> *Child 3:* En den, en might
>
> *Child 4:* The fish might come and eat it.
>
> *Child 1:* The fish might come and eat it.
>
> (Au and Jordan 1981, 128-29)

Au and Jordan (1981) discovered that teacher adjustments in their expectations for participation in reading lessons resulted in the children's increased achievement in reading, as measured by standardized reading tests. Their examples make it clear that divergent home-school norms for interaction may result in children's behaving and talking inappropriately in school, with potentially damaging results. The volume in which Au and Jordan's work appears provides many other examples of such home-school cultural difference.

Cultures also vary in how they view schooling, including what they view as the basic purposes of schooling, student and teacher roles within the classroom, and how teaching and learning occur. Students who have been schooled in one culture may have particular ideas about how schooling should be conducted, and these may differ from their teachers' expectations. As with the rules for talking, differences between mainstream American understandings and expectations and those of students may mean that students do not act as teachers anticipate or expect they will, and do not react to instructional techniques as American students do.

In Miami, for example, many teachers working with Haitian students comment that, even when Haitian students have attained considerable fluency in English, they are often reluctant to participate in class discussions, particularly if those discussions ask students to critique a point of view in a text or disagree with a statement made by the teacher. Haitian educators bring a particular understanding to this puzzlement when they are able to point out that in Haiti students are expected to memorize their lessons and not give their own opinions, particularly if those opinions differ from those of the teacher. For many Haitian students, giving one's own opinions in class is considered culturally inappropriate, and the more open atmosphere of some American classrooms strikes them as chaotic. In addition, students coming from the politically oppressive atmosphere that has characterized Haiti may view the expression of disagreement or dissent as politically dangerous.

In a similar way, many Moslem students from the Middle East have been schooled through the memorization of large portions of material (the Koran), and they have been expected to be able to recite what they have learned, word for word. The purpose of schooling has been to learn the truth as explicated through text. This may mean that American teachers who request oral and written summaries and personal reactions to class material receive instead detailed repetitions of what is in the text with little or no personal interpretation. Students have not had experience in offering their own opinions and interpretations.

In China, languages are taught through the memorization of long lists of words and the repeated writing of each item to be memorized. So Chinese students may be eager to receive lists of words to write and commit to memory, and they may view this as an important way to learn English, even though there is considerable evidence that this practice is of limited value in language acquisition. In fact, worldwide, prescriptive, teacher-dominated rote methods of learning probably predominate, much as they do in the United States. So it is quite possible that second language students may be used to one view of classroom teaching and learning, a view that is in direct conflict with the views presented in this volume.

Given the complexities suggested above, perhaps the most basic, yet striking, classroom implication involves sensitivity to the reality of cultural differences, and to the possible effects these differences may have on instruction. When bilingual/second language learners do not respond to an activity as teachers have anticipated they will, the reason may not be laziness, unwillingness to participate, or language or intellectual deficiency. Cultural factors may play an important role. It may take time and patience for students to learn the new participation rules and to feel comfortable with American ways of schooling. There may also be, as Philips and Au demonstrate, ways the educators can adjust classroom interaction patterns to provide some classroom experiences that are more culturally congruent with varied home patterns. Realistically, the adjustments must work both ways.

Bilingual/Second Language Students Have Individual Needs

While bilingual/second language learners have in common the need to learn English in order to use it for a variety of purposes, they also have individual needs, wants, and interests. Just as do native speakers, bilingual/second language learners bring a variety of personalities, life experiences, and interests with them to school. In the excerpt below, Habib's teacher learns some of what her nineteen-year-old Farsi-speaking student's life has been. Habib has been studying English for seven months:

> *Habib:* OK. I was small guy. OK? My old is, my old was seven. My father is die. OK?
>
> *Teacher:* You were seven when your father died?
>
> *Habib:* Yeah. OK. We was, we don't have anything my family.
>
> *Teacher:* You were very poor.
>
> *Habib:* Yeah. After the two years, the Russians came in my country and they start to fight.
>
> *Teacher:* How old were you when the Russians came into your country?

Habib: Mmm, seven, seven years.

Teacher: Who was living with you?

Habib: My mother, my two sister, and my brother.

Teacher: And your brother was older than you.

Habib: Yeah.

Teacher: How old was your brother?

Habib: My brother? He's twenty-one.

Teacher: So he was taking care of the family.

Habib: Yeah.

Teacher: What was he doing?

Habib: He's, he was come to Iran, he has some business in Iran. But after the three years he come to India and he was have business in there, but he take the money.

Teacher: Did he send you money, in Afghanistan, to your family?

Habib: Yeah. But after the three month, three year, three years he come to the United States.

Teacher: Your brother.

Habib: Yeah, my brother. But, ah, we glad to my brother he come to United States. Every year he take one thousand dollars.

Teacher: That he sent?

Habib: Yeah. There's some. One thousand dollars, one thousand, two, no hundred thousand make it hundred thousand.

Teacher: Hundred thousand what?

Habib: Dollars.

Teacher: You could live for a whole year on one thousand dollars?

Habib: No, only one thousand dollars, hundred thousand dollars Afghanistan money.

Teacher: And that was enough to live on for a whole year?

Habib: Yeah.

Teacher: What happened when the Russians came? What was it like when the Russians came? You said that you were seven years old and the Russians came.

Habib: The Russians came in seven old. But, we was don't have anything. You know. After the two years the Russians came in my country. They started to fight. My brother's come to Iran and he was working out there. And after one year he came to India, he was have business. And every month he help me, and after two years he come to the United States and we are glad to my brother. And after six years, I come too to America. Now we have everything and I love my brother because my brother is not only my brother, he's my father too.[4]

---

[4] I am grateful to Judith Titus for this example.

This conversation reveals some significant facts about Habib's life, including the role that Habib's brother has played and the love and respect Habib feels for him. Habib is not unique among second language learners. Each has a story to tell. For English teachers the old adage of beginning with the learners certainly applies here. Students' abilities to speak English will certainly grow as they share their lives with others. A logical question is: How might this sharing be accomplished?

One response to this question comes from a visit to the Georgia fifth grade introduced earlier. This fifth grade was teamed with another one (a setting colleagues D. Scott Enright and Mary Jane Nations of Georgia State University and I studied for a year). In the two classrooms the bilingual/second language learners represented fifteen different nationalities, and the children differed from each other culturally, linguistically, and individually. Yet the children's teachers learned about and appreciated their students as individuals. The teachers were committed to knowing their students, and they made time for private conversations. The two classes went on an annual four-day field trip to Jekyll Island, and teachers and students involved themselves in fundraising for the trip, including spending many Saturdays together, selling food and drinks at local events to raise money. The teachers told the students about themselves and encouraged reciprocation. One of the teachers often invited students to her house or to the movies. All of these occasions gave teachers and children time to talk and to get to know each other.

The school climate, too, promoted acceptance and indeed interest in differences, a factor which reinforced the teachers' attitudes. The school promoted itself as an international center. Signs and posters around the halls proclaimed pride in the diverse heritages of the students. During International Month each grade adopted a country and learned about it. School programs and holidays reflected the many cultures and languages represented on campus, in songs, dances, folktales, and dress. In this school, students took pride in who they were.

But perhaps of most relevance to English educators, the learners participated in language arts activities which highlighted their diversity and individuality. For example, in addition to individual journals shared with their teachers, the learners carried out a class autobiography project. Following the teachers' examples, the children began by constructing time lines of their own lives. Then, over a period of several weeks, each child wrote and illustrated a chaptered autobiography. During the writing of the autobiographies the children were free to work together, consulting one another and their teachers. Parents, too, were consulted on details. At the conclusion of the project the children shared their autobiographies with their parents, who were invited to a special program.

One of the teachers described this project as "the best thing we did all year." From the point of view of language learning, it certainly may have been, as it asked second language learners to use and develop their English by sharing themselves with others.

Conclusion

This chapter has focused on bilingual/second language learners in English classrooms. The central message is that second language learners have much in common with native speakers, and that good teaching for native speakers is equally appropriate in the bilingual/ second language context. But both individual and cultural differences need to be kept in mind, because they suggest that not all learners will react in the same way to even the most carefully planned activity. Finally, the focus of this chapter is on what bilingual and second language learners bring to the English classroom: their individual life experiences, their customs, their knowledge of other countries and languages, their music, literature, and drama, their dance and other art forms. Taking advantage of this richness, using these resources, can mean enriching language and learning experiences for all the students in the English classroom.

Works Cited

Allen, V. 1986. "Developing Contexts to Support Second Language Acquisition." *Language Arts* 63: 61–67.

Au, K., and C. Jordan. 1981. "Teaching Reading to Hawaiian Children: A Culturally Appropriate Solution." In *Culture and the Bilingual Classroom: Studies in Classroom Ethnography*, edited by H. Trueba, G. Guthrie, and K. Au. Rowley, Mass.: Newbury House.

Ellis, R. 1985. *Understanding Second Language Acquisition*. Oxford, England: Oxford University Press.

Krahnke, K., and M. Christison. 1983. "Recent Language Research and Some Language Teaching Principles." *TESOL Quarterly* 17: 625–49.

Krashen, S. 1982. *Principles and Practice in Second Language Acquisition*. Oxford, England: Pergamon Press.

Lindfors, J. 1987. *Children's Language and Learning*. 2nd ed. Englewood Cliffs, N.J.: Prentice-Hall.

Long, M., and P. Porter. 1985. "Group Work, Interlanguage Talk, and Second Language Acquisition." *TESOL Quarterly* 19: 207–28.

Philips, S. 1983. *The Invisible Culture.* New York: Longman.

Rigg, P., and D. S. Enright, eds. 1986. *Children and ESL: Integrating Perspectives.* Washington, D.C.: Teachers of English to Speakers of Other Languages.

Valdes-Fallis, G. 1977. *Code Switching and the Classroom Teacher.* Arlington, Va.: Center for Applied Linguistics.

18 The Silent Sounds of Language Variation in the Classroom

Jerrie Cobb Scott
Central State University

After a quarter of a century of research and sensitization about dialect differences, many educators remain as ambivalent and confused as ever. On the one hand, there is plentiful evidence that speakers of nonstandard dialects are economically and politically disadvantaged in our society. So the motivation to impart standard dialect skills seems humane indeed. On the other hand, much of the "disadvantage" of nonstandard language is in the ears of the listener. There is no inherent linguistic deficit. So why should teachers and students invest in the frustrating and often fruitless effort to acquire standard speech patterns as a second dialect? When teachers become aware of nonstandard dialect speakers' strengths as communicators, some of the issues that seem so insoluble recede in importance.

The sounds of language variation surround us. A different setting, topic, or audience naturally elicits structural and stylistic variations in the way that we express meaning. To be sure, we all speak a various language. Yet those variations which code lower social class or nonmainstream ethnic group differences alarm us. In the interest of removing stigmatized variants from the speech of nonstandard dialect speakers, some scholars have designed special dialect accommodation programs.

Consider the following dialogue in relation to two of the most widely discussed dialect accommodation models, the eradication and the bidialectal models.

Student 1: You talkin' 'bout celebration time and partying, right?

Student 2: I'm just talkin' 'bout—the majority of people in this room know that when you talkin' 'bout a good time you ain't havin' no good time unless you talkin' 'bout alcohol at the party. (SE gloss: The majority of people in this room associate having a good time with drinking alcohol.)

Student 1: We're talkin' 'bout most of the people, OK. Alcohol is important. We're talkin' 'bout all those things are important. We need to deal with all those things, right? But the thing that is happening with our youth, with our seven-, eight-, and nine-year-olds, right now. Crack, cocaine, trying to sell it and trying to buy it. That's the most critical right now! OK? (SE gloss: We're saying that, while alcohol is a serious problem, other drugs are more serious because they affect young children.)

The dialogue is by African-American students responding to the suggestion that alcohol is a more serious problem than other drugs, but more important, these students were using talk to critique a student-produced videotape on drugs. In this particular case, the dialogue was not interrupted by the teacher. However, it is not difficult to find classrooms in which a teacher would feel compelled to enter the dialogue to correct the students' grammar. According to the dialect eradication model, such behavior would be appropriate. Prior to the 1970s, the dialect eradication model provided the rationale for silencing the sounds of dialect variation in its misguided attempts to match the structural features of low prestige dialects with cognitive limitations. Consequently, teachers were led to believe that the failure to correct students' grammar was harmful because the use of nonstandard English inhibited cognitive growth.

During the 1970s, an alternative to the dialect eradication approach was offered in the form of the bidialectal compromise—the view that dialect differences should be respected, but standard English taught, ideally with a view toward helping students become bidialectal. The proposed pedagogy called for the contrastive analysis of standard and nonstandard features. Using the bidialectal approach, a teacher might have responded to the dialogue above by designing a lesson to show students the differences between, say, "you are talking" and "you talkin'" or "about" and "'bout." The proposed pedagogy failed, however, to adequately address the bidialectal ideal and focused on the teaching of one, instead of several, English-lects. Indirectly, then, the bidialectal approach helps to silence the sounds of language variation. Of importance here is that when we silence the sounds of language variation in our classrooms, we inadvertently discourage the nonstandard dialect (NSD) speaker from participating in classroom dialogue. We have now come to view classroom talk not only as a tool for communication, but also as an essential learning tool. It is therefore critical that we continue the search for effective ways to give vitality and audibility to the sounds of language variation in the classroom.

This means finding alternatives to both the dialect eradication and the bidialectal models discussed above.

The research project that served to inform the ideas in this paper evolved out of an interest in finding alternatives to the models discussed above. Given the evidence that classroom discourse is important, that about two-thirds of the talk in most classrooms is done by teachers (Flanders 1970), and that numerous factors discourage classroom talk by NSD speakers, it was important to design a project that primarily encouraged NSD speakers to talk. By increasing the quantity of talk, it was possible to collect a substantial data base from which to begin abstracting information about how to use the language of NSD speakers to enhance their learning. An oral dialogue project provided an ideal data source. This paper presents observations about classroom discourse and some guidelines for using students' naturally acquired language patterns to enhance their learning.

The oral dialogue project began with a group of middle school students, all members of the school's Leadership Council, who were searching for activities that would allow them to make a positive impact on the school environment. Noting that several critical problems confronted them and their peers, these students wanted a forum for discussing their problems. Convinced that adult-to-student talk was plentiful but insufficient, they moved toward the idea of a student-to-student dialogue. From a pedagogical perspective, my thinking was that these students, predominantly African-American and some lower-income whites, represented a population of youngsters who typically miss opportunities to practice "talking" in the school environment; consequently, their interest in communication and their identification of a communication project for the organization would encourage them to practice talking in the school setting. From a research perspective, my thinking was that they would produce enough talk to allow us to make some observations about their language patterns and the potential uses of their language for enhancing learning. The project evolved into a three-stage videotaping activity.

First, we videotaped students while they were planning what they wanted to talk about. Second, we videotaped the oral dialogue that the students themselves had planned. Third, we videotaped students evaluating the oral dialogue. Thus, students were involved in *planning, producing,* and *critiquing* the oral dialogues. Concerning this process, two observations are worth noting: (1) students' initiation of the project and their involvement in all phases of the activity provided the motivation for effective communication, and as a result of student involvement, (2) the teacher's role automatically shifted from conversation leader to conversation facilitator.

Planning

A closer look at the planning stage shows how the teacher facilitated the exchange of ideas among students. In trying to arrive at topics for discussion, the students brainstormed a number of ideas. It was not until after they agreed upon the intent of the communication that they were able to agree on topics. What they "really wanted to do" was to persuade their peers to stay in school. The topics selected evolved from teacher-guided questions about problems that caused their peers to drop out of school. They identified drugs, teenage suicide, and teenage parenting as the three most serious problems confronting their peers. Only the first two topics were used in this project.

The students also wanted to make their dialogue public by either dramatizing the problem or videotaping the dialogue. As facilitators, the researchers and teachers helped students devise a scheme for doing both. Thus, a student-developed dramatization of the problems was videotaped and used as a prompt to which students participating in the oral dialogue would respond. Next, students had to make a decision about how to format responses to the prompt. Through a series of questions about the message, the teacher helped students arrive at a problem-solution format. This in turn led to the decision to invite college students who could contribute experience-based solutions to the problems posed by the middle school students. The middle school students focused on identifying problems, while the college students focused on offering solutions. It is important to note that the planning stage shows the use of talk to make decisions about discourse planning. And indeed, the conversation flowed naturally toward the identification of aspects of discourse that speakers or writers must consciously attend to: topic, intent, audience, participants, and mode of presentation. By relinquishing control to the students in planning the oral dialogue, the teacher's role shifted to facilitator, a role that was maintained throughout the project. The facilitative role of the teacher not only gave students more talk time, but also created a supportive, nonthreatening learning environment.

What we learned from this phase of the project supports the widely held assumption that the classroom environment, i.e., the type of teacher-talk and the way that teachers and students interact in the classroom, is a key factor in determining how much student talk is found and what kinds of student-teacher interactions enhance learning. In many ways the planning session was free of teacher behaviors known to discourage student participation in classroom discourse.

Studying differences between teachers' interactions with students perceived as high vs. low achievers, Dworkin and Dworkin observed that students perceived as high achievers "receive more response opportunities and are given more time to respond to questions" than low achievers. Further, when high achievers have difficulty expressing their ideas, teachers tend to "delve, give clues, or rephrase the question more frequently than with low achievers" (1979, 712). In essence, our expectations of high achievers seem to trigger communication behaviors that enhance learning. As a strategy for extending these teacher-support strategies to students perceived as low achievers, a perception often associated with nonmainstream students, Kerman (1979) encourages teachers to monitor their communication behaviors to allow all students more response opportunities and to encourage them with affirmations and personal regard statements. (See, also, Scott and Smitherman 1985).

We believe that the probing questions asked by teachers during the planning phase of the project exemplify the kind of facilitative behavior described by Dworkin and Dworkin as well as by Kerman. The classroom environment was highly conducive to talk. Before moving on, we should highlight a second body of literature that speaks to the issue of how students' language differences affect the classroom environment.

Eckerd and Kearney (1981) note that the language typically used by ESL teachers is characteristic of the language that adults use with children. Arguing for a change in teachers' speech style and approach, these authors suggest moving from a teacher-centered to a group-centered approach to language instruction. In a group-centered approach, the authors note, teachers act as facilitators and ESL students are more apt to express themselves freely, make mistakes, and try out new structures.

Heath (1978) also mentions the "Baby Talk" register as a characteristic of teacher-talk; other features include high pitch, exaggerated intonation contours, slow and carefully enunciated words, and simplified grammatical structures. Heath goes on to point out that as the teacher's role shifts from leader to facilitator, the student's role shifts from dependent to independent learner. Our observations, along with those of others, yielded three useful ideas for further instructional planning: (1) the student-to-student format and student involvement help shape the teacher's role as facilitator; (2) the facilitative role of the teacher disallows the enactment of regular classroom routines, including the type of teacher-talk that discourages student participation; and (3) variations from the regular classroom routine can provide a wholesome environment for encouraging talk and using talk to enhance learning. These observations begin to provide an alternative to the dialect eradication and bidialectal approach to dialect-accommodating instruction.

Dialoguing

The dialogue sessions provided information about the kinds of discourse rules and patterns that students naturally use. For example, the dialogue participants began by establishing a set of turn-taking rules. I suspect that because of the mode of presentation—videotape—these students were especially concerned about how they would get the floor. Interestingly enough, they agreed to signal intent to speak by using eye contact and hand raising, one natural and one school-learned turn-taking strategy. Students' conscious awareness of the need for such rules should allow a teacher to move students toward more sophisticated strategies for getting the floor in regular classroom settings. Some of the factors that prevent nonmainstream students from getting a turn to talk in class were discussed above. Suffice it to say that some direct teaching of turn-taking strategies ought to be considered as an important part of language instruction for nonmainstream groups.

We also found that students used a variety of communication strategies to convey their ideas. The two examples presented below, narratives and metaphors, were selected because of their wide use in African-American culture and their recently acknowledged educational value. While prior dialect accommodation models have focused on discontinuities between the home and school languages of nonmainstream students, these forms allow us to focus on potential continuities, a focus that might also be considered an alternative to prior approaches to dialect accommodation instruction.

The following is excerpted from a narrative offered in response to the question, "Have any of you ever had an experience with or thought about committing suicide?" The parts of the narrative are described using Labov's (1972) analysis of the Black English Vernacular narrative structure:

ABSTRACT (summarizes the main point of the story)

Thinking back, I can remember being in high school and one
of the most devastating experiences that I had was when my
best friend tried to kill herself.

ORIENTATION (provides contexts: time, place, person, activities,
situations, etc.)
(Person)
She was overweight and um . . .
she had a sight problem . . .
and she'd always had a bad opinion of herself.
She—she had practically no self-esteem.
And uh . . . I felt sorta like her mentor
because I always tried to cheer her up and
to keep her happy,
But there were times when she felt really low
because she couldn't get the things she wanted
she didn't look the way she wanted;
she couldn't have the guy she wanted.
(Time/Setting/Situation)
And uh . . . there was one particular week . . . um . . .
we were getting close to prom.
And she didn't have a date.
I mean this sounds like something that you'd actually see on
TV,
but she didn't have a date, and she'd really, really tried
her best to look her best
so she could at least attract somebody.
There was one guy in particular who used to play around
with her.
And she knew that he was gonna seriously ask her to go to
the prom.
But he didn't.

STORY EVENTS
She went home.
And she got some lye, some Drano.
She brought it back to school . . . to the chorus room
And she drank it!
I mean she actually drank it!!!
And while she was going down, she was, like, asking,
"Where is he?"
And I was like, "What about the guy? What did you
drink it for?"
And she was like, "I want him to care about me, I want him
to care about me."
She recovered OK, but

CODA (shows the effects of the event on the narrator)
I felt more devastated than she could ever have felt
because she was my friend

and the things she . . . she was feeling inside,
the pain she was going through was . . .
it was, like, magnified within me.
Emotionally, it shook me up
because I loved her.

Using Labov's model, we can see that the story conforms to the narrative structure typically used by African-Americans. The value of the narrative has been described variously—it allows us to translate our personal experiences into dramatic form (Labov 1972); it provides a way to put together our reality (Goffman 1974); the narrative is central to the development of communicative ability (Scollon 1976). Yet there was, until recently, a bias against the use of narratives as a communication medium (Cazden and Hymes 1978) and almost no consideration given to the narrative as a learning device or as a form that provides continuity between home and school uses of language. Opportunities to use and analyze student-produced narratives should be considered for inclusion in language programs for nonmainstream students. Of course, more fine-tuned planning of the instructional use of narratives will be needed, but one can readily identify instructional areas in which the narrative might enhance learning.

To enhance students' awareness of language variation, a teacher might compare the structure of oral narratives produced by students of different ethnic and social groups. Labov's model provides a frame for such an analysis. One problem often mentioned in relation to the written language of NSD speakers is the occurrence of spoken language patterns in writing. To sensitize students to some of the differences between speech and writing, a teacher might compare spoken and written narratives, perhaps adding to the analysis of the structure of the narrative an analysis of the structure of the language used in the narrative. In both literature and composition courses, narratives are used to teach point of view, voice, description, exemplification. Practically any of these concepts can be taught using student-produced narratives and then applying the concepts to models found in text. The point here is that this project allowed us to see that narratives are frequently used by this group as a rhetorical device. Since we also know of the educational value of this structure, it makes sense to find ways to capitalize on the structure to enhance learning.

In response to the suicide narrative, the speaker continues the dialogue by making generalizations about the narrative. Notice the student's use of metaphors, another rhetorical device found frequently in the dialogues:

Actually one has to realize that
you will always have problems;
'Cause life is no cakewalk.
You know, life is . . . life has to go on.
Things may be down for a person right now,
but they'll get better.
You have to keep working at it,
keep punching it out.
And sooner or later, you know,
chips fall as they may.

In the above, life is contrasted to a cakewalk, survival is associated with a fight (keep punching it out), and relief comes by chance (chips fall as they may).

We also noticed that these metaphorical structures tend to occur in chains, initiated by one speaker and successively followed by others. Following the utterances above, the metaphorical chain was continued in the following manner:

You know what's devastating to me now.
When I look back and say, "I was going to kill
myself for that?
You know it—the problem, I mean,
it loses its value. It depreciates.
Put some distance between you and what's actually
happening.
That's how you find your solution.

The dialogue ends with another play on language:
Just remember, suicide is a permanent solution to
a temporary problem.

Recent attention given to metaphors has heightened our awareness of their value. Beyond being a rhetorical device, metaphors are now being viewed as fundamental to the acquisition of knowledge. Lakoff and Johnson, for example, contend that new metaphors have the power to create a new reality (1980). One of the dialogue participants created a new reality for other participants when he said, "Drugs cause the brain to go on holidays." The new reality is sometimes so powerful that such metaphors are repeated, creating what some see as empty formulaic patterns. Hanson, Silver, and Strong (1986) speak of the metaphors that underlie teaching strategies, noting that metaphors "help students see old problems, ideas or products in a new more creative light," but they also "make new, unfamiliar ideas more meaningful" (40).

We could, in a traditional, prescriptive frame, find fault with the metaphors presented above. Or, we could use student-produced metaphors to enhance the students' conscious awareness of their thinking processes, of the role that metaphors play in concretizing one's experiences, of how metaphors come to be labeled as trite expressions, or even how the students create new metaphors in their daily communication. In all, we should not overlook the possibility that metaphors and the play on language typically found in African-American speech patterns have the potential of providing continuities between home and school language (Smitherman 1977).

From phase two of the project, dialoguing, we learned that certain patterns naturally emerge in a setting of free conversation. In order to use talk to facilitate learning, instructional content should include communication patterns and strategies that are already part of students' repertoires. It has become more evident that continuities exist between nonmainstream groups' language and cultural patterns and the skills that we want, or say we want, to teach. The challenge is to find the links.

Critiquing

We turn, finally, to the evaluation phase of the project. When asked to evaluate the dialogues, students responded in a way that reflected a sensitivity to the need to establish evaluative criteria, which, incidentally, were based on function rather than form. One of the dialogue participants described his criteria:

> In watching the videotape, I thought it was interesting. So, I'm going to start off using my communication teacher's three rules: topic, audience, and purpose.

The most systematic criticism of the dialogues was that the ideas were not persuasive enough. More specifically, the dialogues focused on problems and their causes, whereas a focus on solutions and effects, e.g., incarceration, homelessness, disfigurement of body, etc., would have been more persuasive.

> *Student 1:* . . . I think what students need to know is give me some suggestions on how to get out of this situation. Don't tell me it's bad. I know that already. Give some advice. Like, if someone was to come up to me and say do you want to try this, you know, it may be difficult for me to "Just say no" because when somebody comes up to you like that, they're not gonna just say, "Oh, OK." They're

gonna keep at you, and keep at you. So you know, give me a suggestion how I can get out of that situation.

Student 2: OK, how would you deal with this? I'm a dealer and I come up to you. "Would you like to sell? Won't you sell some drugs for me? You can get your own Volvo; you could get some Adidas; you could get all these new things plus an apartment and furniture from Ethan Allen." That's what the videotape shows. Not "Come on and sell for me, but you're not gonna get any sleep; you have to carry a gun all the time. You'll probably have people following you around most of the time. And if you come up short on money, you might get killed, and if we can't find you, we'll kill your mother, or father, or your brother or sister." And I think these are the things that need to be brought out—it's the side effects, the disadvantages, what could happen. . . . So, I think those type of things should be brought out because those things are happening.

Student 3: One thing to make it more convincing is to go out and see some real people. Like I went to the jail . . . and I said, "Sheriff, do you have anybody in here who went through a bad situation from some type of drug situation?" So he got me a lady who had been burned up because she was spaced out on coke to come down and speak to a student. He got another man who had been run out from his manhood because he had went to prison because of drugs. . . . I think these are the type of people who need to be on the tape, people who you can look at and say, "GOSH! I never want to go through that!" Bring out the effects.

These responses show a degree of awareness of the need to establish evaluation criteria. Informally, they established criteria for evaluating the message, but the criteria were more closely aligned with content and function than with form. For these youngsters, what mattered was the message and whether or not it would influence the intended audience. This does not mean that structural patterns should not be treated. Rather it suggests that the most natural response to this language-critiquing task was to attend to content and purpose. As far as NSD speakers are concerned, it might be better to begin with evaluative criteria to which they already assign a high degree of importance. That the students basically overlooked the nonstandard language usage caused concern and warrants further investigation. Did the informal style of the conversation make the structural forms less noticeable? Are nonstandard features acceptable for the setting? Would students pay more attention to nonstandard features if the dialogues had been presented in writing instead of in speech? Speculations aside, we can say that this "talk about talk" provides a mechanism for expanding students' understanding of evaluative criteria— how conventions for language use are formed and used to develop

standards for judging the appropriateness and adequacy of communication and of learning. Based on our data, the use of standards to
evaluate seem to be acquired in a more natural way than we might
assume, rendering evaluation more an object to consciously discover
than to teach anew.

Overall, this project provided convincing evidence that the sounds
of language variation need not be silenced in the classroom, for there
are several factors that can be manipulated so that NSD speakers, like
other students, will benefit from classroom dialogue. First, the classroom environment can be made more conducive to participation by
NSD speakers. In this project, the facilitative role of the teacher was
one of the key factors that encouraged student-talk. Obviously, students need guidance as well as a sense of involvement. Guidance was
provided in the form of teacher-directed questions; students were
involved in the planning, production, and evaluation of an oral
dialogue.

Second, this project showed that NSD students have a repertoire of
rhetorical patterns that can be tapped in order to help students use
talk to enhance learning. The two patterns treated here, narratives and
metaphors, have been noted for their important role in the acquisition
of knowledge. While I offered some examples of how these forms may
be integrated into language/language arts instruction, I also stressed
the importance of these forms for addressing the problem of discontinuities between home and school language.

Third, the students participating in this project seem to have developed a sense of the need to use evaluative criteria for judging effectiveness. The talk in this phase of the project was valued for its potential to develop critical thinking skills. The dialogue had many of the
features associated with argumentative writing. Although most discussions of language variation focus on the structural mismatch between standard and nonstandard English patterns, this work suggests
that evaluative criteria for the more global units of language, e.g., purpose, intent, and effect of communication, may be developed more
naturally by students than criteria for forms.

These observations suggest that, as we rethink the problem of how
best to accommodate language variation in the classroom, we avoid
simply rehashing the old debates. Our views about the importance of
classroom talk have changed so that talk is now perceived not only as
a tool of communication but also as a tool for learning. This shift in
viewpoints adds a new dimension to the whole question of how home-
grown language patterns should be used in the classroom. While prior
models focused primarily on the intrusive effects of nonstandard us-

age on communication skills, newer models must take into consideration the view that talk is a vehicle for acquiring knowledge. Consequently, all students need to be encouraged to participate in classroom
dialogue, regardless of their dialect. If we can, we certainly should find
ways to make audible the silent sounds of language variation in our
classrooms.

Works Cited

Cazden, C., and D. Hymes. 1978. "Narrative Thinking and Storytelling Rights:
A Folklorist's Clue to a Critique of Education." *Keystone Folklore* 22, nos. 1–2:
21–35.

Dworkin, N., and Y. Dworkin. 1979. "The Legacy of Pygmalion in the Classroom." *Phi Delta Kappan* 22 (June): 712–15.

Eckerd, R. D., and M. A. Kearney. 1981. Teaching Conversational Skills in ESL.
Washington, D.C.: Center for Applied Linguistics. Flanders, N. A. 1970.
Analyzing Teacher Behavior. Reading, Mass.: Addison-Wesley.

Goffman, E. 1974. *Frame Analysis.* New York: Harper & Row.

Hanson, R. J., H. F. Silver, and R. W. Strong. 1986. *Metaphorical Problem Solving.*
Moorestown, N.J.: Hanson.

Heath, S. B. 1978. *Teacher Talk: Language in the Classroom.* Washington, D.C.:
Center for Applied Linguistics.

Kerman, S. 1979. "Teacher Expectations and Student Achievement." *Phi Delta
Kappan* 22 (June): 716–18.

Labov, W. 1972. *Language in the Inner City: Studies in the Black English Vernacular.*
Philadelphia: University of Pennsylvania Press.

Lakoff, G., and M. Johnson. 1980. *Metaphors We Live By.* Chicago: University of
Chicago Press.

Scollon, R. 1976. "The Framing of Chipewyan Narratives in Performance: Titles, Initials, and Finals." *Working Papers in Linguistics* (University of Hawaii)
7, no. 4: 97–107.

Scott, J., and G. Smitherman. 1985. "Language Attitudes and Self-Fulfilling
Prophecies in the Elementary School." In *The English Language Today*, edited
by S. Greenbaum, 302–14. Oxford, England: Pergamon Press.

Smitherman, G. 1977. *Talkin and Testifyin: The Language of Black America.* Boston:
Houghton Mifflin.

Editors

Susan Hynds is associate professor in the Reading and Language Arts Center at Syracuse University, where she serves as program director of English Education and director of the Writing Consultation Center. In 1984 her dissertation study was named a finalist in the NCTE Promising Researcher competition. Hynds is currently chair of the NCTE Assembly on Research. She has taught English, speech, and drama on levels from grades 6–12 for nine years. Her research explores the relationships between social understanding and response to literature, as well as the interpersonal dimensions of collaborative writing. Hynds's work has appeared or is forthcoming in *Research in the Teaching of English, The Journal of Teaching Writing, The Reading Teacher, Contemporary Psychology,* and *The Review of Education.* She is coauthor of a forthcoming book, *Developing Discourse Practices in Adolescence and Adulthood* (R. Beach and S. Hynds). Other publications have appeared or are forthcoming in *The Second Handbook of Reading Research* (Barr, Kamil, Mosenthal, and Pearson, in press) and *Beyond Communication: Reading Comprehension and Criticism* (Bogdan and Straw 1990).

Donald L. Rubin is associate professor in the Department of Language Education and the Department of Speech Communication at the University of Georgia. He has contributed essays on oral communication instruction and the relationship between speaking and writing for *Exploring Speaking-Writing Relationships* (Kroll and Vann) and *Speaking and Writing K–12* (Thaiss and Suhor). His chapter on oral communication appears in the first NCTE yearbook, *Consensus and Dissent*. He was project director for a FIPSE-supported program to use oral communication exercises to improve the academic writing of basic writers. The project is described in the NCTE/ERIC monograph *Speaking into Writing*.

Contributors

Phil Backlund is professor of speech communication at Central Washington University. He has been actively involved in developing oral communication curriculum and in promoting increased attention to oral communication skills for public school students. Selected publications include *Assessing Listening Skills, SCA National Guidelines for Essential Speaking and Listening Skills for Elementary Students, Avoiding Bias in Assessing Communication Skills,* and others. He is an active member of the Speech Communication Association and currently chairs its Committee on Assessment and Testing.

Douglas Barnes taught English in secondary schools in the United Kingdom for seventeen years before moving to the University of Leeds, where he became Reader in Education. Formerly chair of NATE, he carried out research into the role played by pupils' and teachers' talk in classroom learning. His main publications include *Language, the Learner and the School* (as coauthor), soon to be issued by Boynton-Cook in a North American edition; *From Communication to Curriculum; Communication and Learning in Small Groups* (as coauthor); *Practical Curriculum Study;* and *Versions of English* (as coauthor).

Lisa D. Delpit is a senior research associate at the Institute for Urban Research of Morgan State University in Baltimore, Maryland, and associate professor of education on leave from Michigan State University. She is currently planning research for a volume on issues of diversity in teacher education. She has lived in Papua, New Guinea, where she executed an ethnographically based evaluation of a mother tongue-medium instruction program, and in Fairbanks, Alaska, where she was a faculty member and researcher at the Unversity of Alaska in the area of language and culture. Other publications include a chapter of *Cross-Cultural Perpsectives on Literacy in the Black Community,* edited by I. McPhail and M. R. Hoover (in press), and articles, "Skills and Other Dilemmas of a Progressive Black Educator" (*Harvard Educational Review* 1986) and "The Silenced Dialogue: Power and Pedagogy in Educating Other People's Children" (*Harvard Educational Review* 1988).

Anne Haas Dyson is associate professor of education in language and literacy at the University of California at Berkeley. A former primary grade teacher, her research concentrates on children's oral and written language use in classroom settings. Among her publications are *Multiple Worlds of Child Writers: Friends Learning to Write* and, with Celia Genishi, *Language Assessment in the Early Years.* She edited the NCTE publication *Collaboration through Writing and Reading: Exploring Possibilities* and, with Genishi, has also edited the "Research Currents" column in *Language Arts.*

Elizabeth C. Fine is associate professor in the Department of Communication Studies and the Center for Programs in the Humanities at Virginia Polytechnic Institute and State University. She received her Ph.D. in communications from the University of Texas at Austin (1978), her M.A. in rhetoric from the University of California, Berkeley (1973), and her B.S. in speech communication from the University of Texas at Austin (1971). Her major research is in performance studies and folklore. She was awarded a Woodrow Wilson Fellowship in 1971, and the Outstanding Dissertation Award from the University of Texas in 1978. Her book, *The Folklore Text: From Performance to Print* was selected by *Choice* as an Outstanding Academic Book of 1985, and was awarded third prize in the Chicago Folklore Competition. Her articles have been published in *Journal of American Folklore, Working Papers in Sociolinguistics, Communication Monographs, Communication Education, Literature in Performance, Annals of Tourism Research*, and *Sprache und Sprechen*.

Lee Galda is associate professor of language education at the University of Georgia, where she teaches courses in language arts and children's literature. She is the author of several articles in journals such as *Research in the Teaching of English* and *Language Arts* and has coauthored a chapter in the forthcoming *Handbook of Research on Teaching the English Language Arts*. She is also the Children's Books Department editor for *The Reading Teacher*, and serves on committees for NCTE and other professional organizations.

Anne Ruggles Gere is professor of English and professor of education at the University of Michigan, where she serves as codirector of the Ph.D. Program in English and Education. She was formerly the director of the Puget Sound Writing Program and prior to that a high school English teacher. Her recent publications include *Roots in the Sawdust: Writing to Learn across the Disciplines, The Active Reader*, and *Writing Groups: History, Theory, and Implications*.

Judith L. Green is professor in the Department of Educational Policy and Leadership (Program Area: Curriculum, Instruction, and Professional Development) at The Ohio State University. She has taught language and reading at the university and public school (K–6) levels. In addition to her journal articles and book chapters, she has edited two books on research in classroom settings: *Ethnography and Language in Educational Settings* and *Multiple Perspective Analyses of Classroom Discourse*. Dr. Green is an editor of a series of books on language and educational processes for Ablex Publishing Corp., and serves on editorial boards for a number of educational journals. She makes presentations regularly at national and international conferences and is actively involved in cooperative projects with public schools.

Muriel Harris is associate professor of English and director of the writing lab at Purdue University. She is the founder and editor of the *Writing Lab Newsletter*, author of *Teaching One-to-One: The Writing Conference*, editor of *Tutoring Writing: A Sourcebook for Writing Labs*, and author of several textbooks, including the forthcoming *Concise Guide to Grammar*. She serves on the editorial board of several journals, on the executive board of the National Writing Centers Association (an NCTE assembly), and as a consultant and outside evaluator in the formation of writing labs. In her workshops and conference presentations at CCCC, NCTE, and regional affiliate conferences, she focuses on (and loudly advocates) individualized instruction in writing in the tutorial setting of writing labs.

Sarah Hudelson is associate professor in the Division of Curriculum and Instruction at Arizona State University, Tempe. She has worked for fifteen years in bilingual/second language teacher education in Arizona, Florida, and Texas. She is a former elementary school teacher. Dr. Hudelson has authored articles on bilingual/second language learners' literacy development in such journals as *Language Arts, The Reading Teacher, TESOL Quarterly,* and the *NABE Journal.* She is the author of a series of English as a second language materials for children titled *Hopscotch,* and she has recently published a monograph through the ERIC Clearinghouse for Languages and Linguistics titled *Write On: Children Writing in ESL.* She has served on the NCTE/TESOL Committee, the NCTE Research Foundation, and as elementary chair for the 1990 NCTE Spring Conference in Colorado Springs.

Judith Wells Lindfors is professor of curriculum and instruction at the University of Texas at Austin, where she specializes in teaching courses on child language acquisition. Her book, *Children's Language and Learning,* now in its second edition, won the Modern Language Association's first Mina Shaughnessy Medal in 1981. A regular presenter at NCTE conferences, she has also served as a member of NCTE's Committee on Research and as a research foundation trustee.

Sara W. Lundsteen is professor of education at North Texas State University. She has taught K–8 English and worked as a language arts consultant. In addition to her many journal articles, book chapters, and twelve previous books, she has recently published a new text, *Language Arts: A Problem Solving Approach,* and collaborated with Eileen Tway on a matching activity book, *Choose Your Own Learning and Teaching Activities for Language Arts.* She makes presentations regularly, for example, at NCTE, IRA, and the International Listening Association.

Nancy Ryan Nussbaum is associate professor of education at Goshen College in Goshen, Indiana. She has experience in teaching grades K–8 in a variety of cultural settings. Nussbaum is currently a Ph.D. candidate at The Ohio State University in the Department of Language, Literature, and Reading. She has collaborated with several colleagues in writing journal articles for publication in professional journals. Her most recent work was done in collaboration with Lisa Puckett for her dissertation research. Their chapter will appear in *Creating Communities of Readers* (edited by Kathy Gnagey Short and Kathryn Mitchell Pierce). She is currently working with teachers in eastern Pennsylvania to develop curriculum resource guides for teaching Bible creatively in their Mennonite elementary schools. She speaks frequently to parents' groups about the importance of reading with children at home.

Cynthia Onore teaches at the City College of New York, where she also directs the programs in English education and language and literacy. She taught junior and senior high school English a number of years ago, but she maintains connections with public school teachers through inservice education projects on language across the curriculum and collaborative learning. She is a member of the NCTE Committee on Language across the Curriculum and a member of the executive committee of the Conference on English Education. Her new book, *Learning Change*, coauthored with Nancy Lester, is a study of the impact of language across the curriculum on individual teachers, their students, and the schools in which they work.

A. D. Pellegrini is professor of early childhood education and a research fellow in the Institute for Behavioral Research, both at the University of Georgia. He has taught both Head Start and fourth grade. For the past fifteen years his research has been on children's play and language. He has edited numerous books and journal articles in these areas. His text, *Applied Child Study: A Developmental Approach*, is in the process of being rewritten for its second edition.

Theresa Rogers is assistant professor of language arts, children's literature, and reading at The Ohio State University. She has taught English and reading at the junior high and high school levels. She has published book chapters, journal articles in *English Quarterly, Elementary School Journal*, and *Journal of Educational Psychology*, and is coauthor of a new edition of *How Porcupines Make Love: Notes on a Response-centered Curriculum*, with Alan Purves and Anna Soter. She is a member of NCRE and presents regularly at NCTE, IRA, and National Reading Conference conventions.

Jerrie Cobb Scott, researcher, educator, and linguist, is director of the Center for Studies of Urban Literacy at Central State University, Wilberforce, Ohio. She was formerly director of composition at the University of Florida and has worked as a public school administrator and teacher. In addition to her journal articles, book chapters, and media appearances, she coedited *Tapping Potential: English and Language Arts for the Black Learner*. Her most recent research, articles, and workshops focus on the connections between visual and print literacy and nontraditional approaches to oral discourse in the classroom.

Stanley B. Straw is professor of education at the University of Manitoba. He has a Ph.D. in reading and language arts from the University of Minnesota and is coeditor of *English Quarterly*, CCTE's research and theory journal. He is also coeditor of two books, *Research in the Language Arts: Language and Schooling* (with Victor Forese), and *Beyond Communication: Reading Comprehension and Criticism* (with Deanne Bogdan). His research interests include analyses of the reading process, particularly aesthetic reading, and the role of collaborative learning in reading and writing.

Betty Jane Wagner is professor in the Department of Reading and Language, Graduate School of Education, and in the English Department of the School of Arts and Sciences at the National College of Education, and is director of the Chicago Area Writing Project and regional director of the National Writing Project. Prof. Wagner has published with James Moffett, *Student-Centered Language Arts and Reading, K–13, A Handbook for Teachers*, and a curriculum, *Interaction*. Her interest in improvisational classroom drama has led to a number of publications, including a book, *Dorothy Heathcote: Drama as a Learning Medium*. Wagner has also published in journals such as *English Journal, Language Arts, The Elementary School Journal, Learning*, and *College English*. Long active in NCTE, she currently chairs the Language across the Curriculum Committee. She is frequently asked to give major addresses at conferences across the nation.